BASS, PIKE, PERCH

AND OTHERS

The Classic Reference Guide to Eastern
North American Game Fish

BY

JAMES A. HENSHALL, M.D.

AUTHOR OF "BOOK OF THE BLACK-BASS," "MORE ABOUT THE BLACK-
BASS," "CAMPING AND CRUISING IN FLORIDA," "YE GODS
AND LITTLE FISHES," ETC.

Skyhorse Publishing

Copyright © 2014 by Skyhorse Publishing, Inc.

All rights reserved. No part of this book may be reproduced in any manner without the express written consent of the publisher, except in the case of brief excerpts in critical reviews or articles. All inquiries should be addressed to Skyhorse Publishing, 307 West 36th Street, 11th Floor, New York, NY 10018.

Skyhorse Publishing books may be purchased in bulk at special discounts for sales promotion, corporate gifts, fund-raising, or educational purposes. Special editions can also be created to specifications. For details, contact the Special Sales Department, Skyhorse Publishing, 307 West 36th Street, 11th Floor, New York, NY 10018 or info@skyhorsepublishing.com.

Skyhorse® and Skyhorse Publishing® are registered trademarks of Skyhorse Publishing, Inc.®, a Delaware corporation.

Visit our website at www.skyhorsepublishing.com.

10 9 8 7 6 5 4 3 2 1

Library of Congress Cataloging-in-Publication Data is available on file.

ISBN: 978-1-62873-625-0
EBook ISBN: 978-1-62873-982-4

Printed in the United States of America

INTRODUCTION

In this volume are included all of the game-fishes of the United States east of the Rocky Mountains, except the salmons and trouts, and the tarpon, jewfish, and other fishes of large size, which are described in other volumes of this series. As a matter of convenience I have grouped the fishes in families, whenever possible, but in their sequence I have been guided chiefly by their importance as game-fishes, and not in accordance with their natural order. The latter feature, however, has been provided for in a systematic list on a subsequent page.

In order not to burden the text with matter that might not be of general interest, the technical descriptions of the fishes of each group are given in small type at the head of each chapter; and that they may be readily understood by the lay reader the following explanations seem necessary.

The length of the head is from the point of the snout to the hindmost point or margin of the gill-cover. The length of the body is from the point of the snout to the base of the caudal fin, the fin itself not being included. The depth of the body is from the highest point of the dorsal line to the lowest point of the ventral line, usually from the base of the first dorsal fin to the base of the ventral fin. The expression "head 5" means that the length of the head is contained five times in the length of the body; the expression "depth 5" means that the depth of the body is contained five times in its length; "eye 5" means that the diameter of the eye is contained five times in the length of the head. In describing the fins the spiny rays are denoted by Roman numerals, and the soft rays by Arabic numerals, and the fins themselves by initials; thus "D. 9" means that the dorsal fin is single and composed of nine soft rays; "D. IX, 10" means that the single dorsal fin has nine spiny rays and ten soft rays; when separated by a hyphen, as "D. X-12," it means that there are two dorsal fins, the first composed of ten spiny rays and the second of twelve soft ones; "A. III, 11" means that the anal fin has three spines and eleven soft rays. The expression "scales 7–65–18" indicates that there are seven rows of scales between the dorsal fin and the lateral line, sixty-five scales along the lateral line, and eighteen oblique or horizontal rows between the lateral line and the ventral line. The number of rays in the fins and the number of scales along the lateral line, as given, represent the average number, and are subject to slight variation; thus in some localities the number of rays in a fin may be found to vary one or two, and the number of scales along the lateral line may vary from one to five, more or less, from the number given in the descriptions.

I have adhered strictly to the nomenclature of the "Fishes of Middle and North America" (Bulletin, U. S. National Museum, No. 47), by Jordan and Evermann, and in the main I have followed the descriptions as recorded in that admirable work; but in many instances I have depended on my own notes.

The suggestions as to angling and the tools and tackle recommended may be confidently relied on, as they are in conformity with my own practice and are based on my personal experience, covering a period of forty years, on many waters, from Canada to the West Indies, and from the Atlantic to the Rocky Mountains.

JAMES A. HENSHALL.

BOZEMAN, MONTANA,
February 1, 1903.

SYSTEMATIC ARRANGEMENT OF THE FISHES DESCRIBED IN THIS VOLUME

FAMILY SILURIDÆ

Ictalurus punctatus (Rafinesque). The Channel Catfish.

FAMILY CYPRINIDÆ

Cyprinus carpio, Linnæus. The German Carp.

FAMILY ELOPIDÆ

Elops saurus, Linnæus. The Ten-pounder.

FAMILY ALBULIDÆ

Albula vulpes (Linnæus). The Lady-Fish.

FAMILY SALMONIDÆ

Coregonus williamsoni, Girard. The Rocky Mountain Whitefish.
Argyrosomus artedi sisco, Jordan. The Cisco.

FAMILY THYMALLIDÆ

Thymallus signifer (Richardson). The Arctic Grayling.
Thymallus tricolor, Cope. The Michigan Grayling.
Thymallus montanus, Milner. The Montana Grayling.

FAMILY ARGENTINIDÆ

Osmerus mordax (Mitchill). The Smelt.

FAMILY ESOCIDÆ

Esox americanus, Gmelin. The Banded Pickerel.
Esox vermiculatus, Le Sueur. The Western Pickerel.

Esox reticulatus, Le Sueur.   The Eastern Pickerel.
Esox lucius, Linnæus.   The Pike.
Esox nobilior, Thompson.   The Mascalonge.

FAMILY HOLOCENTRIDÆ

Holocentrus ascensionis (Osbeck).   The Squirrel Fish.

FAMILY SCOMBRIDÆ

Sarda sarda (Bloch).   The Bonito.
Scomberomorus maculatus (Mitchill).   The Spanish Mackerel.
Scomberomorus regalis (Bloch).   The Cero.

FAMILY CARANGIDÆ

Carangus crysos (Mitchill).   The Runner.
Carangus latus (Agassiz).   The Horse-eye Jack.
Trachinotus glaucus (Bloch).   The Gaff Top-sail Pompano.
Trachinotus goodei, Jordan & Evermann.   The Permit.
Trachinotus carolinus (Linnæus).   The Pompano.

FAMILY RACHYCENTRIDÆ

Rachycentron canadus (Linnæus).   The Cobia.

FAMILY CENTRARCHIDÆ

Pomoxis annularis, Rafinesque.   The Crappie.
Pomoxis sparoides (Lacépède).   The Calico-bass.
Ambloplites rupestris (Rafinesque).   The Rock-bass.
Archoplites interruptus (Girard).   The Sacramento Perch.
Chænobryttus gulosus (Cuvier & Valenciennes).   The Warmouth
     Perch.
Lepomis auritus (Linnæus).   The Red-breast Sunfish.
Lepomis megalotis (Rafinesque).   The Long-eared Sunfish.
Lepomis pallidus (Mitchill).   The Blue Sunfish.
Eupomotis gibbosus (Linnæus).   The Common Sunfish.
Micropterus dolomieu, Lacépède.   The Small-mouth Black-bass.
Micropterus salmoides (Lacépède).   The Large-mouth Black-
     bass.

Family PERCIDÆ

Stizostedion vitreum (Mitchill). The Pike-perch.
Stizostedion canadense (Smith). The Sauger.
Perca flavescens (Mitchill). The Yellow Perch.

Family CENTROPOMIDÆ

Centropomus undecimalis (Bloch). The Snook, or Rovallia.

Family SERRANIDÆ

Roccus chrysops (Rafinesque). The White-bass.
Roccus lineatus (Bloch). The Striped-bass.
Morone interrupta, Gill. The Yellow-bass.
Morone americana (Gmelin). The White Perch.
Petrometopon cruentatus (Lacépède). The Coney.
Bodianus fulvus (Linnæus). The Yellow-Fish.
Epinephelus adscensionis (Osbeck). The Rock Hind.
Epinephelus guttatus (Linnæus). The Red Hind.
Mycteroperca venenosa (Linnæus). The Yellow Fin Grouper.
Mycteroperca microlepis (Goode & Bean). The Gag.
Mycteroperca falcata phenax, Jordan & Swain. The Scamp.
Centropristes striatas (Linnæus). The Sea-bass.
Centropristes ocyurus (Jordan & Evermann). The Gulf Sea-bass.
Centropristes philadelphicus (Linnæus). The Southern Sea-bass.
Diplectrum formosum (Linnæus). The Sand-fish.

Family LOBOTIDÆ

Lobotes surinamensis (Bloch). The Triple Tail.

Family LUTIANIDÆ

Lutianus jocu (Bloch & Schneider). The Dog Snapper.
Lutianus apodus (Walbaum). The Schoolmaster.
Lutianus aya (Bloch). The Red Snapper.
Lutianus synagris (Linnæus). The Lane Snapper.
Ocyurus chrysurus (Bloch). The Yellowtail.

Family HÆMULIDÆ

Hæmulon album, Curvier & Valenciennes.   The Margate-fish.
Hæmulon macrostomum, Gunther.   The Gray Grunt.
Hæmulon parra (Desmarest). . The Sailor's Choice.
Hæmulon sciurus (Shaw).   The Yellow Grunt.
Hæmulon plumieri (Lacépède).   The Black Grunt.
Hæmulon flavolineatum (Desmarest).   The French Grunt.
Anisotremus virginicus (Linnæus).   The Pork-fish.
Orthopristis chrysopterus (Linnæus).   The Pig-fish.

Family SPARIDÆ

Stenotomus chrysops (Linnæus).   The Scup.
Stenotomus aculeatus (Cuvier & Valenciennes).   The Southern
    Porgy.
Calamus calamus (Cuvier & Valenciennes).   The Saucer-eye
    Porgy.
Calamus proridens, Jordan & Gilbert.   The Little Head Porgy.
Calamus bajonado (Bloch & Schneider).   The Jolt Head Porgy.
Calamus arctifrons, Goode & Bean.   The Grass Porgy.
Lagodon rhomboides (Linnæus).   The Pin-fish.
Archosargus probatocephalus (Walbaum).   The Sheepshead.

Family KYPHOSIDÆ

Kyphosus sectatrix (Linnæus).   The Bermuda Chub.

Family SCIÆNIDÆ

Cynoscion nothus (Holbrook).   The Bastard Weakfish.
Cynoscion regalis (Bloch & Schneider).   The Weakfish.
Cynoscion thalassinus (Holbrook).   The Deep-water Weakfish.
Cynoscion nebulosus (Cuvier & Valenciennes).   The Spotted
    Weakfish.
Leiostomus xanthurus, Lacépède.   The Lafayette, or Spot.
Micropogon undulatus (Linnæus).   The Croaker.
Menticirrhus saxatilis (Bloch & Schneider).   The Kingfish.
Aplodinotus grunniens, Rafinesque.   The Fresh-water Drum-
    fish.

FAMILY **LABRIDÆ**

Tautogolabrus adspersus (Walbaum). The Cunner.

FAMILY **EPHIPPIDÆ**

Chætodipterus faber (Broussonet). The Angel-fish.

FAMILY **BALISTIDÆ**

Balistes carolinensis, Gmelin. The Turbot.

FAMILY **PLEURONECTIDÆ**

Pseudopleuronectes americanus (Walbaum). The Flounder.

CONTENTS

CHAPTER I

CHAPTER II

CHAPTER III

Contents

CHAPTER XV

CHAPTER XVI

CHAPTER XVII

THE CHANNEL FISHES

Contents

CHAPTER XVIII

MISCELLANEOUS FISHES

LIST OF ILLUSTRATIONS

BASS, PIKE, AND PERCH

CHAPTER I

THE SUNFISH FAMILY
(*Centrarchidæ*)

THE sunfish family is composed entirely of fresh-water fishes. They are characterized by a symmetrically-shaped body, rather short and compressed; mouth terminal; teeth small, without canines; scales rather large; cheeks and gill-covers scaly; scales mostly smooth; border of preopercle smooth, or but slightly serrated; opercle ending in two flat points, or in a black flap; a single dorsal fin, composed of both spiny and soft rays; anal fin also having both spines and soft rays; the dorsal spines varying from 6 to 13 in the different species, with from 3 to 9 in the anal fin; sexes similar; coloration mostly greenish.

GENUS MICROPTERUS

Micropterus dolomieu. Small-mouth Black-bass. Body ovate-oblong; head 3; depth 3; eye 6; D. X, 13; A. III, 10; scales 11–73–17; mouth large, the maxillary reaching front of eye; scales on cheek minute, in 17 rows; teeth villiform.

Micropterus salmoides. Large-mouth Black-bass. Body ovate-oblong; head 3; depth 3; eye 5; D. X, 13; A. III, 11; scales 8–68–16; scales on cheek large, in 10 rows; mouth very large, maxillary extending beyond the eye; teeth villiform.

GENUS AMBLOPLITES

Ambloplites rupestris. Rock-bass. Body oblong, moderately compressed; head 2¾; depth 2½; eye 4; D. XI, 10; A. VI, 10; scales 5–40–12, with 6 to 8 rows on cheeks; mouth large, maxillary extending to posterior part of pupil; teeth small, single patch on tongue; gill-rakers 7 to 10, on lower part of arch; preopercle serrate near its angle; opercle ends in 2 flat points.

GENUS ARCHOPLITES

Archoplites interruptus. Sacramento Perch. Body oblong-ovate, compressed; head 2⅔; depth 2½; eye 4; D. XII, 10; A. VI, 10; scales 7–45–14; 8 rows on cheeks; mouth very large, maxillary extending beyond pupil; teeth numerous and small, with 2 patches on tongue; gill-rakers 20; opercle emarginate; most of the membrane bones of head serrate.

GENUS CHÆNOBRYTTUS

Chænobryttus gulosus. Warmouth Perch. Body heavy and deep; head 2½; depth 2¼; eye 4; D. X, 9; A. III, 8; scales 6–42–11; 6 to 8 rows on cheeks; teeth small and numerous; gill-rakers 9; preopercle entire; mouth very large; opercle ends in a black convex flap.

GENUS LEPOMIS

Lepomis pallidus. Blue Sunfish. Body short and deep, compressed; head 3; depth 2; eye 3½; D. X, 12; A. III, 12; scales 7–46–16; 5 rows on cheeks; mouth small, maxillary barely reaching eye; teeth small and sharp; opercular flap without pale edge; gill-rakers $x + 11$ to 13.

Lepomis megalotis. Long-eared Sunfish. Body short and deep, the back arched; head 3; depth 2; eye 4; D. X, 11; A. III, 9; scales 5–40–14; 5 rows on cheeks; mouth small and oblique; opercular flap long and broad, with red or blue margin; gill-rakers $x + 8$ or 9.

Lepomis auritus. Red-breast Sunfish. Body elongate; head 3; depth 3; eye 4; D. X, 11; A. III, 9; scales 6–45–15; mouth large, oblique; palatine teeth present; gill-rakers $x + 8$ or 9, quite short; opercular flap very long and narrow; scales on breast very small; 7 rows scales on cheeks.

GENUS EUPOMOTIS

Eupomotis gibbosus. Common Sunfish. Body short and deep, compressed; head 3; depth 2; eye 4; D. X, 11; A. III, 10; scales 6–45–13; 4 rows on cheeks; mouth small, oblique, maxillary scarcely reaching front of eye; pharyngeal teeth paved and rounded; gill-rakers soft and small, $x + 10$; opercular flap rather small, the lower part bright scarlet.

GENUS POMOXIS

Pomoxis sparoides. Calico-bass. Body oblong, elevated, much compressed; head 3; depth 2; D. VII, 15; A. VI, 17; scales 40 to 45; 6 rows on cheeks; mouth large, maxillary reaching to posterior edge of pupil; snout projecting; fins very high, anal higher than dorsal.

Pomoxis annularis. Crappie. Body rather elongate; head 3; depth 2⅓; D. VI, 15; A. VI, 18; scales 36 to 48; 4 or 5 rows on cheek; mouth very wide; fins very high, but lower than *sparoides*.

THE SMALL-MOUTH BLACK-BASS

(*Micropterus dolomieu*)

The generic name *Micropterus* was given to the small-mouth black-bass by the French ichthyologist Lacépède, in 1802, who was the first to describe it The name *Micropterus*, which means "small fin," was bestowed on account of the mutilated condition of the dorsal fin of

the specimen, a few of the posterior rays
of the fin being detached and broken off,
giving the appearance of a short and separate fin.   The specimen was sent to Paris
from an unknown locality in America, and is
still preserved in the Museum of Natural History at Paris, where I personally examined it.
It is a fine example, about a foot in length, and
is remarkably well preserved.   As there was no
known genus to which the specimen with the
curious dorsal fin could be referred, Lacépède
created the new genus *Micropterus*.   He gave
it the specific name *dolomieu* as a compliment
to his friend M. Dolomieu, a French mineralo-
gist, for whom the mineral dolomite was also
named.

Originally, the small-mouth black-bass was
restricted to the Great Lake region, parts of the
Ohio and Mississippi valleys, and along the upper
reaches of streams flowing from the Alleghany
Mountains in the Southern states.   It has, however, been introduced into all of the New England and Middle states, and into many Western
states.   It has a compressed, rather elliptical
body, the dorsal and ventral outlines being nearly
equal; it becomes deeper with age.

As its range, or distribution, is so great and extensive, and the waters it inhabits are so different in hue and character, the coloration of the small-mouth bass varies from almost black to the faintest tinge of green, in different sections of the country. The coloration is so variable that it differs even in fish in the same waters. It is influenced mostly by the hue of the water, character of the bottom, the presence or absence of weeds about the haunts of the bass, and, moreover, the changes in color may occur in a very short time when subject to these various conditions. The general color, however, is greenish of various shades, always darker on the back, and paling to white or whitish on the belly. When markings are present, they form vertical patches or bars, never horizontal. Three bronze streaks extend from the eye across the cheeks. All markings, however, may become obsolete with age.

The natural food of both species is crawfish, which might be inferred from the character of their teeth and wide-opening mouth. There is a popular belief that they are essentially and habitually piscivorous; but this is an error; they are not so black as they are painted. They feed on minute crustaceans and larval forms of insects when young, and afterward on crawfish, minnows, frogs, insects, etc., as do most fishes that have teeth in the jaws. But the teeth of the black-bass are villiform and closely packed, presenting an even surface as uniform as the surface of a tooth-brush. Such teeth are incapable of wounding, and merely form a rough surface for holding their prey securely. All truly piscivorous fishes have fewer, but sharp, conical teeth, of unequal length, like the yellow-perch, pike-perch, mascalonge, and trout, or lancet-shaped teeth like the bluefish.

The black-bass is far less destructive to fish life than any of the fishes mentioned; on the contrary, it suffers the most in a mixed community of fishes, and is the first to disappear. There are small lakes in Canada and Michigan where the brook-trout and black-bass have co-existed from time immemorial without jeopardy to the trout. There are small lakes in Wisconsin where black-bass and cisco, with other species, have coexisted for all time; and while the cisco is as numerous as ever, the black-bass has almost disappeared. It does not follow, however, that black-bass should be introduced in trout waters;

far from it. Brook-trout are being exterminated fast enough, owing to the changed natural conditions of the streams and their surroundings, without adding another contestant for the limited supply of food in such waters.

Both species of black-bass have been introduced into Germany, France, Russia, and the Netherlands. In Germany, especially, they have found a permanent home. It was my privilege materially to assist Herr Max von dem Borne, of Berneuchen, with such advice as enabled him to start on a sure footing in his enterprise, and with such subsequent success in its establishment that he published several brochures on the black-bass to meet the demand for information as to its habits and merits as a game- and food-fish. An effort was made some years ago to introduce the black-bass into English waters, but without success, owing to a want of knowledge as to the proper species to experiment with. The small-mouth bass was placed in weedy ponds or small lakes in which only the large-mouth bass would live.

The small-mouth bass thrives only in comparatively clear, cool, and rocky or gravelly streams, and in lakes and ponds supplied by such streams

or having cold bottom springs. In lakes of the
latter character, in northern sections, it coexists
with large-mouth bass in many instances. In
such cases, however, the small-mouth will be
found usually at the inlet, or about the springs,
and the large-mouth at the outlet or in sheltered,
grassy situations. In winter it undergoes a state
of partial or complete torpidity. In ponds that
have been drained in the winter season it has
been found snugly ensconced in the crevices of
rocks, beneath shelving banks, logs, roots, or
among masses of vegetation, undergoing its
winter sleep. In the spring, when the temperature of the water rises above fifty degrees, the
small-mouth bass emerges from its winter quarters, about which it lingers until the water becomes still warmer, when it departs in search of
suitable locations for spawning. At this time,
owing to a semi-migratory instinct, it ascends
streams, and roams about in lakes or ponds, often
ascending inlet streams, or in some instances
descending outlet streams.

When favorable situations are found, the male
and female pair off and proceed to fulfil the
reproductive instinct. The spawning period
extends from May to July, according to the

section of the country it inhabits, and when the temperature of the water is suitable. The nests are formed on a bottom of gravel or coarse sand, or on a flat rock in very rocky streams. The male fish does the work of preparation by scouring with fins and tail a space about twice his length in diameter, forming a shallow, saucer-shaped depression, in which the female deposits her eggs, which are fertilized by the male, who hovers near by. The eggs are heavy and adhesive, being invested with a glutinous matter that enables them to adhere to the pebbles on the bottom. The number of eggs varies from two thousand to twenty-five thousand, according to the size and weight of the female. The nest is carefully guarded by the parents until the eggs hatch, the period of incubation being from one to two weeks, according to the temperature of the water. The resultant fry are then watched and brooded by the male fish for several days or a week, when they seek the shelter of weeds and grasses in shallow water.

The young fry feed on minute crustaceans and the larval forms of insects. When a month old they are about an inch long, and continue to grow, if food is plentiful, so that they reach a

length of from three to six inches in the fall.
Thereafter they increase a pound a year under
the most favorable conditions, until the maximum
weight is attained, which is about five pounds.
In some instances, however, they have reached a
weight of seven or even ten pounds, where the
environment has been unusually favorable; notably in Glen Lake, near Glens Falls, New York,
where a half-dozen or more have been taken
weighing from eight to ten pounds. One of ten
pounds was twenty-five and one-half inches long
and nineteen inches in girth.

As a game-fish the black-bass has come into
his inheritance. As the French say, he has arrived. With the special tools and tackle now
furnished for his capture, he has proved my apho-
rism, "Inch for inch, and pound for pound, he
is the gamest fish that swims." When I ventured
this opinion twenty-five years ago, there were no
special articles made for his capture except the
Kentucky reel and the McGinnis rod, twelve feet
long and fifteen ounces in weight. In awarding
the palm as a game-fish to the black-bass, I do so
advisedly, in the light of ample experience with
all other game-fishes, and without prejudice, for I
have an innate love and admiration for all, from

the lovely trout of the mountain brook to the giant tarpon of the sea.

In the application of so broad and sweeping an assertion each and every attribute of a game-fish must be well considered: his habitat; his aptitude to rise to the fly; his struggle for freedom; his manner of resistance; his weight as compared with other game-fishes; and his excellence as a food-fish, must be separately and collectively considered and duly and impartially weighed. His haunts are amid most charming and varied scenes. Not in the silent and solemn solitudes of the primeval forests, where animated Nature is evidenced mainly in swarms of gnats, black-flies, and mosquitoes; nor under the shadows of grand and lofty mountains, guarded by serried ranks of pines and firs, but whose sombre depths are void of feathered songsters. However grand, sublime, and impressive such scenes truly are, they do not appeal profoundly to the angler. He must have life, motion, sound. He courts Nature in her more communicative moods, and in the haunts of the black-bass his desires are realized. Wading down the rippling stream, casting his flies hither and yon, alert for the responsive tug, the sunlight is filtered through overhanging trees,

while the thrush, blackbird, and cardinal render
the air vocal with sweet sounds, and his rival,
the kingfisher, greets him with vibrant voice.
The summer breeze, laden with the scent of
woodland blossoms, whispers among the leaves,
the wild bee flits by on droning wing, the squirrel barks defiantly, and the tinkle of the cow-bell
is mellowed in the distance. I know of such
streams in the mountain valleys of West Virginia,
amid the green rolling hills of Kentucky and
Tennessee, and in the hill country where Missouri and Arkansas meet.

The aptitude of the black-bass to rise to the
artificial fly is not questioned by the twentieth-
century angler, though it was considered a matter
of doubt by many anglers during the last quarter
of the nineteenth. The doubt was mainly owing
to a lack of experience, for fly-fishing for black-
bass was successfully practised in Kentucky as
early, certainly, as 1845. I have before me a
click reel made in 1848 by the late Mr. J. L.
Sage, of Lexington, Kentucky, especially for fly-
fishing. I have also seen his fly-rod made by
him about the same time, and used by him for
many years on the famous bass streams of that
state. And I might say, in passing, that black-

bass bait-fishing, as an art, originated in Kentucky a century ago. George Snyder, of Paris, Kentucky, when president of the Bourbon County Angling Club, made the first multiplying reel for casting the minnow, in 1810, and as early as 1830 many such reels were used in that state. The rods employed by those pioneers of black-bass fishing were about ten feet long, weighing but several ounces, cut from the small end of a Mississippi cane, with the reel lashed to the butt. They used the smallest Chinese " sea-grass " lines, or home-made lines of three strands of black sewing-silk twisted together. Those old disciples of Walton would have been shocked, could they have seen the heavy rods and coarse lines that are still used in some sections, for their own tackle was as light, if not so elegant, as any made at the present day.

Another quality in a game-fish is measured by his resistance when hooked and by his efforts to escape. I think no fish of equal weight exhibits so much finesse and stubborn resistance, under such conditions, as the black-bass. Most fishes when hooked attempt to escape by tugging and pulling in one direction, or by boring toward the bottom, and if not successful in breaking away soon give up the unequal contest. But the black-bass exhibits, if not intelligence, something akin to it, in his strategical manœuvres. Sometimes his first effort is to bound into the air at once and attempt to shake out the hook, as if he knew his misfortune came from above. At other times he dashes furiously, first in one direction, then in another, pulling strongly meanwhile, then leaps into the air several times in quick succession, madly shaking himself with open jaws. I have seen him fall on a slack line, and again by using his tail as a lever and the water as a fulcrum, throw himself over a taut line, evidently with the intent to break it or tear out the hook. Another clever ruse is to wind the line around a root or rock, and still another is to embed himself in a clump of water-weeds if permitted to do so. Or, finding it useless to pull straight away, he reverses his tactics and swims rapidly toward the angler, shaking himself and working his jaws, meanwhile, as if he knew that with a slack line he would be more apt to disengage the hook.

I have never known a black-bass to sulk like the salmon by lying motionless on the bottom. He is never still unless he succeeds in reaching a bed of weeds. He is wily and adroit, but at the

same time he is brave and valiant. He seems to
employ all the known tactics of other fishes, and
to add a few of his own in his gallant fight for
freedom.

As a food-fish there is, in my estimation, but
one fresh-water fish that is better, the whitefish
of the Great Lakes. Its flesh is white, firm, and
flaky, with a fine savor, and a juicy, succulent
quality that is lacking with most other fresh-
water fishes. About the spawning period, especially in fish from weedy ponds, it is somewhat
musky or muddy in flavor, like other fishes in
similar situations; but by skinning the fish instead of scaling it much of that unpleasant feature
is removed.

BLACK-BASS TACKLE

The first consideration for the fly-fisher is suitable tools and tackle, and the most important
article of his outfit is the fly-rod. Fortunately,
at the present day, manufacturers turn out such
good work that one does not have to seek far to
obtain the best. And the best is one made of
split bamboo by a first-class maker. Such a rod
necessarily commands a good price, but it is the
cheapest in the end, for with proper care it will
last a lifetime. I have rods of this character that

I have used for thirty years that are still as good as new.   But the angler should eschew the shoddy split-bamboo rods that are sold in the department stores for a dollar.   A wooden rod at a moderate price is far better than a split-bamboo rod at double its cost.   Rods are now made much better, of better material, and considerably shorter and lighter than formerly, and withal they are much better in balance and action.

If any evidence were needed to prove and establish the superiority of the modern single-handed fly-rod over the old-style rod, it is only necessary to refer to the following facts: At the tournament of the New York State Sportsman's Association, in 1880, a cast of seventy feet won the first prize for distance; and at that time the longest on record was Seth Green's cast of eighty-six feet.   At a contest of the San Francisco Fly-casting Club held on October 11, 1902, at Stow Lake, Golden Gate Park, Mr. H. C. Golcher made the remarkable and wonderful cast of one hundred and forty feet, beating the previous record cast of one hundred and thirty-four feet, held jointly by Mr. Golcher and Mr. W. D. Mansfield of the same club.

A suitable fly-rod for black-bass fishing may

be from nine to ten and one-half feet in length, and weigh from six and one-half to eight ounces, according to the preferences of the angler and the waters to be fished.

For an all-round rod for all-round work my ideal is ten and a quarter feet long and weighing seven ounces in split bamboo and eight ounces in ash and lancewood, or ash and bethabara. It should be made in three pieces, with a stiffish back-bone, constituting the lower third of its length, and with most of the bend in the upper two-thirds. A rod constructed on this principle will afford just the requisite amount of resiliency for casting, with sufficient pliancy and elasticity for playing a fish, and embody all the power and strength needed. The reel-seat should be simply a shallow groove in the hand-piece, with reel-bands, instead of the solid metal reel-seat, which subserves no good purpose and is only added weight; moreover, it is now put on the cheapest rods as a trap to catch the unwary. All metal mountings should be German silver or brass. Nickel-plated mountings are cheap and nasty.

A light, single-action click reel of German silver or aluminum of fifty or sixty yards' capacity is the best. A plain crank handle is to be preferred to a balance handle, but in either case there should be a projecting rim or safety band, within which the handle revolves, in order to prevent fouling of the line. My own preference is for the English pattern, with a knobbed handle affixed to the edge of a revolving disk on the face of the reel. A multiplying reel with an adjustable click may be utilized instead of a click reel for fly-fishing.

The enamelled, braided silk line is the only one suitable for casting the fly, and there is no better. A level line will answer, but a tapered one is better adapted for long casts. It may taper toward one end or both ways from the centre, the latter being preferable. From twenty-five to thirty yards is sufficient for all emergencies. It should be thoroughly dried every day it is used. A convenient way is to wind it around the back of a chair.

Leaders may be from three to six feet long, accordingly as one or two flies are used in the cast. It should be composed of single, clear, round silkworm-gut fibre, tapering from the reel line to the distal end. It should not be tested to a greater weight than two pounds, as testing silkworm gut weakens it very materially. It may be stained or not, though there is no advantage in coloring it; I prefer the natural hue. There should be a loop at the small end, and one three feet above it, for attaching the snells of flies. Before using it, it must be soaked in water until soft and pliable. Extra leaders may be carried in a box between layers of damp felt, so as to be ready for emergencies. The best and smallest and most secure knot for tying the lengths of gut together in making the leader is a simple half-hitch, like tying a single knot in a piece of string. When thoroughly soaked, the two ends to be tied are lapped a couple of inches, and a single knot, or half-hitch made in them, pulling the knot tight, and cutting off the loose ends closely.

Snells should be three or four inches long, of good single gut, the shorter length for end fly. If the flies are made with a loop at the head, the snells for same should have a loop at each end for attaching to both fly and leader. If flies are made on eyed hooks, the snell should have but one loop for the leader, and a free end for tying to the eye of hook. The best knot for the purpose is made by passing the end of snell through the eye of hook, then around the shank just below the eye, and then between the shank and snell and draw tight, forming a jam knot. Where the snell is tied to the fly, it should likewise have a loop for attaching to the leader. It should also be reinforced by a piece of gut an inch long at the head of the fly to strengthen it and prevent chafing. Snells, whether separate or tied to flies, should be carried like leaders between layers of damp felt.

Most flies made for black-bass fishing are too large. The largest trout flies tied on hooks Nos. 4 to 6 are big enough. As just mentioned, they are tied directly to the snell on tapered hooks, or made with a small gut loop at the head of the fly, which is much the best way. Since the introduction of the eyed hook, or rather a revival of it, for trout flies, they are now utilized for bass flies also. As between the Pennell hook with turned-down eye and the Hall hook with turned-up eye, there is not much choice. Both patterns are based on the old Limerick hook. I prefer the Sproat or O'Shaughnessy to either, with gut loop at the head of the fly.

If the black-bass is not color-blind, he seems to have a penchant for brown, gray, black, and yellow, as flies embodying these colors seem to be more attractive to him than others. One can judge in this matter, however, only from experience. And even then the deduction of one angler is often at variance with the inference of another.

The most successful bass flies, like salmon flies, are not made in imitation of natural insects. This is true also of some of the "general" trout flies that have proved particularly pleasing to the black-bass, as the professor, grizzly king, king of the waters, Montreal, coachman, etc. True, the black, gray, red, and yellow hackles, which are supposed to be imitations of caterpillars, are very useful on nearly all waters; but their resemblance to any known larval forms is very slight.

There is a well-known rule in regard to the size and color of flies to be used at particular states and stages of the water, and in accordance with the time and character of the day. It is to use small and dark flies on bright days, with low and clear water; and larger and brighter flies on dark days with high or turbid water, and at dusk. This rule is hoary with age. It has come down to us through past centuries with the indorsement of thousands of intelligent and observant anglers, and should be respected accordingly. It is in the main reliable and trustworthy. Of course there will occur exceptions to prove the rule. And some iconoclastic anglers at this late day, in view of the exceptions, declare that it is entirely valueless as a guide; but they offer nothing better. It is true, nevertheless, and a safe rule to follow.

FLY-FISHING

To be a successful fly-fisher for black-bass the angler must know something of the habits of his quarry, or at least of its haunts and favorite places of resort. On streams these places are in the eddies of rocks or large boulders, in the deeper water above and below riffles, under shelving banks and rocks, among the submerged roots of trees on the bank, near weed patches, driftwood, and logs, and in the vicinity of gravelly bars and shoals. Except in cloudy weather the angler may rest during the noon hours, as the most favorable time is in the morning and late afternoon until dusk. If wading, the angler should fish down-stream, and when the shadows are long, should endeavor to keep the sun in front. He should move slowly and cautiously, making as little noise as possible, casting to the sides and in front over every likely spot. Casts of thirty or forty feet are usually sufficient. The flies should be allowed to float down-stream, with tremulous motions, sidewise, to imitate the struggles of a drowning insect, and then permitted to sink several inches or a foot at each cast.

Whipping the stream is sometimes quite successful where the bass does not respond to ordinary casting. This is done by casting in quick succession and repeatedly over one spot, allowing the flies merely to touch the water, until several such casts are made, when they should be permitted to sink, for a few seconds, as before. In making up the cast, two flies should be selected of different combinations of colors, as polka and professor. If necessary, changes should be made until two are selected that seem to meet the fastidious fancy of the fish.

If a taut line is maintained, the bass usually hooks himself, but the angler should strike quickly upon feeling the slightest tug, or when seeing the swirl of the fish. One cannot strike too quickly. By striking is meant a simple turning of the hand sidewise, with a perfectly tight line; this is amply sufficient to set the hook. Should the line be slack and lifeless at the moment, a more vigorous movement is required, but even then it is usually too late. When a bass is hooked, the contest should be between rod and fish, rather than between the reel and fish. It is the spring of the rod that conquers him, not the giving and taking of line. If the rod is held firmly, at an angle of forty-five degrees, with the thumb on the spool of the reel, there is no likelihood of a good rod breaking. Line should be given grudgingly, and the fish kept on the surface as much as possible. When exhausted he should be drawn over the landing-net and lifted out quickly, at the same time releasing the thumb from the reel to relieve the strain on the rod.

In fishing from the bank in deeper streams, or from a boat on small lakes, whereby the fish is better enabled to see the angler, longer casts are necessary, or the angler must screen himself from observation by trees or bushes on the bank. The boat should be kept in the deeper water and the casts made toward the shallows of bars, shoals, and weed patches. The best time for boat fishing on lakes or ponds is from near sundown until dark.

CASTING THE MINNOW

The live minnow, shiner preferred, is by far the best bait for the black-bass, as it is more easily seen, and the best way of presenting it is by casting from the reel. For this purpose a rod eight or nine feet long is much better than a shorter or longer one. After a long series of experiments with rods from six to twelve feet, I arrived at the conclusion that the one now known as the Henshall rod, eight and one-fourth feet long and from seven to eight ounces in weight, fulfils all the requirements of casting, hooking, and playing a black-bass. It is light, strong, and of beautiful proportions. In first-class split bamboo it may be as light as six and one-half ounces, but should not exceed seven and one-half ounces. In ash and lancewood, or bethabara, from seven to eight ounces is the correct weight.

A multiplying reel is indispensable. It may be two-, three-, or four-ply, but the best work and the most effective casting can only be done with the most perfect reel. It should be as light as possible, in a fifty- or sixty-yard reel. German silver is the best material, though brass is fully as serviceable, and costs less. Some very good reels are made of hard rubber and metal.

Only braided lines should be used, as twisted ones kink too much in casting. Undressed silk, of the smallest caliber, size H, is best. Braided linen is stronger, but of larger caliber, and not so suitable for good casting. Neither can effective casting be done with oil-dressed or enamelled lines.

Snelled hooks on single-gut snells, size No. 1 or No. 2, Sproat preferred and O'Shaughnessy next, are the best in any method of bait-fishing for black-bass. There are several other styles of hooks used, but, everything considered, those named are the most faultless, and for shape, strength, and general excellence cannot be excelled.

No leader is used, as the minnow must be reeled up to within a foot or two of the tip of the rod in casting. The snell of the hook is attached to the reel-line by the smallest brass box-swivel, or it may be tied directly to the line. The casts are made from right or left and underhand, not overhead as in casting the fly. Casts of 160 feet have been made in this way. The chief factor in this style of casting is the proper control of the reel by the thumb — by a gentle but constant and uniform pressure on the revolving spool, to prevent over-running of the line during the cast, and a stronger pressure to stop the reel at the end of the cast. The thumb must be thoroughly educated to this work, and, once acquired, the rest is easy, as but little muscular effort is required. The novice must begin with short casts and increase their length as he becomes more proficient in the management of the reel. Perfect casting from the reel is more difficult than casting the fly, and more artistic.

In wading a stream the casts are directed to the same likely places mentioned under the head of fly-fishing. The minnow is allowed to sink to half the depth of the water and reeled in slowly, which gives a lifelike motion to the bait when hooked through the lips. If there is no response, the next cast should be made to another spot, as a bass, if inclined to take the lure at all, will usually do so upon its first presentation.

In fly-fishing it is imperative to strike as soon as the bass seizes the fly, otherwise he ejects it at once, if not hooked by a taut line, for he is conscious of the deception as soon as the fly is taken into his mouth. With natural bait it is different. The bass first seizes the minnow crosswise or tail first, turns it in his mouth, and swallows it head first. This takes a little time. Usually he holds it in his mouth and bolts away from other fish, or rushes toward a secure hiding-place — hence the vigorous initial dash and taking of line. If stopped before being hooked, he gives several tugs in quick succession, when he should be given line slowly. The angler, with thumb on the spool of the reel, can feel every motion of the fish. When he pulls steadily and strongly and increases his speed, the hook should be driven in by striking in the opposite direction to his course, or upward. A vigorous "yank" is not needed. With the strained line a movement of the tip of the rod a foot or two is sufficient with a sharp hook.

If fishing from a boat, where the angler is more apt to be seen, it should be kept in deep water and the casts made toward the haunts of the bass in shallow water. Should the hooked bass break water on a long line, the slight straightening of the bent rod that ensues will tend to keep it taut, and there is nothing more to do. On a short line, however (the bend of the rod being maintained), he should be followed back to the water by a slight lowering of the tip, but it should again be raised as soon as he touches the water. The critical moment is when he is apparently standing on his tail, shaking himself, with wide-opened jaws. If he is given any slack line at this time, the hook is likely to be thrown out.

Lowering the tip to a leaping fish is a good

old rule when done understandingly. It has been ridiculed by some anglers who do not seem to have a clear conception of it. They claim that by lowering the tip it gives sufficient slack line to enable the fish to free himself. But if the rod is bent, as it should be, the simple lowering of the tip with a short line merely relieves it somewhat from the weight of the fish; there is no slack line, nor could there be unless the rod is lowered until it is perfectly straight, which no wide-awake angler would permit. As the fish is in the air but a second or two, the careless angler simply does nothing, which is, perhaps, the best thing that could happen for him.

Trolling is practised from a moving boat along the edges of weeds or rushes, or in the neighborhood of gravelly shoals and bars or rocky ledges. The bait may be a minnow or a very small trolling-spoon; if the latter, it should have but a single hook. The revolving spoon is itself the lure, and any addition of a bunch of feathers, a minnow, or a strip of pork-rind does not add to its efficiency in the least, and moreover savors of pot-fishing. A rod and reel should always be used, as trolling with a hand-line is very unsportsmanlike.

Still-fishing is practised from the bank or from an anchored boat. If the bait is live minnows, no float is necessary; but if crawfish, helgramites, cut-bait, or worms are employed, a very small float is useful to keep the bait off the bottom. The boat should be anchored in close proximity to the feeding-grounds of the bass, and the angler should keep as still as possible. Contrary to the popular opinion, fish hear sounds, not only those made in the water, but those in the air as well, otherwise they would not be provided with so delicate an auditory apparatus; because they do not always notice sounds made in the air is no proof that they do not hear them. The suggestions already made as to the hooking and playing and landing the bass apply to still-fishing as well. The minnow is best hooked through both lips, but if they are very small, they may be hooked just under the dorsal fin.

THE LARGE-MOUTH BLACK-BASS
(Micropterus salmoides)

The large-mouth black-bass was also first described by the French ichthyologist Lacépède, in 1802, from a drawing and description sent to him from South Carolina by M. Bosc, under the local

name of "trout-perch." Owing to the vernacular
name, he gave it the specific name of *salmoides*,
"salmon-like" or "trout-like." Thirty years before, pressed skins of the large-mouth bass had
been sent to Linnæus by Dr. Garden from Charleston, South Carolina, under the name of "fresh-
water trout," but Linnæus failed to describe or
name it. The black-bass is called "trout" to this
day in the Southern states.

The large-mouth black-bass is very similar in
appearance to the small-mouth bass. It is not
quite so trimly built, being somewhat more
"stocky" and robust. Its mouth is larger, the
angle reaching behind the eye. It has larger
scales, and those on the cheeks are not much
smaller than those on the body, while in the
small-mouth bass the cheek scales are very small
compared with its body scales. The large-mouth
is more muscular, and has a broader and more
powerful tail.

Its distribution is perhaps wider than that of
any other game-fish, its range extending from
Canada to Florida and Mexico, and, through
transplantation, from the Atlantic to the Pacific. It has also been introduced into Germany,
France, Russia, and the Netherlands, where it is

greatly esteemed both as a game-fish and food-fish.

The coloration of the large-mouth bass is often of the same hue as the small-mouth bass, though usually it is not so dark, being mostly bronze-green, fading to white on the belly. When markings are present, they tend to form longitudinal streaks of aggregated spots, and not vertical ones, as in the small-mouth.

Its habits of feeding, spawning, etc., are very similar to those of the small-mouth. It prefers stiller water, and is more at home in weedy situations, and will thrive in quiet, mossy ponds with muddy bottom where the small-mouth would eventually become extinct; on the other hand, the large-mouth can exist wherever it is possible for the small-mouth to do so. It is better able to withstand the vicissitudes of climate and temperature, and has a wonderful adaptability that enables it to become reconciled to its environment. The feeding habits of the two black-basses are much the same, though they differ as to their haunts. The large-mouth favors weedy rather than rocky places, and though its food is also much the same, the large-mouth is perhaps more partial to frogs and minnows, in the absence of crawfish, which, like the other species, it prefers.

In the Northern states it hibernates, and reaches a maximum weight of six or eight pounds, while in the Gulf states, where it is active the year round, it is taken weighing twenty pounds or more. In Florida I have taken it on the fly up to fourteen pounds, and up to twenty pounds with natural bait. In waters where it coexists with the small-mouth bass there is no difference in their excellence as food-fish. I have often eaten the large-mouth bass from the clear-water lakes of Utah and Washington, that, with the single exception of the whitefish of Lake Superior, were the best of all fresh-water fishes. And I can truly say the same of those from some of the large rivers of Florida, notably the St. Lucie, St. Sebastian, and New rivers.

It prefers to spawn on gravel or sand, but if such situations are lacking, it makes its nest on a clay or mud bottom, or on the roots of water-plants; or in ponds of very deep water without shallow shores, it will spawn on the top of masses of weeds, in order to get near enough to sunlight. In other respects its breeding habits are similar to its cousin the small-mouth, the time of incubation and the guarding of the eggs and young being about the same.

As to the much-mooted subject of the gameness of the large-mouth bass I have no hesitation in saying, from an experience of nearly forty years, covering all sections of the country, that where the two species coexist there is no difference in their game qualities. The large-mouth is fully the equal of the small-mouth where they are exposed to the same conditions. Many anglers profess to think otherwise, but their deductions are drawn from a comparison of the two species when subject to totally different environment; for it is altogether a matter of environment and not of physical structure or idiosyncrasy that influences their game qualities. A small-mouth bass in a clear, rocky stream, highly aerated as it must be, is, as a matter of course, more active than a large-mouth bass in a quiet, weedy pond.

With others the opinion is merely a matter of prejudice or hearsay, a prejudice that is, indeed, difficult to account for. It does not make the small-mouth bass a gamer fish by disparaging the large-mouth. As I have said elsewhere, if the large-mouth bass is just as game as the small-mouth, the angler is just that much better off.

As prejudice and ignorance go hand in hand, we are not surprised when we hear persons — I do not style them anglers — call the small-mouth the "true" black-bass, implying that the large-mouth is not a black-bass, but is, as they often say, the Oswego bass, which is, of course, absurd. I am glad to add, however, that the prejudice against the large-mouth bass is dying out among observant anglers, who know that a trout in a clear stream is more vigorous than one in a weedy, mucky pond.

From my own experience I am prepared to say that the large-mouth bass is more to be relied on in rising to the fly than the small-mouth, which fact should be taken into consideration when the gameness of the two species is compared. The remarks concerning fly-fishing for the small-mouth bass are also applicable to the large-mouth, as both are fished for in the same way, and with the same tackle, except that the rod may be a little heavier. For the large bass of the Gulf states the rod should be fully eight ounces in weight, and the flies a trifle larger, on hooks Nos. 2 to 6; otherwise the tackle should be the same.

Minnow-casting for the large-mouth need not differ from that described for the small-mouth bass. The tackle likewise may be the same, though for the heavy bass of Florida the rod may be eight, or even nine ounces, if preferred. Hooks may also be employed of a larger size, say Nos. 1 to 1–0, or even 2–0, as larger minnows are used for bait.

Some anglers of the Middle West have adopted a very short rod of six feet or less for casting the live frog or pork-rind overhead, in the same way as casting a fly. This is a very primitive style of bait-casting, being the same as practised by bucolic boys and Southern negroes using a sapling pole without a reel. The frog is reeled up to within a few inches of the tip and propelled like a wad of clay from a slender stick as we were wont to do as boys. The frog is projected with great accuracy, but not without a smack and splash on the water. With such a rod most of the pleasure of playing a bass to a finish is lost. Presumably the end justifies the means, but this method does not appeal to the artistic angler. If bait must be used, a small minnow, lightly cast from a suitable rod, is more in accordance with the eternal fitness of things and the practice and traditions of the gentle art. In very weedy ponds and lakes, however, where there is not open water enough

OSWEGO (LARGE-MOUTH) BASS

to play a bass, and where it must be landed as soon as possible, this rod and style of casting answer a good purpose.

Still-fishing is the same for either species of black-bass, but as it is usually done from an anchored boat on Northern lakes, where the large-mouth bass is of greater size and weight than the small-mouth bass, somewhat heavier tackle may be used than recommended for the small-mouth.

Trolling with the live or dead minnow, or a small spoon with a single hook, is a very successful method on lakes, ponds, and broad, still rivers. A greater length of line can be utilized in trolling, whereby the fish is not so apt to see the angler. More ground can also be covered than in any other style of fishing. The boat should be propelled slowly along the borders of rushes and weed patches, over shoals and gravelly banks, and near projecting points of the shore. Considerable care should be exercised to move as noiselessly as possible, avoiding splashing with the oars or paddle, or making any undue noise with the feet or otherwise in the boat, as such sounds are conveyed a long distance in so dense a medium as water. In trolling, the line may be lengthened to fifty yards, if necessary, though from twenty to thirty yards will usually be sufficient, especially when a good breeze is blowing.

Bobbing for the large-mouth bass is much in vogue in the Gulf states, but is more often practised in Florida. The conventional "bob" is formed by tying a strip of deer's tail, with or without a piece of red flannel, around a triangle of hooks, the hairs completely investing the hooks. A single hook, however, answers fully as well or better. The hook is of large size, Nos. 3–o to 5–o. The method of procedure is as follows: The boat is propelled by a single-bladed paddle, the paddler being seated in the stern. The boat is moved silently and cautiously, skirting the edges of water-lilies and bonnets, which grow thickly along the margin of the channels. The angler is seated in the bow with a very long cane rod, to which is affixed a short line of a few feet, not to exceed six. As the boat advances, the angler dances the bob as far ahead as possible. It is held a few inches or a foot above the water, into which it is "bobbed" at short intervals. Sometimes the bass leaps from the water to seize it. When hooked, the fish is landed without any ceremony and as soon as possible, keeping it meanwhile on the surface, to prevent its taking to the weeds. Bartram described bobbing as practised in Florida, for black-bass, nearly a century and a half ago.

Although bass fishing dates back to the middle of the eighteenth century, when bobbing, skittering, and still-fishing were common methods in the extreme Southern states for the large-mouth bass, and though the dawn of the nineteenth century saw bait-fishing and fly-fishing for the small-mouth bass in Kentucky, it is surprising how little was known in the Northern and Eastern states about the black-bass and bass fishing a century after Bartram described bobbing for that game-fish in the narrative of his travels. Even so late as 1871, when the *Forest and Stream* was established, very little appeared in its pages anent bass fishing. Indeed, a few years later, a discussion lasting a year or more appeared in its columns from week to week, as to whether the black-bass would rise to the fly. Previous to the publication of the writer's " Book of the Black-bass " in 1881, no work on angling gave any but the most meagre account of black-bass or bass fishing. The " American Angler's Guide," published in 1849 by John J. Brown, states that the black-bass has rows of small teeth, two dorsal fins, and a swallow-tail. In the same work the large-mouth bass of the Southern states is classified under the head of " brook trout," the author being misled apparently by its Southern name of " trout," and goes on to say that they "grow much larger than Northern trout," and that they "are fished for with the same arrangement of tackle as the striped bass or salmon." A contributor to the work, however, from Buffalo, New York, treats briefly and vaguely of still-fishing with minnows and crawfish. Brief notes also from Southern and Western anglers give fair descriptions of the appearance and habits of both species of black-bass. Frank Forester (Henry W. Herbert) knew no more of the black-bass than Mr. Brown, and acknowledges that he never caught one. That old Nestor of angling, Uncle Thad Norris, in his "American Angler's Book," 1864, gives the descriptions of Louis Agassiz and Dr. Holbrook for the black-bass, and then relates his only experience as follows, " I have taken this bass in the vicinity of St. Louis, on a moonshiny night, by skittering a light spoon over the surface of the water, while standing on the shore." Genio C. Scott in his " Fishing in American Waters," 1869, has less to say, and evidently knew less of the black-bass than any of the earlier writers. He gives just three lines concerning black-bass fishing, saying, " This fish is taken by casting the artificial fly, or by trolling with the feathered spoon, with a minnow impaled on a gang of hooks, and forming spinning tackle." Of all the angling authors prior to 1870, Robert B. Roosevelt is the only one who knew anything about black-bass or black-bass fishing, having fished for it in the St. Lawrence basin. He says, " They will take minnows, shiners, grasshoppers, frogs, worms, or almost anything else that can be called a bait." Also, " They may be captured by casting the fly as for salmon or trout, and this is by far the most sportsmanlike way, but the most destructive and usually resorted to is trolling." The only personal experience he gives of black-bass fishing, unfortunately, is by trolling with large flies. In his " Game Fish of the North," 1862, he devotes five pages to the black-bass, but apparently does not discriminate between the two species. In " Superior Fishing," 1865, he devotes two pages to the black-bass of Canada and the Great Lakes, in a general way, but gives two instances of fishing as follows, " Pedro soon hooked a splendid black-bass, and landed him after a vigorous struggle of half an hour; he weighed three pounds and three-quarters, and was thoroughly game." And again, "That evening was again devoted to the black-bass, which took both the fly and spoon greedily."

During the period covered by the authors named, from 1849 to 1869, the anglers of the South and Middle West were using light cane rods, Kentucky reels, and the smallest sea-grass lines for bait-fishing, and trout fly-rods and trout-tackle for fly-fishing, rods and tackle as light, to say the least, as those in use to-day.

In 1866 I removed to Oconomowoc, Wisconsin, where there were thirty lakes within ten miles abounding in black-bass of both species, with pike, rock-bass, crappies, perch, etc. On my home grounds was a large shallow pond fed from Fowler Lake. Becoming much interested in the black-bass, and finding but little information available in the books of that day concerning their habits, I determined to give some study to the subject. Accordingly I cut a ditch from the pond to the lake, with suitable screens, and stocked it with black-bass of both species. During their spawning period in the summer I watched them faithfully and constantly from a blind of bushes on the bank. This I did for several years, turning the adult bass into the lake when the fry were large enough to look out for themselves, and turning the fry out also in the fall.

I extended my observations of the bass during their breeding season to the many lakes near by. I found a difference of several weeks in the time of their spawning in these lakes, owing to the difference in temperature, caused by their varying depth. The appearance of the bass also differed slightly in the various lakes, so that it was possible, from a close study of their variations in color, size, and contour, to determine in what particular lake any string of bass was taken.

About the same time, from 1868 to 1870, Mr. Cyrus Mann and Mr. H. D. Dousman established their trout hatchery and ponds not far from Oconomowoc, and Colonel George Shears, of Beaver Lake, a few miles away, also began hatching trout on a smaller scale. These establishments presented an opportunity to study the artificial propagation of brook-trout, and I soon became familiar with the *modus operandi*. This was before the institution of the United States Fish Commission, though the state of Wisconsin already had an able and efficient Fish Commission, Mr. H. D. Dousman being one of the commissioners. Colonel Shears also experimented with black-bass culture, and between us we reared many thousands to the age of three months, before turning them out. Near my pond was a shallow, marshy cove to which the pike resorted in early spring to spawn, giving me an opportunity to study their breeding habits, also. There being so many lakes and ponds in the vicinity, and their being so well supplied with fishes of various kinds, my opportunities for the observation of fish life were as great as fortunate.

The differences of opinion among anglers, of all men, pertaining to the practice of their art, has become axiomatic. Some will differ even to the estimation of a hair in the legs of an artificial fly, while it is averred others will go so far as to "divide a hair 'twixt south and southwest side," as Butler has it. But, seriously, there are several moot points which I have endeavored to discuss in the following piscatorial polemic.

Two friends went fishing. Both were famous black-bass anglers, with the enthusiasm born of a genuine love and an inherent appreciation of the gentle art so common among Kentucky gentlemen. One was a fly-fisher, the other a bait-fisher. Each was a devotee to his especial mode of angling, though generously tolerant of the other's method. They had fished together for years when the dogwood and redbud blossomed in the spring, and when the autumnal tints clothed the hillsides with scarlet and gold.

They differed in their methods of fishing from choice, or from some peculiar, personal idiosyncrasy, for each was an adept with both bait and fly. But this difference in their piscatorial practices, like the diversity of nature, produced perfect harmony instead of discord. Each extolled the advantages and sportsmanship of his own method, but always in a brotherly and kindly manner; never dictatorial or opinionated in argument, or vainglorious and boastful as to his skill, for both were possessed of the generous impulses of gentlemen and the kindly influences of the gentle art. Moreover, they were innately conscious of a common aim, and differed only as to the ways and means of best attaining that end, which, while dissimilar, were not inharmonious.

And so the Silver Doctor and the Golden Shiner, as they dubbed each other, went trudging along the bank of the merry stream together.

The Doctor, lightly equipped with only rod, fly-book, and creel, sometimes relieved the Shiner by toting his minnow bucket or minnow net. They were fishing a rocky, gently flowing river, characteristic of the Blue Grass section.

They stopped at a broad, lakelike expansion of the stream, caused by a mill-dam, and, in a quiet cove at the entrance of a clear brook, Golden Shiner proceeded to fill his minnow bucket with lively minnows, using for the purpose an umbrella-like folding net. This he attached to a long, stout pole, and, after baiting it with crushed biscuit, lowered it into the water. In a short time he had all the bait necessary — chubs, shiners, and steelbacks.

" The golden shiner is the best of all," said he, " especially for roily or milky water; but the chub and steelback are stronger and livelier on the hook, and for very clear water are good enough."

They then proceeded below the mill-dam, where there was a strong riffle, with likely-looking pools and eddies.

" The proper way to hook a minnow is through the lips," continued Golden Shiner, " especially for casting. One can give a more natural motion to the minnow on drawing it through the water. For still-fishing, hooking through the tail or under the back fin will answer; but even then I prefer my method, unless the minnow is less than two inches in length." And he made a long cast toward the eddy of a large boulder.

"For the same reason," acquiesced Silver Doctor, "artificial flies are tied with the head next the snell,"—industriously casting to right and left over the riffle.

"But some flies are tied with the tail next to the snell," ventured Shiner.

"That is true, but it is unnatural. I never saw an insect swim tail first up-stream. Nature is the best teacher, and one should endeavor to follow her lead." Just then the Doctor snapped off his point fly. Upon examination he found that the snell was dry and brittle next to the head of the fly, though he had previously soaked it well in a glass of water. He discovered that a drop of shellac varnish had encroached beyond the head of the fly for perhaps the sixteenth of an inch on the snell. This portion, being waterproof, remained dry and brittle — a very common fault with cheap flies.

"This fly," said the Doctor, "was given to me for trial by Judge Hackle. He tied it himself.

The broken end of the snell still shows a portion of shellac coating."

" I never thought of that before," remarked Shiner. " No doubt many flies are cracked off from the same cause."

" Without a doubt, as you say. I know a lady," continued the Doctor, " who, as Walton says, ' has a fine hand,' and who superintends an extensive artificial fly establishment — and who has written the best book ever published on the subject of artificial flies — who personally inspects every fly turned out by her tyers. And, moreover, she varnishes the head of every fly herself, in order that not the least particle of shellac may touch the snell. Such careful supervision and honest work, to quote Walton again, ' like virtue, bring their own reward,' " and the Doctor resumed his casting with another fly.

" Well, Doctor, I sympathize with you; but my snells are clear-quill and no varnish. I may throw off a minnow once in a while by a very long cast, but it is soon replaced, and costs nothing. And, speaking of casting, I observed that you made half a dozen casts to reach yonder rock but sixty feet away, while I placed my minnow, by a single cast, a hundred feet in the other direction. Moreover, I reel my line toward me through undisturbed water, while you whipped the entire distance by several preliminary casts."

"That is necessarily true," answered the Doctor; "but while you must recover all of your line for a new cast, I can cast repeatedly with the extreme length of my line in any direction; so I think honors are easy on the question of casting."

"But," persisted Shiner, "with my quadruple multiplying reel, it is only a matter of a few seconds to prepare for a new cast. Then again, I have better control of a hooked fish, and can give and take line much faster than you with your single-action click reel."

"While I grant your reel has a great advantage in speed, I hold that a single-action click reel is all-sufficient to play and land a hooked fish. Your reel is intended particularly to make long initial casts, and it is admirably adapted for that especial purpose; but in playing a bass it has no advantage over a click reel; in fact, I prefer the latter for that purpose. Really, the engine of destruction to the hooked fish is the rod. Its constant strain and yielding resistance, even without a reel of any kind, will soon place him *hors de combat*."

Golden Shiner was not slow to perceive the

force of the Doctor's arguments and held his peace. In the meantime both anglers had suc- ceeded in killing some half-dozen bass, the larg- est ones falling to the rod of the bait fisher, as is usually the case. The sun was now climbing toward the zenith, and the Doctor's flies seemed to have lost their attractiveness for the wary bass, while the Shiner, seeking deeper water, was still successful in his efforts. The day, however, was becoming uncomfortably warm.

"You will admit, Doctor, that you must cast your flies early in the day or late in the afternoon to insure much success, while I can fish during the middle of the day in deeper water and still have a measure of reward, which I consider quite an advantage of bait over fly."

"Granted. Fish rise to the fly only in com- paratively shallow water, and are found in such situations in bright weather only early and late in the day. But I prefer to fish at just those times. I do not care to fish during the middle portion of the day in summer." And the Doctor proceeded to reel in his final cast.

Just then his friend hooked the largest fish of the morning's outing. It was an unusually gamy bass, and leaped several times in rapid succession from the water, shaking itself violently each time. But the Shiner was equal to " his tricks and his manners," and soon had him in the landing-net.

" Doctor, why does a hooked bass break water and shake his head? Is it through fear or rage? "

" It is to rid his jaws of the hook. He can neither pick his teeth with a fin, nor remove a foreign substance from his mouth with his tail. His mouth is his prehensile organ. A horse, cow, dog, or fowl will shake the head violently to rid its mouth of an offending object. But a fish, having no neck to speak of, can only shake his head by shaking his body, and that only in a lateral direction. As a bass cannot shake himself energetically enough beneath the water to dislodge the hook, owing to the resistance of the denser medium, he naturally leaps into the air for that purpose; and he always does so with widely extended jaws, as you have seen time and again this morning. He probably also fortifies himself at the same time by taking in oxygen from the air. He does so, at all events, willy-nilly."

" How high can a black-bass leap from the water, do you think? "

" A foot or two at most, as you well know,"

replied the Doctor. " In rocky streams like this, one has a good gauge for measuring the leap. I never saw a bass leap as high as yonder boulder, which is about three feet above the water; and as you have taken several fish in its eddy, you might have proved it by your own observation, as I did myself."

" I distinctly remember, now," affirmed Shiner, "that my last catch — the big fellow — leaped several times very near that same rock, and he did not go half as high."

The two friends then repaired to a cool spring beneath a spreading beech, to enjoy a luncheon and a quiet pipe, — well satisfied with their morning's sport, — and to continue the *argumentum ad hominem* anent fly and bait, with the usual result that

> " A man convinced against his will,
> Is of the same opinion still."

THE ROCK-BASS

(*Ambloplites rupestris*)

In the same family with the black-bass are a number of other sunfishes that will next be considered, merely as a matter of sequence, and not on account of their importance as game-fishes.

The rock-bass was first described by the French naturalist, Rafinesque, in 1817, while travelling in America. His specimens were from New York and Vermont, which he named *rupestris*, "living among rocks." In the Northern states it is generally known as the rock-bass, but in Kentucky and other states of the Middle West it is called red-eye, goggle-eye, etc.

Its original habitat was from Canada and Lake Champlain southward along the Mississippi Valley to Louisiana and Texas, but its range has been extended to many other states east and west by transplantation.

In its general appearance it resembles somewhat the black-bass, but it is a deeper fish and is more compressed. Its dorsal and anal fins are comparatively larger and stronger. It has a large eye and a capacious mouth well filled with small teeth, some on the roof of the mouth being rather sharp.

The color is of various shades of olive-green, with brassy or coppery reflection, more or less mottled with black, forming broken and indistinct lines along the sides. The iris of the eye is scarlet, hence "red-eye"; there is a black spot on the angle of the gill-cover and dark mottlings on

the soft dorsal, anal, and caudal fins.   It prefers
clear streams and lakes, and congregates in small
schools about rocky situations, gravelly bars, about
mill-dams, and in the vicinity of weed patches
in ponds.   It spawns in the spring and early summer, making and guarding its nest like the black-
bass, and feeds on crawfish, small minnows, and
insect larvæ.   In size it usually runs from a half-
pound to a pound in streams, though reaching
two pounds or more in lakes.   It is a good pan-
fish for the table, and is well thought of in the
Mississippi Valley, though held in lighter esteem
in the St. Lawrence basin, where it coexists with
larger and better fishes.

The rock-bass is an attractive-looking fish, and
for its size is very pugnacious.   It will take the
artificial fly, or natural or artificial bait.   It bites
freely at small minnows, grubs, grasshoppers, cut-
bait, or angle-worms.   It is capable of affording
considerable sport with light tackle, owing to its
large and strong fins, and its habit of curling its
sides in opposition to the strain of the rod.

With a light fly-rod of four or five ounces, and
corresponding tackle, and trout flies on hooks
Nos. 5 to 7, the rock-bass is not a mean adver-
sary.   It rises to the various hackles, and to such

flies as coachman, brown drake, gray drake, and stone fly, especially toward evening. The flies must be allowed to sink with every cast after fluttering them awhile on the surface. For bait-fishing a trout bait-rod of the weight just mentioned, with a reel of small caliber and the smallest braided silk line, will be about right. Sproat hooks Nos. 3 to 4 on light gut snells tied with red silk are the best. Live minnows about two inches long, carefully hooked through the lips, are to be lightly cast and allowed to sink nearly to the bottom and slowly reeled in again. Or if a float is used, the minnow may be hooked just under the dorsal fin. A small float is necessary when white grubs, crawfish, cut-bait, or worms are used as bait. On lakes it is readily taken by trolling with a very small spoon, about the size of a nickel, with a single Sproat or O'Shaughnessy hook No. 1 attached.

A rod nine or ten feet long cut from the small end of a native cane pole, weighing but a few ounces, with a line of sea-grass or raw silk about the length of the rod, will answer very well for bait-fishing. This is the tackle mostly used by boys in the Middle West, and it might be profitably employed by boys of larger growth.

A dozen "red-eyes," gleaming with green and gold, on the string of the boy angler, is something to be proud of. He gazes with fond admiration on the wide-open crimson eyes, which to him seem more precious than rubies. He admires the bristling fins, the gracefully sloping sides, the gaping mouth and forked tail, with boyish enthusiasm and appreciation. Although hot and tired, and with many a scratch and bruise on hands and feet, such trifles are lighter than air, and do not admit of a moment's consideration. Seated on a rock at the margin of the stream, with the string of fish in the water, he feasts his eyes on the finny beauties with the conscious pride of well-earned success and the happy culmination of his outing. In imagination the battles are all fought over and over again. He knows just where and under what condition and circumstance each fish was caught, as, with bare toes, he separates and indicates the individual on the string. That largest one was hooked under the dam beside the big rock. The next in size was taken among the roots of the old sycamore at the bend of the creek. Another and still another from the deep hole under the rocky cliff. Oh, the joyous days of youth and going a-fishing in the glad springtime of life! And then, having laved his swollen feet in the cooling stream, he washes the blood and scales from his hands, scrapes the mud and slime from his well-worn clothes, shoulders his lánce of elm, and starts for home, bearing his trophies with as proud a mien as a warrior of old returning with the spoils of war.

THE SACRAMENTO PERCH
(*Archoplites interruptus*)

The Sacramento perch is closely allied in structure to the rock-bass, and is the only perchlike fish in fresh water west of the Rocky Mountains. It was collected by the Pacific Railroad Survey and described and named *interruptus* by Girard, in 1854, owing to the interrupted character of the vertical markings. It inhabits the Sacramento and Joaquin rivers in California, and is much esteemed as a food-fish, but unfortunately it is being rapidly exterminated by the carp and cat-fish that are said to infest its spawning grounds. In its conformation it is almost identical with the rock-bass, but differs in having more teeth on the tongue and more gill-rakers. In coloration, however, it differs very much, being sometimes uniformly blackish or brassy, but usually the black coloration is disposed in several vertical bars or markings of an irregular shape. It has a black spot on the angle of the gill-cover.

I have had no experience in angling for the Sacramento perch, which is said to be taken with the hook in large quantities for the market. I have no doubt but the tackle recommended for the rock-bass would be just as effective for this fish, with similar baits.

THE WARMOUTH PERCH

(*Chænobryttus gulosus*)

The warmouth perch, also known as the black sunfish in the North, was first described by the French naturalists, Cuvier and Valenciennes, in 1829, from specimens from Lake Pontchartrain, Louisiana. They named it *gulosus*, "large-mouthed," owing to its big mouth. There is a slight variation between the Northern and Southern forms. It abounds in all coastwise streams from North Carolina to Florida and Texas, and sparingly in Lake Michigan and the upper Mississippi Valley. In its general shape and appearance it is not unlike the rock-bass, though in the radial formula of its fins and in its large mouth it approaches nearer the black-bass than any other species of the family. It has a large head and deep body, almost as deep as long, and is nearly symmetrical in outline. Its teeth are in brushlike bands on the jaws, with patches on the tongue. The Southern form has one or two less soft rays in the dorsal and anal fins.

It is dark olive on the back, lighter on the sides, with blotches of blue and coppery red, and the belly brassy or yellowish. Iris red, ear-flap black, bordered with pale red, with three dusky red bars radiating from the eye across the cheeks. Fins mottled with a darker color, and a black blotch on the last rays of the soft portion of the dorsal fin.

It is not so gregarious as the rock-bass, but otherwise is similar in its habits, though not so partial to rocky situations, rather loving deep pools and quiet water. It feeds on minnows, tadpoles, frogs, insects, and their larvæ. It spawns in the spring. It is a good pan-fish, and grows to eight or ten inches in length and a weight of nearly a pound. For its size, it is the gamest member of the family except the black-bass, and is more like that fish than the others. It is a favorite game-fish in the South, rising well to the fly, and is a free biter at natural bait.

In angling for the warmouth, the same rods and tackle mentioned under the head of rock-bass are well suited.   In the Southern states a light native cane rod, ten or twelve feet long, and a line of the smallest caliber, sea-grass or twisted silk, is the favorite style of tackle, with hooks Nos. 2 to 3 tied on light gut, and a quill float and split-shot sinker.   The usual bait is the black cricket, or the catalpa worm or caterpillar. The white grub found in decayed stumps, and other larvæ, crawfish and small minnows, are all useful.   Of these the minnow is the best.   On streams a small float is necessary to keep the bait from the roots of overhanging trees.   In the stillness of Southern streams, under the moss-draped trees, I have idled away many a dreamy hour in the pleasure of fishing for the warmouth, but at the same time fully alive to the weird sur-roundings.   Occasionally the splashing of a hooked fish on the surface entices an alligator from his lair in expectation of a fishy morsel. The echoes are awakened time and again by the pumping of the bittern, the hoarse cry of the crane, or the hooting of an owl in the dark re-cesses of the cypress swamp.   The solitudes of those waters are very fascinating to the lone fisher. The novelty of the situation appeals very strongly to the angler-naturalist whose experiences have been on the clear, sparkling, tumbling streams of the North. There Nature is ever bright and joyous; here she is quiet and sombre and subdued. But the fishes know no north or south or east or west, — always the same creatures of interest and beauty, and ever responding to the wiles of the angler.

I was once fishing on St. Francis River, in Arkansas, where the warmouths were both large and gamy. One day I went through the woods and cane-brakes to the banks of Mud Lake, situated in the midst of a cypress swamp. The lake was much smaller than it had been formerly, as was apparent from the wide margins of the shores, which were of considerable extent between the timber and the water. On this margin was a group of four cypress trees that in size exceeded any that I had ever seen, and I think worthy of mention. They were from twenty to twenty-five feet in diameter, or sixty to sixty-five feet in circumference, three feet above the ground. They were buttressed like the wall of a mediæval stronghold. In comparing notes with many naturalists and travellers, they have de-

clared the size of those cypress trees to be both
unique and wonderful.

THE BLUE SUNFISH

(*Lepomis pallidus*)

The blue sunfish was first described by Dr.
Mitchill from the waters of New York in 1815.
He named it *pallidus*, meaning "pale," as it was
more sober in hue than the other brilliantly
colored sunfishes. It is the largest of the sunfishes, so-called, as the black-bass, warmouth,
and crappies are not popularly regarded as
"sunfishes."

The blue sunfish has a wider distribution than
any other member of its family except the black-
bass. Its range extends from the Great Lakes
through the Mississippi Valley to Texas, and
along the South Atlantic states to Florida. In
the Middle West it is known as blue gill and in
the South as blue bream and copper-nosed bream.
It has a medium-sized head and very deep body,
its depth varying from one-half its length to almost
as deep as long, in which case, barring head and
tail, it is almost round in outline. It is much
compressed. The ear-flap is quite black, without
the pale or red border usual in the other sunfishes.

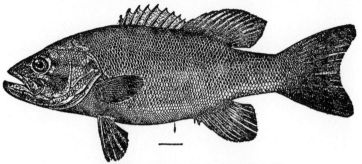

THE SMALL–MOUTH BLACK–BASS
Micropterus dolomieu

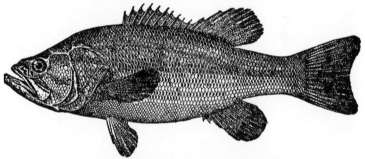

THE LARGE–MOUTH BLACK–BASS
Micropterus salmoides

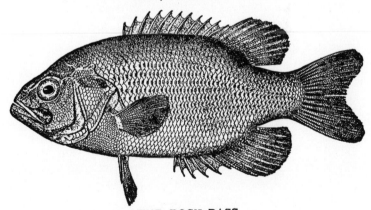

THE ROCK–BASS
Ambloplites rupestris

As might be inferred from its extensive range, its coloration varies greatly. In large and old examples it is sometimes of a uniform slaty hue with purplish reflections. In others it is olive-green or bluish green, darker above, with the breast and belly coppery red. Young specimens are more brilliantly colored, with silvery reflections and various chainlike markings. It thrives alike in stream, pond, or lake, adapting itself to almost any environment. It feeds on insects and their larvæ, very small minnows, and other small aquatic organisms. It spawns in the spring and early summer, and its manner of nesting and guarding its young is similar to that of the other members of the family. It grows to six or eight inches in length usually, but often to a foot, especially in large waters. It is quite a favorite game-fish in most localities, and with such tackle as recommended for the rock-bass it gives considerable sport, especially in localities that are lacking in larger and better game-fishes. It rises well to the fly, and will take any of the baits recommended for the other sun-fishes.

In those states of the Middle West, where the brook-trout does not exist, the "blue gill" is greatly esteemed and much sought after, as it furnishes the opportunity to employ light trout tackle in its capture, and with such gear it affords fine sport. I have taken the blue sunfish in all waters from Wisconsin to Florida. In the latter state many years ago I fished a fresh-water lake on Point Pinellas, near St. Petersburg, Florida, though there were but two houses there at that time. I was using a very light rod, and the fish were as large and round as a breakfast plate, and moreover the gamest and most beautiful in coloration of any blue gill I had ever met. The characteristic blue was replaced by a deep, intense, and brilliant purple, shot with silvery and golden reflections. While playing one on the surface, an osprey sat on a dead pine watching with apparent concern and eagerness. The fish made a stubborn resistance, with much splashing. Then a strange thing happened. The fish-hawk swooped down and seized the fish and attempted to fly away with it. Perhaps the hook became fast to his claw, but at any rate he circled around and around the pond, tethered to my line. It was the first, last, and only time that I did the aerial act of playing a bird on the wing. After a few seconds of this exciting and novel sport the osprey broke away, carrying both fish and hook.

THE LONG-EARED SUNFISH

(*Lepomis megalotis*)

This species was first described by Rafinesque in 1820 from streams in Kentucky. He named it *megalotis*, meaning " large ear," owing to its large and conspicuous ear-flap. It is one of the handsomest sunfishes in its brilliant coloration, and a great favorite with the youthful Waltonians of the Mississippi Valley. It inhabits small streams in Michigan and the Mississippi Valley, and the Atlantic slope from South Carolina to Florida and Mexico, and is very abundant in Kentucky, where it is sometimes called " tobacco-box," owing to its "lid-like " opercle.

Its body is short and deep, with quite a hump or arch anteriorly, making the profile of the face quite steep in old specimens. The ear-flap is very long and wide, blackish in color, with a border usually of pale bluish or a reddish hue; its back is blue, with chestnut or orange belly; sides with red spots and bluish lines; iris of eye red; lips blue. The soft rays of the dorsal fin are blue, with orange between. Ventral and

anal fins are dusky blue. The top of the head
and nape is dark. The coloration is very brilliant
and varies in different localities. Its habits of
feeding and spawning are similar to those of
the blue sunfish, though it usually inhabits smaller
streams; it grows to a length of from six to eight
inches, and is regarded as a good pan-fish by
many.

It is an eager biter at angle-worms, which is
the bait *par excellence* of juvenile anglers, who
greatly enjoy fishing for "sunnies." The only
tackle needed is a light cane rod very fine line,
and small hooks, Nos. 6 or 8, split-shot sinker,
and, of course, a float, for no boy would care
to fish without a "bob" or "cork." Half of the
pleasure of the young angler is in watching
the float.

But the fly-fisher may also obtain sport to his
liking with a rod of a few ounces' weight and
midge flies on No. 10 hooks, for at the close of
the day the long-eared sunfish rises well. In
the absence of better fishing this is not to be
despised.

I once saw a boy fishing for "tobacco-boxes"
from a rock beneath a mill-dam on a Kentucky
stream. He hooked one of good size, and in

his eagerness to secure it tumbled into the pool, which was quite deep, much over his head. After some little delay we got him out, almost drowned, and in a very limp and exhausted condition. When finally he was restored and capable of speech he exclaimed, " I saved my tobacco-box, anyhow!" During all the struggle he held on to his rod, and still clutched it when "landed." Whether he did so from the desperation with which drowning men are said to cling to straws, or from an inherent sporting instinct, deponent sayeth not. A clergyman, who knew nothing of fish, but who was attracted to the scene, said to the dripping boy, " My lad, let this be a solemn warning to you : throw away the tobacco-box you have saved and give up chewing; it may drown you yet."

THE RED-BREAST SUNFISH

(*Lepomis auritus*)

This handsome sunfish was the first of its family to receive the recognition of a naturalist, being described by Linnæus in 1758. He named it *auritus*, or " eared," from its conspicuous ear-flap. His specimen was credited to Philadelphia, and was, presumably, from some neighboring water. It is a fish of the Atlantic slope, with a range extending from Maine to Florida, and is also found in Louisiana. It is very abundant in the South Atlantic states.

Its form is similar to the long-eared sunfish, but with a more prominent snout and a depression in front of the eye. Its ear-flap is as long but not so broad; its color olive or bluish above; sides bluish with reddish spots; breast and belly orange or red; blue stripes on the front of the head. The southern form has a dusky blotch on the last rays of the dorsal fin, which is lacking in those of northern waters.

Its habits are similar to those of the other sunfishes proper, as to food, spawning, etc. It grows to a length of from eight to ten inches. It is a favorite food- and game-fish in the South, where it is known as red-breast bream and red-bellied perch. The same remarks as to angling mentioned under the head of warmouth perch will apply to this fish as well.

My angling career really began with the capture of "silversides" with a paste of bread crumbs, but was inaugurated with taking this "sunny" and the "punkin-seed" on the artificial fly. An old English gamekeeper, in the employ of our family as gardener and hostler, taught me to tie a fly and cast it with a willow wand when but five years of age. At the feet of that Gamaliel in corduroy I imbibed a love of angling that has constantly grown with the lapse of years. But increased knowledge of fishes and a wider experience in angling have not lessened my affection for my first love—the "sunny." This acknowledgment is due one of the humblest and least important, but also one of the prettiest species of the finny tribe.

THE COMMON SUNFISH

(*Eupomotis gibbosus*)

This is the pumpkin-seed or "sunny" of fragrant memory. It is enshrined in the heart of many an American angler as his first love, when with pin hook, thread line, and willow wand he essayed its capture in the nearest brook or millpond.

Looking backward over an angling career of half a century, the gamesome "sunny" with its coat of many colors shines out as a bright particular star among those of greater magnitude. It is here set down, then, mainly as a matter of sentiment and to keep its memory green.

The little "sunny" was christened by the greatest naturalist that ever lived, Linnæus, who in 1758 named it "*gibbosus*," owing to the gibbous outline of its little body.   His specimens were from South Carolina.

It inhabits the Great Lake region, and the Atlantic seaboard from Maine to Florida, and the northern portion of the Mississippi Valley. In outline it is not unlike a pumpkin-seed, hence one of its popular names.   This is well expressed in its specific name *gibbosus*.   It has quite a small mouth, but large eye.   In coloration it rivals the gayly-tinted fishes of the coral reefs in tropical seas.   The predominating colors are yellow and blue, being bluish on the back, paling on the sides to a lighter shade, with yellow blotches and coppery reflections, and belly bright orange-yellow; the cheeks are yellow with blue streaks; rays of dorsal fin blue, the connecting membrane yellow; ear-flap black, ending in a scarlet border; lips blue; iris of eye scarlet.

Its habits of spawning, nest-making, and care of eggs and fry are similar to those of the other sun-fishes mentioned.   It is partial to clear water, with sandy or gravelly bottom, in the vicinity of weed patches.   It feeds on insects and their larvæ and minute crustaceans, and is especially fond of the eggs and fry of other species. It grows to a size of eight inches, though usually from three to six inches.

Like all the sunfishes, it is an eager biter, and with very light tackle much real pleasure can be enjoyed by the angler who is not too particular as to his preferences. It rises readily to small dark flies, as the several hackles, black gnat, etc., on hooks Nos. 10 to 12. For bait-fishing nothing is quite so good as earthworms on hooks Nos. 8 to 10.

There are quite a number of other sunfishes belonging to this family, but those named are the most important. In the Southern states, where the sunfishes are known generically as "bream" or "brim" and "perch," they are more appreciated than in the Northern states, where the brook-trout is the favorite among the smaller species. If fished for with very light and suitable tackle, there is a great measure of enjoyment to be derived from bream-fishing, north or south. Certainly for beauty of coloration they are not excelled, and as pan-fish they are preferred by many to the dainty brook-trout.

There is a certain fascination in fishing with

a float, or "cork," or "bob," as the boys have it.
And among us "old boys" there is a certain
undefined feeling, it may be a reminiscent affection, connected with the float, much the same as
that with which we regard the powder-flask and
shot-pouch of the days of yore.   And I am not
sure but that the old things and old ways were
best, or at least more enjoyable.   One can heartily
agree with Alonzo of Aragon in his preferences
for old wood to burn, old wine to drink, old
friends to trust, and old authors to read.

What old angler does not remember the eagerness and expectancy with which he watched the
"cork" in days gone by?   How well he knew and
understood every motion of it, responsive to the
nibbling "sunny": first a gentle spinning, then
a preliminary bobble, then a premonitory start
away an inch or two, and then — O joy! — its
swift and sudden disappearance beneath the surface.   The lapse of time cannot wither nor
modern custom stale the pleasures of youthful
fishing.   To be sure, it was not all piscatorial
cakes and ale; there were a few thorns with the
roses; there were the bruised fingers and toes,
the wet and torn clothes, and the impending
and dreaded "dressing down" when home was

reached; but these disagreeable concomitants were soon forgotten, and are now scarcely remembered, while the pleasures are laid up in the lavender of sweet recollection.

The old-time zest of fishing with a float can still be gratified; we can renew our youth by fishing for "sunnies" in the old-fashioned way. In the wooded streams of the Southern states the float is a *sine qua non* for bream-fishing, owing to the many tangled roots of trees on the banks, and the mosses, grasses, and other aquatic plants that grow so luxuriantly in the sluggish waters. Then here's to the float and the sunny and the bream!

THE CALICO-BASS

(*Pomoxis sparoides*)

The calico-bass was first described by Lacépède from specimens sent to France from South Carolina. He named it *sparoides* from a fancied resemblance, either in its scales or compressed body, to those features in fishes belonging to the family *Sparidæ*.

Owing to its wide distribution it has received many names, more or less descriptive. In the Northern states it is variously called crappie, croppie, strawberry-bass, grass-bass, bank lick bass, silver-bass, big-fin bass, Lake Erie bass, razor back, bitter-head, lamplighter, etc., while in the Southern states it is known as speckled perch, goggle-eyed perch, chincapin perch, bridge perch, etc.

As the calico-bass and the next fish to be described, the crappie, belong to the same genus of the sunfish family, and resemble each other very much, the vernacular nomenclature is much confused, and in some instances is interchangeable. Some years ago I proposed to call them northern and southern crappie; but as the name calico-bass has obtained considerable currency, it is best to adopt that name for the northern species, leaving the name crappie for the southern form.

The calico-bass is found in the Great Lake region and the upper Mississippi Valley, and along the Atlantic slope from New Jersey to Florida and Texas. Its range has been considerably extended by transplantation, even to France, where it thrives well as a pond fish. It is a handsome fish, resembling in its general features and shape the sunfishes, but with a thinner body and larger fins. It has a long head and a large mouth, with thin lips and projecting lower jaw. The eye is large with a dark, bluish iris. Its fins are large and strong. It grows usually to eight or ten inches in length, weighing from half a pound to a pound, but occasionally reaches a foot in length and two or three pounds in weight. Its color is bright olive-green, with silvery reflections, darker on the back, and paling to the belly. In some localities it is of a much darker and purplish hue with brassy lustre. It is profusely covered with dark spots or blotches, as large as the finger-tips or "chincapins." The fins are mottled with pale spots on a darker or olive ground. It is gregarious, being usually found in schools, and prefers clear water. It is especially adapted to pond culture, and spawns in spring or early summer, according to locality; it prepares its nest in sand, gravel, or on a flat rock in the same way as the sunfishes. Its food is the same, also, though it is more partial to young fish. It is an excellent pan-fish but does not excel as a game-fish, for though a very free biter, it does not offer much resistance when hooked. However, with very light tackle it affords considerable sport, as it does not cease biting, usually, until most of the school are taken.

The usual method of angling for this fish is

from an anchored boat on ponds or small lakes, or from the bank. At times it rises pretty well to the fly, and trolling with a very small spoon is also successful on lakes. The lightest rods and tackle should be employed, with hooks Nos. 3 to 5 on gut snells. A small quill float is useful in very weedy ponds with mossy bottom. The best bait is a small minnow, though grasshoppers, crickets, crawfish, cut-bait, or worms are all greedily taken. Fly-fishing is more successful during the late afternoon hours until dusk. The flies should be trout patterns of coachman, gray drake, black gnat, Henshall, or any of the hackles on hooks Nos. 4 to 5.

I first became acquainted with the calico-bass during my residence in Wisconsin, many years ago. In the vicinity of Oconomowoc it was known as the silver-bass, though summer visitors from St. Louis, confusing it with the kindred species, the crappie, called it "croppie," as the real crappie is known at Murdoch Lake near that city. Owing to its greedy, free-biting habits it was a prime favorite with youthful anglers and the fair sex; for once a school was located, the contest was free, fast, and furious until, perhaps, the entire school was captured. It was frequently taken by black-bass fishers when casting the minnow or trolling, much to their disgust. Of course it is always the unexpected that happens, in fishing as in other affairs of life, and the angler who was casting a fine minnow for a black-bass, viewed with disdain if not anger the unlucky "pickerel," rock-bass, perch, or calico bass that appropriated — or, as the English angler has it, "hypothecated" — the said choice shiner.

I was once fishing with General Phil Sheridan and General Anson Stager for black-bass on a lake near Oconomowoc. When the great telegrapher, after a beautiful cast near a bed of rushes, hooked a calico-bass, and was anathematizing the "measly silver-bass" with all the dots and dashes of the Morse alphabet, Sheridan quietly remarked, "Oh, let up, Stager, it is one of the fortunes of war; better luck next time!" Stager smiled, gently unhooked the offending fish, and returned it to the water, saying, "Goodby, croppie, my regards to the rest of the family; but don't monkey with my minnow again."

When cruising on the St. Johns, or camping on some of the fresh-water lakes of Florida, I have greatly enjoyed both the fishing with light tackle and the eating of this fine pan-fish. It is there known as the perch, silver perch, or speckled perch. It may not be out of place to say that the generic term "bass" is connected only with salt-water fishes in the Southern states. Fishes that are known in the Northern states as bass of some kind become, generically, "perch" in the South; and the black-bass becomes a "trout" or jumping-perch. If bait-fishing, one is never at a loss for bait on the lakes of Florida. The black-bass and calico-bass lie in open water, adjacent to the patches of lily-pads or bonnets. Among the latter frequent the minnows and small fry. To catch your minnow the bait is also handy. In the stems of the lilies and bonnets there lies concealed a small worm, which is readily seen by splitting the stems. With the worm first catch your minnow, which is transferred to your bass hook, which is next cast into clear, deeper water, to be taken by a black-bass or "speckled perch." What a simple and admirable arrangement for the lazy fisherman!

My old friend, Dr. Theodatus Garlick, who with Dr. H. A. Ackley were the fathers of fish-culture in America, having succeeded in hatching brook-trout as early as 1853, relates the following instance of the remarkable tenacity of

life in the calico-bass: "A specimen from which
a drawing was made, was wrapped in a piece of
paper when taken from the water, and carried in
my coat pocket for over four hours, and when
placed in a bucket of water soon revived, and
seems at the present time to enjoy excellent
health. In warm weather, however, it would not,
in all probability, survive so severe a test of its
vital powers." I imagine that this circumstance
happened in winter, and that the fish became
frozen before or after being placed in his pocket;
otherwise I doubt if the fish could have survived
so long, unless the piece of paper was very large
and very wet. I know of many instances occur-
ring with myself and others where freshly caught
fish have been revived after being frozen for
several hours.

THE CRAPPIE

(Pomoxis annularis)

The crappie was first described by Rafinesque
in 1818 from specimens collected at the Falls of
the Ohio, near Louisville, Kentucky. He named
it *annularis*, "having rings," as it was said to
have "a golden ring at the base of the tail,"
but I have never seen it; it does have a gold

ring, however, around the iris of the eye, and this
was probably the occasion of the name.

Like the calico-bass, the crappie has received
a great many local names. In the northern
region of its range it is variously known as
white croppie, crappie, barfish, bachelor, etc., and
in Kentucky as newlight, Campbellite, and tin-
mouth, while farther south it is called silver perch,
speckled perch, goggle-eye, sac-a-lait, shad, etc.
It inhabits the Ohio and Mississippi river basins
from Kansas to Louisiana and Texas, and is
more abundant in Kentucky and other Southern
states than farther north. Its range, however,
has been extended by transplantation to many
states. In general features it resembles the
calico-bass very much, though to the trained eye
the differences are very apparent. It is not quite
so deep nor so robust as the calico-bass. The
mouth is somewhat larger, and the snout more
prominent or projecting on account of a depression or indentation in front of the eye. The eye
is a little larger, and the membrane of the jaws
is quite thin and transparent, hence one of its
names, — "tin-mouth." The crappie has but six
spines in the dorsal fin, whereas the calico-bass has
seven, whereby they may be readily distinguished.

It grows to about the same size and weight as the calico-bass, ten or twelve inches, though under favorable conditions it grows larger, reaching a weight of three pounds. I have frequently taken it as heavy, or a little heavier, in Kentucky, where many ponds and streams seem peculiarly fitted for it. In coloration it is much paler than the calico-bass, and the markings are not so dark or in such large spots or blotches. It is silvery olive-green, much mottled with a darker shade of same color, especially on the back, the lower sides and belly being more silvery and seemingly translucent. The dorsal and caudal fins are much mottled with shades of green, though the anal fin is almost plain. The iris of the eye is dark, with a silvery or golden border.

It is found in clear streams and likewise in still, weedy ponds and bayous, or in all situations adapted to the large-mouth black-bass, with which fish it is nearly always associated. It is admirably suited for pond culture. It is quite gregarious and loves to congregate about the submerged top of a fallen tree or sunken brush, and about mill-dams. It feeds on all small aquatic organisms and insects and their larvæ, and the fry of other fishes, tadpoles, etc.

While a very free-biting fish, its game qualities, when hooked, are not remarkable. It is pulled out with scarcely a struggle. It is rather a shy fish, withal, and must be fished for cautiously, and with little noise or confusion. When these precautions are observed, and with very small minnows for bait, nearly the entire school can be captured in a short time. It is an excellent pan-fish, and on this account is a prime favorite.

For still-fishing, a light rod of a few ounces in weight, and a line of the smallest caliber, size H, should be used. Hooks for bait-fishing should be about No. 3, as the crappie has a large mouth; they should be tied on gut snells. A quill float is useful in weedy places, or about brush and logs. The best bait is a very small minnow, hooked under the dorsal fin, care being taken not to injure the spinal cord. Soft crawfish, cut-bait, or earthworms may be substituted where minnows are scarce. A reel is not necessary for bait-fishing, but a short leader should always be used, and where required a split-shot sinker is heavy enough.

For fly-fishing, the lightest trout fly-rod and the smallest click reel should be employed, with a braided, enamelled silk line of the smallest caliber, and dark or grayish flies of small size, on hooks No. 4, on gut snells, with a fine leader. The most useful flies are gray, red, and black hackles, black gnat, blue dun, gray and brown drake, and stone fly; but far the best fly that I have ever used is the Henshall of a small size. It has a body of green peacock harl, hackle of white hairs from a deer's tail, gray wings, and tail of a fibre or two from the tail feather of a peacock; they will rise to this fly when no other will tempt them to the surface. Toward sunset, with the tackle named, on a breezy summer day, the angler will be amply rewarded, for under these conditions fly-fishing for the crappie is a sport not to be despised.

It has been alleged that the name "Campbell-ite," by which the crappie is sometimes known in Kentucky, was bestowed because the fish first appeared in Kentucky streams about the same time that the religious sect founded by Alexander Campbell became established in that state. This may have been the origin of the name, but I am inclined to doubt it from the fact that the crappie has probably always inhabited Kentucky streams, inasmuch as it was first described by Rafinesque in 1820 from Kentucky waters. He gave gold ring and silver perch as the common names then in vogue for it at Louisville. I think it more likely the name originated in this wise: among the many names given to this fish is "newlight," probably owing to its bright and apparently translucent appearance; and as this name was also bestowed by some on the religious sect referred to, the names newlight and Campbellite became interchangeable for both fish and sect. It is, however, seldom called Campbellite, while newlight is the most universal name for it in central Kentucky.

The name crappie, or croppie, has an unknown derivation; perhaps it comes from the French *crêpe*, a "pan-cake," from its shape or deliciousness when fried, for it was always a great favorite with the French of St. Louis and the creoles of Louisiana. In the latter state it is also known as *sac-à-lait*, "bag for milk" (?).

Great numbers of crappies are annually seined from the shallow bayous and sloughs bordering the Illinois and Mississippi rivers by the United States Fish Commission, and planted in suitable waters. If allowed to remain in the sloughs, which dry up in the summer and fall, they would eventually perish.

CHAPTER II

THE BASS FAMILY

(*Serranidæ*)

THE bass family is composed mostly of marine fishes, nearly all of which are good game- and food-fishes. These will be described among the fishes of the East Coast and Florida in subsequent pages. It is the most typical group among the percoid (perchlike) fishes. Only two species of the family inhabit fresh water, — the white-bass and the yellow-bass.

The fishes of this family are characterized by an oblong body, large mouth, brushlike or bristlelike teeth, sometimes with canines; one or two dorsal fins, the first always composed of spiny rays; the anal fin, always with three spines; scales adherent and rough (ctenoid); preopercle usually serrate; opercle with flat points or spines; cheeks and opercles always scaly; premaxillary protractile; dorsal and ventral outlines do not always correspond; caudal fin not deeply forked; its peduncle stout.

85

THE WHITE-BASS

(*Roccus chrysops*)

Roccus chrysops. The White-bass. Body oblong, deep, and compressed; head $3\frac{1}{2}$; depth $2\frac{1}{2}$; eye 5; D. IX–I, 14; A. III, 12; scales 10–60–15; mouth moderate, maxillary reaching middle of pupil; a patch of teeth at base of tongue, and a patch on each side; preopercle serrate; subopercle with a deep notch; lower jaw somewhat projecting; dorsal fins separate; gill-rakers long and slender, $x + 14$.

Morone interrupta. The Yellow-bass. Body oblong, ovate, the back arched; head 3; depth $2\frac{2}{3}$; eye $4\frac{1}{2}$; D. IX–I, 12; A. III, 9; scales 7–50–11; dorsal fins slightly joined; jaws subequal; no teeth on base of tongue; gill-rakers moderate, $x + 13$ to 16; preorbital and suprascapula serrate.

The white-bass was first described by Rafinesque in 1820 from the falls of the Ohio River, near Louisville, Kentucky. He named it *chrysops*, or "gold eye," owing to the golden hue of the iris. It is known also as white lake-bass and fresh-water striped-bass. It is abundant in Lake Erie, Lake Michigan, and upper Mississippi River, especially in Lake Pepin, and in Lake Winnebago, Wisconsin. It was formerly not uncommon in the Ohio River, but is now rare. Its body is compressed and rather deep, with the back arched; its head is rather small, but the mouth is large, with the lower jaw protruding; the eye is large; teeth brushlike, without canines. The color is silvery white, greenish above, golden below, with six or more narrow dusky lines along the body, most conspicuous above the lateral line; those below broken, or not continuous. The white-bass is found in water of moderate depth, preferring those that are clear and cool, as it does not resort to weedy situations. It is essentially a lake fish, except in spring, when it undergoes a semi-migration, entering the tributaries of lakes in large schools. It spawns usually in May. It feeds on small fishes, crawfish, insects, and their larvæ, etc. Its usual size is a pound or a little less, but occasionally it grows to three pounds. It is a food-fish of much excellence, its flesh firm, white, flaky, and of good flavor.

It is one of the best fresh-water game-fishes, being a bold biter, and on light and suitable tackle affords much sport to the appreciative angler. For fly-fishing, the best season is during the spring, when it enters the tributary streams of lakes. At this time the fly-fisher will be successful at any hour of the day. He may fish from the bank or from an anchored boat, the latter plan being the best. As the fish are swimming in schools, either headed up or down stream, no particular place need be selected, though off the points at the edge of the channel, or in the narrowest portions of the streams, are perhaps the best. In the summer and fall the fish are in the lakes or deeper water, when the fishing will be more successful during the late afternoon hours until sundown, and the angler may be guided by the conditions followed in black-bass fly-fishing, as mentioned in a previous chapter.

A trout fly-rod of six or seven ounces, with the usual trout click reel and corresponding tackle, will subserve a good purpose. When the fish are running in the streams the most useful flies are gray drake, green drake, stone fly, brown hackle, gray hackle, Henshall, and Montreal, of the usual trout patterns, on hooks Nos. 5 to 7.

For bait-fishing, a light black-bass or trout rod, with multiplying reel, braided silk line of the smallest caliber, a leader of small gut three feet long, and hooks Nos. 3 or 4 tied on gut snells, will answer well. The best and in fact the only bait that can be successfully used is a small minnow, hooked through the lips. The fishing is done from an anchored boat on lakes or the deep pools of streams, either by casting or still-fishing.

No fish will rise to the artificial fly except in comparatively shallow water, or when near the surface, and this is especially true of the white-bass when it resorts to the depths after the spring run is over. I remember a striking instance of this that once occurred in Wisconsin. I was fishing for black-bass in the Neenah channel of Lake Winnebago during the May-fly season, when the black-bass were taking the artificial fly right along, being near the surface feeding on the natural flies, though the water was quite deep, with a rocky bottom. A party of bait-fishers anchored near my boat, and began fishing with heavy sinkers, as the water was very swift, and with small minnows for bait. The white-bass were not slow in taking the proffered minnows, and they caught a goodly number, but not a single black-bass; nor did I take a single white-bass during several hours of fishing, for they were lying among the rocks at the bottom.

In the rocky coves about the Bass Islands of Put-in-Bay, on Lake Erie, I have had really good sport, in the summer months, bait-fishing for white-bass, with light tackle, the fish running about two pounds; but with the fly my success was generally *nil*, as they were in deep water, and nothing but minnows would attract them. But in the upper Mississippi, notably on Lake Pepin, the case was different. About the rocky points of that beautiful lake, and in the clear water of the river below, I have enjoyed royal sport fly-fishing for white-bass. This was years ago. Afterward I made a trip in a steam yacht from Cincinnati to St. Paul, traversing the Mississippi from Cairo to the head of navigation, and also going up the St. Croix River to Taylor's Falls. On this trip the white-bass fishing was not so good as in former years, though the black-bass seemed to have held their own pretty well. I might remark, in passing, that the upper Mississippi is one of the most beautiful and scenic rivers in the world, and is unsurpassed for black-bass fly-fishing. At one time the islands of that river furnished superb woodcock shooting in summer, which could be varied with fine fishing.

THE YELLOW-BASS

(*Morone interrupta*)

The yellow-bass was first described by Dr. Theodore Gill in 1860. His type specimens were from the lower Mississippi River in the vicinity of St. Louis and New Orleans. He

named it *interrupta*, in allusion to the broken or
"interrupted" lines along its sides. It is also
known as brassy-bass. It belongs to the same
genus as the white-perch of the East Coast. It
is found only in the lower Mississippi River and
its tributaries, sometimes extending its range a
short distance up the Ohio River.

The yellow-bass might be called a cousin of
the white-bass, though it belongs to a different
genus. It takes the place of that fish in the
lower Mississippi Valley. Compared with the
white-bass it has a somewhat longer head, with
a body not quite so deep; otherwise the general
shape is much the same. The mouth is a little
larger, though the snout does not project quite so
much, and the profile of the head is straighter,
and it has a larger eye. The posterior border of
the cheek-bone is finely serrated.

The general color is brassy or yellowish,
darker on the back and lighter on the belly.
There are about half a dozen very distinct and
black longitudinal lines along the sides, the lower
ones broken or "interrupted," the posterior portions dropping below the anterior, like a "fault"
in a stratum of rocks.

It is fond of the deeper pools in the rivers and

clear-water bayous, and the foot of rapids and
riffles.   It is partial to the same character of food
as the white-bass, small minnows constituting the
greater part.   It likewise spawns in the spring,
and grows to a pound or two in weight, sometimes reaching three pounds.   It is an excellent
food-fish.

I have had good sport with the yellow-bass
on St. Francis River in Arkansas, and at the
head of the Yazoo Pass, in Mississippi, with the
same tackle and by similar methods as recommended for the white-bass on a prior page.   As
with the two black-basses and the two crappies,
the white-bass and yellow-bass having similar
habits and kindred tastes, the same tackle and the
same modes of angling are as well suited for one
as for the other.   This will apply to both fly-
fishing and bait-fishing.

I was once, one autumn, with a party on a river
steam yacht on the lower Mississippi when geese,
ducks, deer, and turkeys were more plentiful than
they are now.   Up the St. Francis River, in the
" sunk lands " of Arkansas, the yacht was moored
at Cow Bayou, near a steep clay bluff, on the top
of which was a dilapidated tent occupied by a
young man and his wife, who were building a

shanty boat in which to float down to sunnier
climes for the winter, as the man was "nigh
gone" with consumption. One morning I was
out early fishing for yellow-bass after a rainy
night. As I was landing a fish I saw the woman
at the top of the bluff, looking for a way down to
the yacht. She was quite a fresh and comely-
looking woman, too. She started down very
carefully, for the wet clay was quite slippery. I
became interested to see how she would succeed.
Suddenly her bare feet slipped from under her,
and she came down with a rush, her one garment,
as I soon discovered, an old calico gown, slipping
back over her head, disclosing her nude form,
which appeared very white in contrast to the red
clay. Then I looked the other way just as she
flopped over from a prone to a supine position.
When she reached the river side she looked like
a sculptor's model in clay. She quietly adjusted
her gown as if nothing unusual had occurred,
and asked: "Has you-uns got any matches?
We-uns' matches all got wet in the drizzle last
night, and I want to cook my old man's break-
fus." I pulled ashore and handed her my match-
box, and scarcely knowing what to say, I remarked,
"You had better change your dress before you

cook breakfast." She replied, "I hain't got another one."

While the boys were eating their breakfast of
fried fish, deer steak, and broiled duck, I related
the " toboggan " episode, and mentioned the " one
frock." When the meal was concluded the boys
overhauled their belongings and chipped in several
pairs of slippers, long woollen stockings, under-
clothing, and blankets, and the " skipper " threw in
some calico and muslin from the yacht's stores.
These were made into bundles and carried to the
top of the bluff by a more circuitous route. Proceeding to the tent they deposited their offerings,
together with some ducks and venison. The
man and woman were overcome with gratitude,
but the boys said they were glad to get rid of the
stuff. The skipper had taken his camera along to
get a snap-shot at the tent and its occupants, which
being made known to them the woman said,
" Wait a minnit ! " She went into the tent, but
immediately reappeared wearing a large sun-
bonnet, in which she was " took " with her " old
man." I have often wondered since why she put
on that sun-bonnet. My excuse for this digression
may be found in the memorable words of George
Dawson, " It is not all of fishing to fish."

CHAPTER III

THE BASS FAMILY (*CONTINUED*)

(*Serranidæ*)

In addition to the fresh-water species of this family and those of the East Coast are the groupers, cabrillas, etc., of Florida waters, to be noticed later. The family name is founded on Cuvier's genus *Serranus*, from the Latin *serra*, or "saw," in allusion to the serrated edge of the cheek-bones, common to all fishes of this family.

Roccus lineatus. The Striped-bass. Body rather elongate, little compressed; head 3¼; depth 3½; eye 6; D. IX–I, 12; A. III, 11; scales 8–67–11; back little arched; head subconical; mouth large, maxillary reaching middle of orbit; lower jaw projecting; teeth on base of tongue in two parallel patches; preorbital entire; preopercle weakly serrate; margin of subopercle entire; suprascapula entire; gill-rakers long and slender, 4 + 15; dorsal fins separate; caudal fin forked.

Morone americana. The White-perch. Body oblong, ovate, the back moderately elevated; head 3; depth 2½; eye 4; D. IX–I, 12; A. III, 8; scales 8–50–12; head depressed above eyes; snout rather pointed; mouth small, maxillary not reaching middle of orbit; preorbital entire; base of tongue without teeth; head scaled; dorsal fins connected at base; gill-rakers 4 + 16.

Centropristes striatus. The Sea-bass. Body robust, elevated anteriorly, somewhat compressed; head 2⅔; depth 2⅔; eye 5; D.
X, 11; A. III, 7; scales 5–55–17; head large and thick, naked
on top; mouth rather large, lower jaw projecting; teeth in
broad bands, the canines small; preopercle serrate; gill-rakers
long, about $x + 18$; scales on cheeks in 11 rows; caudal fin
double concave or three-lobed.

THE STRIPED-BASS

(*Roccus lineatus*)

The specific name *lineatus*, or "striped," was
bestowed by Bloch in 1792. North of the Delaware River it is universally called striped-bass,
but in more southern waters it is known as rock
or rockfish, from its habit of foraging on rocky
shores in search of crustaceans and small fishes.
From this vernacular name comes the generic
name *Roccus*. It is found from the Gulf of St.
Lawrence to Florida, but is most abundant from
Buzzards Bay to Cape Hatteras, North Carolina.
It has been successfully transplanted to the Pacific
coast, where it is now common near San Francisco.

The form of the striped-bass varies considerably
with age. Young specimens are rather slender
and symmetrical in outline, the depth being about
a fourth of the length. The depth increases
with the weight of the fish, while the back be-

SURF–FISHING FOR BASS

comes more arched, and the belly more pendu-
lous. The head equals in length the depth of the
body usually. The mouth is large, opening obliquely; the snout is rather sharp, and the lower
jaw projects. The color is olivaceous, often
bluish on the back, sides with silvery lustre, fading to white on the belly. There are six to eight
horizontal rows of dark spots, forming interrupted
stripes, four or five running from head to caudal
fin, with three shorter ones below; the fins are
pale and usually unmarked. It is found within
the range given during the entire year, though
it frequents certain situations at different seasons.
The largest fish resort to the rocky shores of the
bays and indentations of the coast between the
shores and outer reefs, those of smaller size frequent the estuaries and tideways, and still smaller
ones seek the shallower and quieter waters.

It spawns in the spring, usually in May, in
both fresh and brackish water. Large schools
ascend rivers for long distances in the spring,
more particularly those rivers resorted to by
the shad, which they seem to follow, perhaps for
the purpose of feeding on shad spawn, as they
are said to do. Others follow the smelt up certain rivers farther north. A large female will

deposit from a million to two million eggs, which are about one-seventh of an inch in diameter, are free, transparent, and semi-buoyant, and hatch in a few days. Owing to a large oil-drop in the front part of the yolk-sac, the young fry at first swim with the head toward the surface of the water, and not in the horizontal position usual with the fry of most fishes.

Its food consists of small fishes, crabs, lobsters, shrimps, squids, sandworms, and other marine invertebrates. It grows to a very large size, being frequently taken by anglers from thirty to sixty pounds, and in the nets of fishermen as heavy as one hundred pounds or more. In the city of Baltimore, in boyhood days, I often went to the fish markets on Saturdays to see and admire the various kinds of fishes. On one occasion there were several large rockfish being weighed on the old-time balance, consisting of a beam and two large, flat, wooden scales supported by chains. The largest fish did not weigh quite two fifty-six-pound weights. A man then asked me how much I weighed, and I replied one hundred and three pounds. I was then placed on the scale instead of the weights, with the result that the fish outweighed me perhaps a pound or two. At all events it weighed between one hundred and three and one hundred and twelve pounds — probably one hundred and five pounds. It was as long as an average man.

The striped-bass is a food-fish of fine quality, and the markets of the eastern cities are well supplied with it during summer and fall, and to a certain extent during the winter. It is very active from early spring until late in the fall, when it resorts to the back-waters and bayous of tidal rivers for the winter. It is said by some to hibernate, but this is doubtful. The opinion is probably due to the fact that it is more sluggish and listless while in winter quarters, and refuses to respond to the wiles of the angler.

That the striped-bass is a game-fish of high degree goes without saying. It is rated by some enthusiastic anglers as being superior even to the salmon in game qualities. This opinion, however, is hardly correct when the two are compared weight for weight. In surf-fishing the first rush of a large fish, upon feeling the hook, is something to be remembered. It is probably longer and stronger than that of a salmon of equal weight, for the reason that while the latter fish is leaping from the water in its efforts to escape, the bass is making his furious dash for liberty beneath the surface, and exerting every ounce of his muscular fibre in the effort. But this immense strain cannot long be continued, and as he seldom breaks water like the salmon, and does not sulk, he resorts to strategy and finesse to free himself.

After making several desperate but ineffectual rushes to escape, he may endeavor to chafe or part the line against sharp rocks, or to foul it among the kelp or sea-weeds. Sometimes, but not often, he dives toward the angler to obtain slack line, which is a dangerous move if the reel does not respond quickly in taking up the loose line. When it is considered that all of these manœuvres of a monster bass to free himself occur amidst the rolling and tumbling of the surf, or in the dashing of foam-crested combers, while the angler often has but a precarious footing on a slippery rock, and perhaps with a half gale of wind blowing, some idea may be formed of the skill and good judgment required to subdue and land so valorous a fish. And under such conditions it is very natural for the angler to rank his noble quarry with the salmon.

When a Baltimore boy I thought there was no

CATCHING SEA-BASS OFF NEWPORT

better sport than still-fishing for rockfish running
from a half to a pound or two, on the flats off
Fort McHenry, the Lazaretto, or up the Patapsco
River near the Long Bridge. It was good sport,
too, for the fish were plentiful in those days, and
from an anchored boat, with light cane rod and
shrimp bait, I was often on the ground to catch
the young flood tide at sunrise, or before, on
summer mornings, and seldom failed to be rewarded with a full basket of small striped-bass.

Still-fishing in summer is best practised in
comparatively shallow water in the estuaries, at
the edge of the tideways, near the mouths of
rivers, or up streams of good size as far as the
tide reaches. In some cases the fishing may be
done from bridges, piers, wharves, or from the
bank, but usually from an anchored boat. In
the estuaries and at the mouths of rivers the
first of the flood and the last of the ebb are usually the best stages of the tide. In the shallow
bays and lagoons, or far up the rivers, the full
tide is the most favorable time. For this fishing
the rod should be light, pliable, and not more
than nine feet in length. A black-bass rod can
be utilized to good advantage. The best rod for
the purpose, however, is the " Little Giant," a

modification of the Henshall black-bass rod. It
is in two pieces, seven and one-half feet long, and
weighs eight ounces in ash and lancewood, or
seven ounces in split bamboo. It is stiffer than
the Henshall rod, so that a two- or four-ounce
sinker can be used with it whenever necessary.
A good multiplying reel must be employed with
black-bass rods. The line should be fifty yards
of braided linen, smallest size, with a three-foot
leader of single gut; Sproat or O'Shaughnessy
hooks Nos. 1 or 2 on gut snells are large enough
for bass up to two or three pounds. A small
float is useful on grassy bottom with shrimp or
crab bait, and sinkers of weights in accordance
with the strength of the tidal current must be
employed, also a landing-net.

Shrimps, soft or shedder crabs, soft-shelled
clams, sandworms, small minnows, silversides,
spearing or killifishes, are all good baits in their
season. Shrimp is perhaps the best all-round
lure. It should be hooked under the back plates,
and a single shrimp is sufficient for small bass.
Shedder or soft crab should be cut in small
pieces. The scallop is likewise an attractive
bait, especially in the fall, when clam bait may
also be used to advantage. Early in the spring

shad roe may be used in quiet waters, or at slack tide, but it is a difficult and unpleasant bait to handle.

The bait should be from one to three feet above the bottom, and should be kept in motion. Even crab bait should not be allowed to lie on the bottom, as some anglers advise. To maintain the proper position and depth of the bait the angler may employ a float, with or without a sinker, as the exigencies or conditions demand.

Very often hand-lines or stiff cane poles are used in estuary fishing, and the bass, even when of several pounds in weight, are yanked out of the water into the boat at once. But with the tackle recommended above the pleasure of the angler is enhanced, and the fish given a chance for his life in the brief struggle that follows.

In trolling for fish of from three to ten pounds a natural bamboo rod, eight or nine feet long, answers well with one hundred yards of braided linen line, size E or F, and Sproat hooks No. 2–o to 3–o on gut snells. Where the bass run larger, two hundred feet of line, size E, with hooks Nos. 5–o to 6–o may be required, also a heavier rod. The baits for trolling are bloodworms of large size, a minnow hooked through

the lips, the natural squid or an eel-tail; also
the artificial squid of bone or block tin, or a
trolling-spoon or spinner with a single hook.
When the spoon or artificial squid is used it is
not necessary or advisable to add sandworms
or other natural bait, as is often done. Employ
one or the other, but never both in combina-
tion. The artificial baits are sufficiently attractive in themselves, and the additions mentioned
do not enhance their effectiveness. The boat
should be rowed alongshore, or over rocky
reefs or shoals, and about the eddies of rock
pools. As the fish always hooks itself in trolling, it only remains for the angler to play and
land his quarry in good form, always having a
large landing-net or gaff in the boat.

Casting menhaden bait from the rocky shores
of the coast requires tools and tackle of great
excellence and strength, as the largest bass are
taken in this way. The most approved rod is
a first-class split-bamboo, eight or eight and
one-half feet long, and weighing from twelve to
sixteen ounces. A more serviceable rod, that is,
one that will admit of harder usage, is made of
greenheart, lancewood, or bethabara, of the same
length, but somewhat heavier. A cheaper rod,

but one that will give good satisfaction, and withal is lighter than a wooden rod, is made of natural male Calcutta bamboo, and is known as a "chum" rod. Rods of eight or eight and one-half feet in length should be made in two or three pieces, or if not exceeding seven and one-half feet may be made of one six-foot piece with a handle of eighteen inches. They should have double bell-mouth guides and funnel top. The more expensive rods should have the guides, or at least the funnel top, lined with agate.

The reel must be a first-class multiplier, made expressly for surf-fishing, with jewelled or steel bearings, with a capacity of two hundred yards of from twelve- to eighteen-thread Cuttyhunk line. The hooks should be knobbed Sproat or O'Shaughnessy, Nos. 5–0 to 7–0, and attached to the line by two half-hitches, the loose end turned up and secured by another half-hitch. A long-handled gaff-hook of good steel and very sharp is indispensable. A chum knife and spoon are also necessary, and a woollen thumb-stall will be needed for thumbing the reel, or a piece of leather may be affixed to one of its bars as a brake.

The bait for casting may be the tail of a lobster, cleaned of every vestige of shell, but menhaden bait is generally used. After scaling the fish, a slice of several inches is cut from its side, tail end, and scored on the flesh side longitudinally with a sharp knife, to admit of its being more readily folded along the hook, which it should envelop completely. The small end of the bait is affixed to the head of the hook by a half-hitch or two, its bend and barb being concealed by the broader end of the bait. This is the conventional method of baiting, though I have had good success in more southern waters by using an entire bait of mullet or other silvery fish, five or six inches in length, and hooked through the lips.

The residue of the menhaden, after the baits are cut off, is chopped fine, and is known as "chum." This is thrown in the water to attract the bass. It is called "chumming," and causes an oily "slick" that spreads over the surface for a long distance. The pieces of cut fish thrown in are soon swallowed by scup, cunners, bass, and other fishes, leaving nothing but the oily slick on the surface. The bluefish, being a surface feeder, is probably attracted by the slick, but it is questionable if it is noticed by the striped-bass, a bottom and mid-water feeder. And even if the common belief were true, it is not likely that the bass would be tolled directly toward the angler through a slick covering many acres. The real attraction is in the chopped menhaden that sinks below the surface.

Casting the menhaden is quite an art. It is somewhat in the nature of casting a minnow for black-bass as described on a previous page, though the rod is a two-handed one and the bait much heavier. The bait is reeled up to within a foot or two of the rod tip, and the rod grasped by both hands, one just above and one below the reel, with the thumb of the lower hand resting on the spool of the reel, and protected by a woollen or leather thumb-stall. With the rod at one side, it is given a preliminary whirl, or swing or two, and the bait cast, underhand, much like striking at a hip-high or shoulder-high ball with a bat. The cast is made from either side, and while some anglers place the right hand below in casting from both sides, it is not the best way. In casting from the right side the left hand should be below, and the reel controlled by the left thumb; while in casting from the left side the right hand should be below. The thumb should maintain a gentle and uniform pressure on the spool as it revolves, to prevent backlashing, and by a stronger pressure stop the revolution of the spool as the bait reaches the water.

As long a cast is made as possible, and when the bait settles it should be reeled in again very slowly and the cast repeated until the bait is taken by a bass. When the water is very rough, so as to churn the bait and keep it in constant motion, fewer casts are necessary, as the bait can be left in the water for a longer time before making a new cast. When the fish is hooked and starts on his initial rush, line should be given, the thumb always on the spool to check him when it can be done without endangering the tackle. His first rush will probably be his strongest, and he must then be killed on the rod and reeled in to the gaffer. During the struggle of playing the fish, great care must be observed to prevent the cutting or chafing of the line against sharp rocks, and to keep the fish away from weeds, timbers, or other obstructions.

As the bass may weigh anywhere from ten to fifty pounds, the utmost skill and precaution are necessary to land him safely. Very often the angler has not only to contend with the fish, but with the strength and undertow of the tide and the tossing of breakers — factors that are by no means to be despised or neglected. But once fairly gaffed, the angler may feast his eyes on the grand fish, weighing, perhaps, thirty pounds or more, and congratulate himself on a great achievement.

When the bass are running far up the freshwater streams in the spring, they will often take the artificial fly. As the fish do not run much heavier than black-bass, the rod and tackle used in fly-fishing for that fish can be utilized, employing such flies as oriole, polka, coachman, red ibis, or other showy creations. The fishing is more successful about sundown.

Many years ago the striped-bass was planted in the waters of the Pacific coast by the United States Fish Commission. It has multiplied exceedingly, so that bass-fishing is now a favorite sport with San Francisco anglers, who fish the neighboring bays, rivers, and sloughs with great success. The baits commonly used are clams and the trolling-spoon. The sport has culminated in the formation of several striped-bass clubs, with quite a large membership.

THE WHITE-PERCH

(Morone americana)

The white-perch was described, but not named, by Shöpf, in 1788, from the waters near New York. From his description Gmelin named it, in the same year, *Perca americana*, or " American perch." The genus *Morone* was established for it in 1814 by Dr. Mitchill, as owing to structural differences it could not properly be placed in the genus *Perca.*

The white-perch is one of the most abundant fishes of the brackish waters on the Atlantic coast, its range extending from Nova Scotia to South Carolina, but more especially from Cape Cod to Cape Hatteras. It is also landlocked in fresh-water ponds at various places along the coast.

It is a handsome fish, symmetrical in outline, and well proportioned. Its body is compressed, its depth is not quite a third of its length. Its head is as long as the depth of the body, depressed above the eyes, and with a somewhat pointed snout. The mouth is rather small; the teeth are small, without canines; there are a few teeth on the edge of the tongue, but none on its base.

There are two dorsal fins, though they are connected at the base.

Its color is olivaceous, or green of various shades on the head and back, with silvery or greenish sides, and silvery white belly. Sometimes the color is bluish on the back and head. Those confined in ponds are always darker in hue.

The white-perch is one of the best and most esteemed pan-fishes of the eastern coast. It grows to a foot or more in length, occasionally weighing three pounds; but the usual size is from six to nine inches, and from one-half to a pound in weight in brackish water. Smaller ones ascend the streams to fresh water. It is usually found associating with small striped-bass, and their habits are much alike, feeding on the same food, as small minnows, young eels, shrimp, etc. It spawns in the spring, usually in May, in shallow, weedy situations in both fresh and brackish water. The eggs are quite small, about forty thousand to a fish, and hatch in three or four days.

As a boy I was very fond of fishing for white-perch, which were then very abundant in the Spring Garden branch of the Patapsco River, at Baltimore, from Ferry Bar to the mud-flats near the Long Bridge, and also above the bridge on the main river in brackish water. Being gregarious, it was found in large schools, and was a free biter at shrimps, shedder-crab, small minnows, and earthworms. At the time of which I write it was very plentiful at the mouths of all tidal rivers emptying into Chesapeake Bay. I have seen great wagon loads brought ashore in one haul of a long market seine. And in camping along the Bay, during my summer vacations, they seemed to be as plentiful as blackberries. There was never any dearth of fried white-perch or other fishes in our camp, and we never tired of them. We feasted on them daily, with terrapin, soft-shelled crabs, oysters, green corn, tomatoes, cantaloupes, and watermelons, and all to be had for the mere catching or asking.

Any light rod may be used for white-perch, with or without a small multiplying reel, with a line of braided linen, smallest size, and hooks Nos. 6 to 8. Most anglers use two or three hooks, but I would advise a single hook for all kinds of fishing. A short leader of single gut, about three feet long, is an advantage, and hooks should be tied on gut snells.

In quiet water, with small, live minnows for

bait, a sinker or float need not be used. In tidal waters a sinker is necessary to keep the bait at mid-water, or a few feet from the bottom, especially when shrimp, crab, or earthworms are used for bait. The weight of the sinker must be adapted to the strength of the tide. The best season is during late summer or autumn in brackish water, from an anchored boat, at half-flood or half-ebb tide; up the tidal rivers at high tide. At low water they must be looked for in the deep holes, among the rocks. Wherever found the white-perch will not disappoint the angler, but is ever ready to respond to his baited hook.

It rises pretty well to the artificial fly, especially when landlocked in ponds, or far up the streams. Trout tackle and trout flies are just right, on hooks Nos. 7 or 8; and as the most favorable time for fishing is toward dusk, light-colored flies are the best, as coachman, gray drake, red ibis, oriole, etc.

I was once fishing for white-perch on Gunpowder River, in Maryland, with a companion who happened to lose one of his hooks through a defective snell, which, however, he soon recovered by catching the perch that had stolen it.

We were perfectly sure that it was his, as he had tied his hooks himself with a peculiar shade of sewing silk. He then marked the fish by clipping off a portion of one of the spines of the dorsal fin, and returned it to the water, only to be retaken three times, twice by my friend and once by myself. The lips of the perch being then quite ragged from the frequent hooking, it was humanely killed and deposited in the basket.

From my experience with both wild and domesticated fish I am quite sure that cold-blooded animals, like fishes and batrachians, are not very sensitive to pain. Owing to the very small brain and the gelatinous character of the spinal marrow of fishes, it is very doubtful if they suffer much, if any, pain from the infliction of so slight an injury as the pricking of a fish-hook. If it were otherwise, I do not think a hooked fish would offer so much resistance and pull so hard upon the hook if it caused much pain. Nor does it seem reasonable that a fish would repeatedly subject itself to the same experience if its mouth felt at all sore, as all experienced anglers know they do, time and again. The mouth and throat of a fish cannot be very sensitive when it is considered that it swallows, whole, such prey as

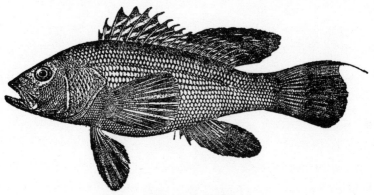

THE SEA–BASS

Centropristes striatus

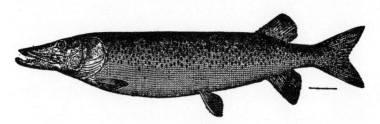

THE MASCALONGE

Esox nobilior

THE PIKE

Esox lucius

sunfish and catfish fry, bristling with sharp fins and spines, and those of the catfish are always erect, even if swallowed head first. Marine fishes also swallow crabs, lobsters, prawns, besides mollusks, sea-urchins, and other creatures that would be exceedingly irritating and painful to a sensitive throat.

THE SEA-BASS

(*Centropristes striatus*)

The sea-bass is known in various localities as black sea-bass, black will, black harry, hannahills, humpback, and also by names belonging rightly to other well-known fishes, as blackfish, bluefish, and rock-bass. The name sea-bass, however, is in most general use, and is the most distinctive and appropriate. Linnæus described it briefly, in 1758, and named it *striatus*, or "striped." He afterward received specimens from South Carolina, which in 1766 he named *atraria*, or "blackish," but the older name must hold according to the law of priority.

It is confined to the Atlantic coast, with range extending from Cape Cod to Florida, but it is most abundant along the coast of New Jersey. It has a robust body, its depth not quite

a third of its length; the back is elevated over
the shoulder, the "hump" being more prominent
in males during the breeding season. The head
is large and thick, with a large, oblique mouth,
leathery lips, and projecting lower jaw. The fin
rays are long and slender, and the caudal fin is
double concave.

Its color is bluish black, sometimes greenish
black or dusky brown on the back and top of the
head, lighter on the sides and belly. The edges
of the scales being dark, give a mottled, streaked,
or reticulated appearance. The dorsal fin has
several series of bluish white elongated spots;
the other fins are bluish or dusky, and are more
or less mottled. Young specimens have a broad
dusky band or stripe along the sides, which later
becomes broken up, forming cross shades.

The sea-bass, as its name implies, is a sea fish,
seldom entering brackish water. It congregates
in large schools about the offshore rocky reefs
and shoals, and about old wrecks, feeding on
crabs, shrimps, and other marine organisms,
often in company with the tautog and porgy.
It is a deep-water fish, and of course a bottom
feeder. It spawns in summer, between May and
August, depending on the temperature of the

water, but usually in June. The eggs are quite small, about twenty-five to the inch, and hatch in from four to six days. Its usual weight is from one-half to two or three pounds, occasionally weighing ten or twelve pounds. It is very voracious and will take almost any kind of bait that is offered. It is taken in large numbers by market fishermen on hand-lines and clam bait. It commands a ready sale, being a good food-fish, with firm, flaky flesh of a fine savor, and is highly valued for chowders. It is a hard-pulling fish on the line, boring toward the bottom with vicious tugs.

A light cane chum rod is very suitable, or perhaps the Little Giant rod is better. It is seven and one-half feet long and weighs eight ounces, and will bear the strain of such sinkers as must be used. The line should be braided linen of small caliber, and a multiplying reel should always be used. A short leader of three or four feet, and Sproat hooks, Nos. 1–0 to 3–0, on silk-worm fibre and a sinker adapted to the strength of the tide, make up the rest of the tackle. As the fishing is done from an anchored boat a land-ing-net should be provided. With the tackle just mentioned, at slack tide, and with clam, shedder-crab, sandworms, or shrimp bait, the angler can enjoy a good measure of sport with the sea-bass. Where the tide runs very strong, compelling the use of heavy sinkers of from three to six ounces, a striped-bass rod should be employed, especially in water from fifteen to thirty feet deep.

Great crowds of men, women, and children patronize the excursion boats from New York and Philadelphia, in the summer season, to catch bass, porgies, tautog, and flounders on the various fishing banks off the Jersey coast, where they use hand-lines and clam bait. While such fishing is greatly enjoyed by the uninitiated, it does not appeal to the angler.

THE SOUTHERN SEA-BASS

(Centropristes philadelphicus)

This species was described by Linnæus in 1758, and named *philadelphicus*, under the impression that his specimen was from the vicinity of that city. Afterward he received specimens from the South Carolina coast, which, in 1766, he named *trifurca*, meaning "three-forked," in allusion to its "triple-tail." The older name, unfortunately, must stand.

Its color is olive-gray, darkest on the back, whitish below, with seven oblique dusky and diffuse bars along the upper portion of the sides. The three-forked appearance of the caudal fin is more pronounced than in the northern sea-bass; otherwise there is no structural difference, except in coloration. Its habits are similar. The same remarks apply equally to the following species, except that it has a few less gill-rakers than the northern species. They may eventually all prove to be the same species, or geographical varieties. The directions as to fishing apply as well to both these southern forms as to the northern sea-bass.

THE GULF SEA-BASS

(*Centropristes ocyurus*)

This species was described from the "snapper banks," off Pensacola, by Jordan and Evermann in 1886, who named it *ocyurus*, or "swift tail." It has not been recorded from any other locality. It agrees with the northern sea-bass, except as mentioned, and in its coloration, which is grayish or pale olive, darker on the back, with three longitudinal rows of black blotches along the sides. It is called "tally-wag" by the snapper fisherman.

CHAPTER IV

THE PIKE FAMILY

(*Esocidæ*)

THE fishes of this family have a long body, not much compressed, and not elevated. The head is long, with a flattened and prolonged snout; a very large mouth filled with long and very sharp, cardlike teeth on the jaws and roof of the mouth, and with smaller teeth on the tongue. They have a single dorsal fin composed entirely of soft rays, and situated very far back and opposite to the anal fin, which is likewise composed of soft rays. The scales are small; the cheeks and gill-covers are more or less scaly; the head is naked above. All are greedy, voracious fishes, marauding tyrants, living almost entirely on other fishes. There is but one genus, *Esox.*

Esox nobilior. The Mascalonge. Body elongate; head $3\frac{2}{3}$; depth 6; eye 5; B. 17 to 19; D. 17; A. 15; scales 150 along the lateral line; cheeks and opercles naked below, scaly above; in about 8 rows.

THE MASCALONGE OF THE WEEDS. TROLLING WITH
HAND–LINE

Esox lucius. The Pike. Body elongate; head 3⅓; depth 5; eye 6; B. 14 to 16; D. 16 or 17; A. 13 or 14; scales 125; cheeks entirely covered with scales; lower half of opercles naked, upper half with scales.

Esox reticulatus. Eastern Pickerel. Body elongate; head 3½; depth 6; eye 8; B. 14 to 16; D. 14; A. 13; scales 125; cheeks and opercles entirely covered with scales.

Esox vermiculatus. The Western Pickerel. Body elongate; head 3¼; depth 5 to 6; eye 6; B. 12; D. 11 or 12; A. 11 or 12; scales 105 along the lateral line; cheeks and opercles entirely covered with scales.

Esox americanus. The Banded Pickerel. Body elongate; head 3½; depth 5½; eye 5; B. 12 or 13; D. 11 or 12; A. 11 or 12; scales 105; cheeks and opercles entirely covered with scales.

As some anglers find it difficult to distinguish a large pike from a mascalonge, or a pike from a pickerel, owing to the similar shape and appearance, the several species can be easily identified by means of the following artificial key:

The mascalonge (*Esox nobilior*) has the upper part of both the cheeks and gill-covers scaly, while the lower half of both cheeks and gill-covers is naked; it has from 17 to 19 branchiostegal rays (the branchiostegals are the rays on the under side of the gill-cover, that, like the ribs of an umbrella, assist in opening and closing it during breathing). Its coloration is of a uniform grayish hue, or when marked with spots or bars they are always of a much darker color or shade than the ground color.

The pike (*Esox lucius*) has the cheeks entirely scaly, but only the upper part of the gill-cover, the lower half being naked; it has from 14 to 16 branchiostegal rays; its coloration is a bluish or greenish gray, with elongated or bean-shaped spots covering the sides, and which are always of a lighter hue than the ground color.

The eastern or reticulated pickerel (*Esox reticulatus*) has both the cheeks and the gill-covers entirely covered with scales; it has from 14 to 16 branchiostegal rays; its coloration is shades of green, with sides of golden lustre, and marked with dark reticulations, mostly horizontal. It is rarely or never found west of the Alleghanies.

The little western pickerel (*Esox vermiculatus*) has both cheeks and gill-covers entirely scaly, as have all the pickerels; it has from 11 to 13, usually 12, branchiostegal rays; its coloration is greenish or grayish, with curved streaks on the sides forming bars or reticulations; the color is quite variable, sometimes plain olive. It is found only west of the Alleghanies.

The banded or American pickerel (*Esox americanus*) has, like the other true pickerels, both the cheeks and the gill-covers entirely covered with scales; it has 12 or 13 branchiostegal rays; coloration dark green, sides with many distinct black curved transverse bars; a black bar below the eye, and one from the snout through the eye to the gill-cover. It is found only east of the Alleghanies.

THE MASCALONGE

(*Esox nobilior*)

The specific name *nobilior*, long current for the mascalonge, and the one based on its earliest accurate description, was conferred by Rev. Zadoc Thompson in 1849 in "Notes on Certain Vermont Fishes," in the Proceedings of the Boston Society of Natural History, Vol. III, published July 18, 1849, and later he described it fully in the "History of Vermont," 1853, Part I. It is an excellent and appropriate name, and one that has become familiar to anglers. I have retained it, inasmuch as it was discarded, I think, for a very insufficient reason.

The specific name *masquinongy*, which has recently been given to this species in the books, is supposed to have been given to the mascalonge by Dr. Mitchill in 1824. His description, however, cannot now be found. It is alluded to by De Kay in his "Fishes of New York," in 1842, who gives its reference as "Mirror, 1824, page 297"; but I have searched for it in vain, as have others. De Kay merely says: "According to Mitchill, who describes a specimen 47.0 long and weighing thirty pounds, the fin rays are as follows: 'D. 21; P. 14; V. 11; A. 17; C. 26.' But this radial formula is just as applicable to Richardson's *E. lucius:* 'D. 20; P. 16; A. 18,' also given by De Kay. The size and weight of the alleged specimen of Mitchill would seem to indicate the mascalonge, but the great northern pickerel, *Esox lucius*, occasionally reaches a like size and weight. I once caught one weighing twenty-five pounds in northern Wisconsin, and saw several a little heavier, one of fully twenty-eight pounds.

Dr. Kirtland, in 1838, had, previous to De Kay, applied Mitchill's name *masquinongy* to a specimen from Lake Erie, and it is upon this evidence, principally, that this name has been adopted as the specific title of the mascalonge.

But afterward Dr. Kirtland used Thompson's name *nobilis* (meaning *nobilior*) and Le Sueur's name *estor* for the mascalonge. He also subsequently described the mascalonge from Lake Erie as *atromaculatus*, and one from the Mahoning River, Ohio, as *ohiensis*. From this it would appear that Dr. Kirtland, although a good naturalist in his day, was not at all clear in his estimation of the mascalonge.

There has been considerable controversy concerning the common or vernacular name of the mascalonge. Some claim it is from the French, and derived from the words "masque" and "allonge," which virtually mean "long face," and which is certainly nearer to the common pronunciation of mascalonge or muscalunge. Others claim it is an Indian name from the Ojibwa language, as "mash," meaning "strong," and "kinoje," meaning "pike." "Mash" is also said to mean "spotted" and "deformed." From mash and kinoje come "maskinonge," as it appears in the statutes of Canada. The name has been spelled in numerous ways, as evidenced in the Century

Dictionary, which gives the following variations: maskalonge, mascalonge, maskalunge, maskallonge, masquallonge, masq'allonge, mascallonge, muscalonge, muskalonge, muskalinge, muskellunge, moskalonge, moscononge, maskinonge, maskanonge, maskenonge, maskenozha, maskinoje, and maskenonge, to which might be added muscalinga, mascalinga, etc. There is no authority or precedent for the name " muskellunge " as used by some writers and anglers, as neither the original French or Indian words have the letter " u " in either the first or last syllable. Moreover, the term " lunge " is in some sections applied to the lake trout. I am aware, of course, that the name has obtained considerable currency, but in much the same way that the black-bass is called " trout " in the South, and the pike-perch is denominated " salmon " in certain localities.

Rev. Zadoc Thompson, who was the first to call attention to the scaling of the cheeks as a diagnostic character, gives the vernacular name "masquallonge," and attributes it to French derivation, to which opinion I am inclined. As the most prominent writers on fish and fishing give it as " mascalonge," that name should be universally adopted, no matter what its origin, or whether derived from the French Canadians or the Chippeway Indians; that question is more interesting to philologists than to anglers. As an instance of inconsistency, or of the irony of fate, the books give the scientific name of the subgenus as *mascalongus*, from the French, and the specific name as *masquinongy*, from the Ojibwa.

The mascalonge is common in the St. Lawrence basin and the Great Lakes, more abundant in the lakes of northern Wisconsin, less common in the upper Mississippi River, Chautauqua Lake, New York, and Conneaut Lake, Pennsylvania, and rare in the upper Ohio River and tributaries. It has a long body, somewhat compressed, its depth being about one-fifth of its length; the head is large, about a fourth of the length of the body, and flattened, with the lower jaw projecting. It has a terrible array of teeth of assorted sizes. On the edge of each side of the lower jaw are several long, bayonet-shaped teeth, from one-half to an inch apart; in the front part of the tip of the projecting lower jaw are a few short but sharp teeth, recurved; in the front part of the upper jaw are three clusters of long, fanglike teeth, standing out amidst the smaller, cardlike teeth; on the edge of the forward half of the upper lip is a row of small, but very sharp, recurved teeth; back of these on the roof of the mouth (vomer and palatines), and extending back from the fangs in front to the throat, are three rows of cardlike teeth, recurved and very sharp.

The coloration and markings vary so much that several varieties have been needlessly established, as the variations are found in every locality, and do not seem to depend on habitat or environment. The usual color is dark gray, greenish or brownish, always darker on the back, lighter on the sides, and belly white or whitish. The fins usually have dusky or slate-colored spots or blotches; the lower fins and caudal fin are often reddish. The markings of the body vary a great deal. In the young the upper half of the body is covered with small, round black spots, which usually disappear or change their shape as they grow old. In mature fish the spots are more diffuse, sometimes enlarging to an inch or more in diameter, or by coalescing form vertical broad bands, while in others there are no distinct dark markings. And while all of these various markings are found in fish from the same locality there is no apparent structural difference.

I have examined and compared specimens from the St. Lawrence and Indian rivers, New York, Lake Erie, the Wisconsin lakes, Lake Pepin, Chautauqua and Conneaut lakes, Scioto and Mahoning rivers, in Ohio, and have seen preserved heads of large ones from Ohio, Kentucky, and Tennessee, and found that they all agree so well in the number of branchiostegals, squamation of cheeks and opercles, in dentition, fins, and in measurements, that they must all be considered as one and the same species. At the Chicago Columbian Exposition there were some twenty very large specimens of mounted skins from Canadian waters, in the exhibit of the Ottawa Museum, which showed well the variation in markings. Some still showed the dark spots on a gray ground; others were more or less distinctly barred with broad or narrow bands; others showed both bars and diffuse spots; and still others were of a uniform slate or grayish coloration, without markings of any kind. In the museum of the Cuvier Club, in Cincinnati, there are quite a number of mounted skins of mascalonge from the Wisconsin lakes, mostly large ones, that also show all of the various markings, as well as those of a uniform coloration.

About 1890 I donated to the Cincinnati Society of Natural History a specimen from Lake Erie; and in 1892 I donated to the United States National Museum two specimens from Lake Erie, and one from a tributary of the Muskingum River, in Ohio. All of these Ohio fish were from eighteen inches to two feet long, and all showed similar markings, being profusely covered with round black spots from an eighth to a quarter of an inch in diameter. Where the spots become diffused, and the bands are inclined to spread and coalesce, they are always more distinct toward the tail. In a mascalonge of less than a foot in length the spots are very black, very round, and quite small, not exceeding a sixth or an eighth of an inch in diameter.

Various appellations have been bestowed on the mascalonge to denote its rapacity, as the shark, wolf, or tiger of the waters, all of which are well merited by that fierce marauder. It subsists entirely on fish, frogs, snakes, and even the young of aquatic mammals and water fowl. Nothing in the shape of food comes amiss to him. He is solitary in his habits, lying concealed among the water plants and rushes at the edges of the streams or channels and along the shores, or beside shelving rocks or banks in clear lakes, from whence he darts open-mouthed upon the luckless fish that approaches his lair. The number of fishes swallowed by a mascalonge during a single summer is almost incredible; and they are not minnows and small fry alone, such as are devoured by other predaceous fishes, but such as are old and large enough to reproduce their kind. It is fortunate that the mascalonge is comparatively a rare fish. As it is now being artificially propagated in some states, great care and judgment should be exercised as to the waters planted, so as not to jeopardize other and better game-fishes.

It spawns early in the spring and in very shallow water, where most of the eggs are devoured by frogs, turtles, fishes, and water fowl — a wise provision of nature when it is considered that the female deposits from one hundred thousand to three hundred thousand eggs. The eggs are quite small, about ten or twelve to an inch, and hatch in about two weeks. The mascalonge is the most valuable food-fish of its family, and is pronounced by some as being really excellent; but I consider it much inferior to the whitefish, lake-trout, pike-perch, black-bass, or brook-trout. While possessing no especial flavor, its flesh is firm and flaky, more so than that of the pike or pickerel, and it commands a ready sale in the markets.

It grows occasionally to an enormous size. I have taken it up to forty pounds, good weight. The late Judge Potter, of Toledo, Ohio, an angler of the old school, informed me that he had seen, in early days, many that weighed from fifty to seventy-five pounds. Mr. L. H. McCormick, formerly of Oberlin College, Ohio, saw one taken in a pound net that weighed seventy-two pounds. The late Dr. Elisha Sterling, formerly of Cleveland, Ohio, a contemporary of Judge Potter and the late Dr. Garlick, the father of artificial fish-culture in America, told me of one he once speared in Lake Erie that weighed eighty pounds, and said that those of fifty to sixty pounds were common in the forties.

The mascalonge is the best game-fish of its family. When of large size, from twenty to thirty pounds, it exhibits a bull-like ferocity when hooked, making furious dashes for liberty, and if not stopped in time will eventually take to the weeds. It exhibits great powers of endurance, but little finesse or cunning in its efforts to escape. It depends on main strength alone, swimming swiftly in straight lines, as might be inferred from its shape. Its long body does not admit of the quick doublings of the black-bass or brook-trout. If kept on the surface with a taut line it sometimes leaps into the air; but if allowed its own sweet will it bores toward the bottom, or endeavors to reach the refuge of weeds or rushes. One of less weight than twelve pounds, when hooked, can scarcely be distinguished from the pike or pickerel in its manner of resistance, and exhibits but little more gameness.

A black-bass rod of eight or nine ounces is sufficient for the largest mascalonge one is likely to encounter in these days. I caught one on the St. Lawrence, many years ago, that weighed thirty-two pounds, on an eight-ounce Henshall rod, and gaffed it in twenty minutes. Others have done the same even with a lighter rod. But it must be remembered that the weight of the fish, added to his fierce lunges, is very trying to a light rod, and I should not recommend one of less weight than eight ounces, which will answer for all emergencies in skilled hands. A good multiplying reel, a braided silk or linen line, size E or F, and Sproat or O'Shaughnessy hooks Nos. 3–0 to 5–0 on gimp snells, with brass box-swivel for connecting snell and line, constitute the rest of the tackle.

The best season for mascalonge fishing is in May or June, and in September and October, the latter months preferable. The most favorable hours are in the early morning and late afternoon. The middle of the day may be fished with a better prospect of success on cloudy, lowering days, with a brisk wind.

The best bait is a large minnow, either alive or dead, though a frog answers very well; and in the absence of either, a trolling-spoon, No. 4, with a single hook, may be utilized for casting. Rowing along in water from five to ten feet deep, the bait should be cast as far as possible to the edge of weed patches, reeling it again very slowly, or if the bait is alive it may be allowed to swim outside of the water-plants for a short time. By moving along continuously, and making frequent casts, this method is much more successful than still-fishing. When the wind is just right, or when the current is strong enough and the wind not contrary, it is a good plan to allow the boat to drift while casting.

As soon as a fish is struck and hooked the boat should be moved to deeper and open water at once, in order to give free play to the fish and lessen the probability of its taking to the weeds. In open water the angler has a better chance successfully to play and land his quarry, which should be kept on the surface as much as possible. He can be aided very much in his efforts by the careful and judicious management of the boat by a skilful oarsman.

When the mascalonge shows signs of weakness and can be drawn alongside, it should be gaffed at once. Not by striking at it with quick and violent motions, which serve only to frighten the fish and endanger the angler's tackle, but the gaff should be kept below the fish until it can be drawn over it, and then by raising it slowly and cautiously, until near enough, when, by a quick upward and drawing motion, the point of the hook should be driven into the throat or breast of the fish, and by the same motion the fish should be lifted into the boat. It should then be killed by a smart stroke on the head, as a wound from its sharp teeth is no trifling matter. In the absence of a gaff-hook the fish should be more thoroughly exhausted before bringing it alongside the boat, when it should be struck a stunning blow on the head before being taken in.

The bait or spoon may be trolled along the edges of the channel, just outside of the weed patches, from a moving boat, with a line of thirty to fifty yards. In trolling, the revolving spoon, glistening and shining, is the attractive lure, and any addition of a minnow, or strip of fish or pork-rind, or other bait, as is often resorted to by some, is entirely unnecessary. It adds nothing to the chances of hooking a fish, and should never be practised by the consistent angler. He may use pork-rind if he wishes, but let it be used alone, on its own merits. A spoon is bad enough in any case, but it only makes it more reprehensible and repulsive, to the angler at least, to handicap it with bait of any kind; even the bunch of feathers that usually adorns the spoon should be discarded, as it is of no practical use.

Most mascalonge are taken, I am sorry to say, by trolling with a hand-line of heavy braided linen, size B or C, and a spoon of very large size, as large as No. 8, which seems to be the favorite size with hand-trollers. In this method of fishing the mascalonge hooks himself when he strikes the spoon. It is then drawn in, hand over hand, as the sailors say, with might and muscle. And as might be supposed, those who practise this method are loudest in their praise of the mascalonge as the "king of all game-fishes." A quick pull, a strong pull, and a pull all together, with the hauling aboard as soon as possible of the struggling fish, amidst much splashing and floundering, seems to be their estimation of gameness in a fish.

The foregoing remarks apply to fishing on lakes and quiet, weedy streams of the Northern states. In the clear and swifter waters of the upper Ohio, and its tributaries, the mascalonge lies in the deep pools during summer and fall, where it is taken by still-fishing. A large sucker, weighing from half a pound to a pound, is the favorite bait, with suitable rod and reel. The fish is given plenty of time to gorge the bait before striking, and this is quite important with so large a bait. Many large mascalonge, there called "pike," have been taken in this manner in those waters, events to be long remembered and talked about, while the head is carefully preserved for the admiration and envy of future generations of anglers.

Once when returning from a fishing trip to northern Wisconsin when mascalonge were much more in evidence than at the present day, I was carrying the head of a forty-pounder that just filled an ordinary tin bucket. At Appleton, while waiting for the train to Green Bay, the big head was the centre of an admiring group of anglers. Then came the natural and inevitable query, "Where did you catch it?" In order to avoid a long recital, which only could have done justice to the subject, and expecting the train at any moment, I replied, "An Indian speared it on Lake St. Germain." They looked at me as if I had seven heads; then one said: "Well! well! It requires an awful lot of moral courage to make such an admission." But I killed it, all the same, on a nine-ounce rod, and my Indian canoe-man gaffed it.

THE PIKE

(*Esox lucius*)

The pike is more generally known in the United States as "pickerel," and sometimes as the great northern pickerel to distinguish it from the pickerel, properly so-called. In England the young pike is a pickerel, an older one a jack, and the mature fish a pike. In England and continental Europe the pike (*E. lucius*) is the only species of the family inhabiting their waters, while there are five species of the family in America, which makes it all the more confusing when the name "pickerel" is applied indiscriminately to all, — even the mascalonge being sometimes alluded to as an "overgrown pickerel."

The range of the pike in America is from Lake Champlain, the Great Lake region, and the upper Mississippi River, north to Alaska; it is rare in the Ohio Valley.

Next to the mascalonge the pike is the most important and largest member of the pike family. It has a long body, somewhat compressed, its length being a little more than five times its depth. The head is large, somewhat more than a fourth of the length of the body, with a long, flattened, and projecting snout; the teeth are similar, but not quite so large or numerous as in the mascalonge.

The coloration and markings of the pike are quite constant, not varying so much as in others of the family, and is very different from those of the mascalonge or any of the pickerels. The ground color is grayish or greenish gray, darker on the back and fading to silvery white on the belly; the sides, from head to tail, are profusely covered with irregular, oblong, or bean-shaped whitish spots or blotches, much lighter than the ground color; the dorsal, anal, and caudal fins are marked with dark spots or blotches. It is somewhat more gregarious, and is more of a rover than the mascalonge; otherwise its habits are very similar, and it coexists with that fish in many waters, especially in the region of the Great Lakes. It feeds on fish, frogs, and water-snakes. Its usual weight reaches fifteen pounds, though it occasionally grows to four feet in length and a weight of twenty-five or thirty pounds.

As a food-fish it is variously estimated. Some consider it to be very good, and it sells well in the markets, — which, however, is not always a fair criterion. It is much better in the fall and winter than in summer. Most people who know it best, and I agree with them, think it inferior to any fresh-water fish for the table except the carp and sucker. Its flesh is soft and dry, and unless of large size is not flaky, and it is, moreover, very full of small bones. One of ten pounds, stuffed with a savory dress-ing and baked, is not unpalatable, but cannot be compared favorably with the whitefish, black-bass, or trout.

The pike when of large size is a good game-fish. Its weight and strength, added to its bold rushes when hooked, are very trying to light tackle. One of fifteen pounds is worthy of the angler's most serious attention on an eight-ounce rod. Its manner of fighting is similar to that of the mascalonge, though in a lesser degree, and it does not continue its resistance so long. After a few frantic rushes it weakens very materially, and if kept away from weeds soon gives up the struggle for freedom.

In England, where game-fishes are much scarcer than in this country, the pike is considered a fine game-fish and is much sought after by bait-fishers, and with a wonderful array of murderous traces, minnow-gangs, and spinning tackle. In the United States, where there are so many better game-fishes, it is not often made the object of special pursuit. Most pike are caught by anglers in northern waters when fishing for black-bass.

Ordinary black-bass rods and tackle are very suitable for pike fishing, though where they run large, eight to fifteen pounds, an eight- or nine-ounce rod is to be preferred to a lighter one. A good multiplying reel, a braided line, either silk or linen, size F, and Sproat hooks,

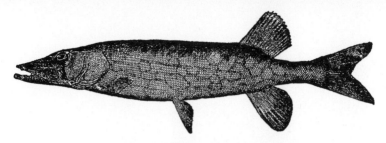

THE EASTERN PICKEREL
Esox reticulatus

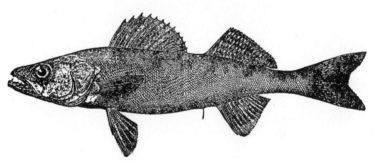

THE WESTERN PICKEREL
Esox vermiculatus

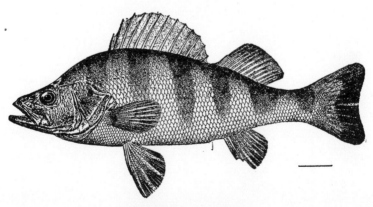

THE PIKE–PERCH
Stizostedion vitreum

THE YELLOW–PERCH
Perca flavescens

Nos. 2–0 to 3–0, are better suited to large pike than black-bass.

A minnow, or a trolling-spoon of small size with a single Sproat or O'Shaughnessy hook, may be employed in casting from a boat along the edges of weed patches, lily-pads, and wild rice, and along the shoals and bars. The same tackle can be utilized for trolling in the same situations. Where the conditions are favorable it is advisable to allow the boat to drift, in order to dispense with the noise and confusion of rowing or paddling. The directions already given for black-bass fishing, as to playing and landing the fish, will answer just as well for the pike.

As the pike seems to suggest the trolling-spoon, this is a good place to say a few words concerning that little-understood article of fishing tackle. In the first place, it should never have more than a *single* hook, and that should never be handicapped by adding a minnow, frog, or strip of fish or bacon-skin, as is so often done. The hook should be left free to perform its function, untrammelled by extraneous and useless appendages. If the angler pins his faith to them, by all means give them a fair chance on a hook without a spoon; it is not only more logical, but more sportsmanlike. Give the fish a chance, also, and of two evils let it choose the least by using them separately. Seriously, the spoon is a most alluring and attractive bait in itself. Its bright and shining appearance when spinning and glancing through the water is well-nigh irresistible to a predaceous fish, and is in itself all that could be desired as an effective lure.

The original trolling-spoon (made by Buell) was the bowl of a dessert spoon, with a hole in the broadest end for the line, and a single hook soldered to the narrow end. It is as effective as the best trolling-spoon made to-day. With a single hook, either loosely attached or soldered to the spoon, one is more apt to hook his fish, and more certain of landing it, to say nothing of the cruel and inhuman practice of using the triangle of three hooks usually attached to most trolling-spoons.

Manufacturers generally affix a triangle of hooks to trolling-spoons, disguised by a bunch of red and white feathers that are worse than useless. The spoon is made of many shapes and of various sizes, and often of two or three spoons combined. They seem to vie with each other as to who can turn out the most ridiculous contrivance, for the farther it departs from the original spoon the more useless it becomes. Manufacturers are not all anglers, and endeavor to produce what is most novel and attractive to the prospective customer. Such appliances sell to the uninitiated and unwary, but do not catch many fish, or even anglers of experience.

And the same remarks will apply in a measure to the gang or trace of several hooks, usually employed in trolling or spinning the minnow. A minnow, hooked through the lips — and it may be a dead one — with a single hook, will move more lifelike, and be really more attractive to the fish, than the whirling, wabbling one, bristling with a dozen hooks. It is cruel and heartless to employ so murderous a device. I have seen the mouths of bass and pike and lake-trout lacerated and mutilated, sometimes the lips and upper jaw torn completely off, by the triangle of the spoon or the half dozen or more hooks of the gang or trace. If their use cannot be dispensed with on the score of inutility, a single hook being far more successful, their employment should be relinquished in the name of humanity.

The pike will not often rise to the artificial fly,

but will take it if allowed to sink a foot or two after casting. Many years ago, in Wisconsin, I devised the "polka" black-bass fly, and on its first trial, at the very first cast, it was seized by a pike of six pounds. The polka has a body of red floss silk, with spotted wings of the guinea fowl. I have frequently taken the pike with other red-bodied flies, as the Abbey, red ibis, king of the water, and Montreal, but the polka was always the favorite. Flies with bodies of peacock harl, as coachman, Henshall, Governor Alvord, etc., are very useful, as well as some with yellow bodies, as professor, queen of the water, and Lord Baltimore. The afternoon hours, especially toward sundown and until dusk, are the most promising for fly-fishing. Large flies are also successfully used in trolling for pike, from a rather slow-moving boat. For fuller instructions for fly-fishing the reader is referred to those given for the black-bass, which will answer very well for the pike, especially where the two fishes inhabit the same waters.

Fishing through the ice for pike or pickerel has quite a fascination for some persons, even for those who never fish in any other way. And there is a certain kind of enjoyment in it, though actual fishing, as we understand it, has but little to do with it. If the ice is glare and free of snow, one can vary the amusement with skating. The bracing, nipping air on a clear day, with the sun shining brightly on the winter landscape, has its charms, and fishing through the ice is a good pretext for a winter outing. A dozen or more holes are cut through the ice in a circle, its diameter extending over the feeding grounds of the pike, whether small or great in extent. A fire may be built in the centre, if far from the shore on a lake, or on the shore itself if convenient to the holes. The holes being cut and a fire made for comfort, the next thing to do is to place the "tip-ups," as they are called, and bait the hooks, when there is nothing more to be done but to fill one's pipe and wait by the fire for the anticipated event — the rising of a signal proclaiming a "bite."

Tip-ups are made in several ways, but the simplest plan, which is as good as any, is to provide a piece of thin board, say two or three feet long and two or three inches wide. A few inches from one end a hole is bored, through which is thrust a round stick, like a section of a broom-handle, and long enough to extend well across the hole in the ice. A short line, usually three or four feet long, with suitable hook and sinker, is tied to the short end of the thin board, through a small hole bored for the purpose. The hook is then baited, placed in the water, and the thin board is laid down on its edge, with the short end at the middle of the hole in the ice, and the round stick straddling it. It will be readily understood that a fish pulling on the line at the short end of the thin board, or lever, will raise the long end, thus indicating to the watcher the looked-for event. The long end of the lever may be shaved to a point, to which a signal flag may be affixed. Where the fish are plentiful it will keep one pretty busy running from one hole to another to take off the pike or rebait the hooks.

When residing at Oconomowoc, Wisconsin, I found that fishing through the ice for pike and yellow-perch was a favorite sport. I indulged in it once for pike and several times for perch, for the latter is a firm, sweet, and delicious pan-fish in the winter. Driving over La Belle Lake in my sleigh to the " pickerel grounds," where my man had cut the holes the day before, the tip-ups and lines were soon arranged and the hooks baited with live minnows. A fire was then built on the shore, near at hand, to warm the chilled fingers. It was pretty tame when considered from the angler's point of view; but with the keen, crisp winter air, and the bright sun sparkling on the pure white snow, on which I occasionally took a spin in the sleigh, it was quite an enjoyable experience. In the course of a few hours several pike were taken and left lying on the snow, where they soon became frozen stiff. Upon my arrival at home they were placed in a tub of cold water, when all but one or two revived and began to swim about; the latter were probably too thoroughly frozen or may have been dead before being frozen. Apropos of this: I had some minnows in a live box, at the edge of the lake near my home, that thawed out alive in the spring after being frozen all winter. They were evidently the same minnows, as there were no dead ones, and the live ones could hardly have got into the box from the lake.

The mediocrity of the pike as a game-fish is doubtless a just estimation in a majority of cases, but once in a while one will exhibit game qualities that will surprise the most doubting and contemptuous angler, compelling his admiration, and forcing him to admit that there are exceptions

to all rules, but more especially in fishing. I was
once one of a party of black-bass fishers on a lake
in Wisconsin. In one of the boats was a lady of
Milwaukee, who was justly considered one of the
most expert and level-headed anglers in the party.
She always stood up in her boat, was a marvel in
casting the minnow, and played a bass to a finish
in a style both graceful and artistic after a short,
sharp, and decisive contest. She used the lightest rods and tackle, and the best. On this occasion, after landing a number of gamy bass and
logy pike, she hooked a pike of about six pounds
that put her six-ounce rod to the severest test,
and gave her twenty minutes of the liveliest
work that a fish is capable of. It leaped repeatedly from the water, and rushed not only straight
away, but twisted and turned and doubled in a
manner that would have done credit to the gamest bass. Finally she brought it to the landing-
net in triumph, though she was, to use her own
expression, "completely tuckered out." I venture
to say that no man of the party would have been
successful in landing that pike, with the same
tackle, in the same length of time.

A woman who is an expert angler will risk
her tackle to greater lengths than a man, and will

take more chances in subduing a fish within a reasonable time. This is not because of recklessness, or because she does not understand or appreciate the tensile strength of her rod. On the contrary, she knows her tackle well, and has the utmost faith in its potentiality. I knew a lady friend who was never more than thirty minutes in bringing to gaff any salmon of from twenty-five to thirty pounds. And my Kentucky friend, Mrs. Bachmann (formerly Mrs. Stagg), killed her tarpon of two hundred and five pounds in eighty minutes.

THE EASTERN PICKEREL

(*Esox reticulatus*)

The eastern pickerel, also called chain pickerel in the North, and jack in the South, was first described by Le Sueur, in 1818, from the Connecticut River. He named it *reticulatus*, owing to the "reticulations" or the netted character of the markings on the body.

Its range extends from Maine along the coastwise streams to Florida and Louisiana. West of the Alleghanies it has been reported from the Ozark region of Missouri and Arkansas, but I am rather inclined to doubt it.

In its general form the pickerel resembles a small pike, though it is more slender, has a larger eye, and its coloration is quite different. The ground color is either olive-brown or some shade of green, the sides with a golden lustre, and the belly white. The sides are marked with many dark lines and streaks, mostly oblique and horizontal, forming a kind of network. There is a dark vertical bar below the eye; the dorsal fin is plain; the lower fins sometimes reddish; the caudal fin occasionally has a few dark spots or blotches.

In its habits of feeding and spawning it is similar to the pike, spawning in the early spring. It is found in weedy ponds in the North, and in the quiet, grassy reaches of southern streams. It feeds mostly on small fishes and frogs. It grows to a foot in length, usually, sometimes to two feet and weighing seven or eight pounds, though its usual maximum weight is three or four pounds.

In the New England states it is regarded by many as not only a fine game-fish, but an excellent food-fish as well. Others despise it on both counts, and there you are. To many a Yankee boy fishing for pickerel was the highest ideal of angling, but with the larger experience of mature years his idol has been thrown from its pedestal, and he, too, has learned to look askance at the friend of his youth. But while the pickerel is not a game-fish of high degree, it is capable of furnishing a fair amount of sport with light black-bass tackle in waters not too weedy.

Ordinary black-bass rods and tackle are quite suitable for pickerel fishing, either with bait or fly, though the hooks should be larger, about 1–0 to 2–0, on gimp snells or heavy silkworm fibre. Where the weeds are too thick to admit of playing the fish a reel can be dispensed with, and a plain, light bamboo or cane rod, in its natural state, can be substituted for the jointed rod. It should be long enough to furnish considerable elasticity, say twelve feet, as its flexibility must subserve, somewhat, the purposes of a reel.

The pickerel will take a sunken fly in shallow water, after it has been fluttered on the surface awhile. The red ibis, soldier, Abbey, polka, Montreal, and coachman are all good pickerel flies, if cast toward the dusk of evening.

Skittering is a favorite method of fishing for the pickerel in weedy ponds. It is practised with a long cane rod, and line of about the same length as the rod, with or without a reel. A spoon bait, frog, or a piece of white bacon-rind cut in the semblance of a fish, or a frog's hind legs, skinned, are skittered or fluttered on the surface near the lily-pads and pickerel weeds. The fish should be kept on the surface if possible, when hooked, and drawn into open water; otherwise it may become entangled in the weeds and lost.

The pickerel may also be taken by still-fishing from a boat with the live minnow or frog. On open water, a very successful way is trolling with a small spoon and single hook, or a dead minnow. For these methods the reader is referred to pike or black-bass fishing on previous pages.

I have found the pickerel as far south as eastern Florida, where it is known as "pike," though it is rarely met with, and owing to its rarity is held in pretty fair esteem as a game-fish. In the marshes and rice ditches of South Carolina, and some sluggish streams of southeast Georgia, it is rather more plentiful, though usually of inferior size and dusky coloration. I once caught several on the Cooper River in South Carolina when fishing with very light tackle for "bream," which were unusually active and strong, and which impressed me as entitled to a better reputation as a game-fish than is commonly accorded to it by anglers. On the whole, the eastern pickerel is not half a bad fish, as English anglers would say. One might go farther and fare worse.

THE WESTERN PICKEREL

(Esox vermiculatus)

The western pickerel was first described by Le Sueur from the Wabash River. He named it *vermiculatus*, owing to the "wormlike" appearance of its markings. He collected it about 1818, but his description was not published until 1846. It inhabits the Mississippi Valley, south to Arkansas and Mississippi, and the tributaries of Lakes Erie and Michigan. It is not found east of the Alleghanies.

It is formed on the same general lines as the other members of the pike family, but is rather more slender and rounder, with a shorter head, proportionally, but a larger eye. Its color is olive-green, or grayish green, darker on the back, and belly white. The sides are covered with many dark curved streaks, inextricably mixed, or forming reticulations. The coloration is quite variable in different waters. A dark vertical bar is usually present below the eye ; the sides of the head are variegated.

It is common in the grassy streams of the Middle West and weedy bayous of the Southwest, never exceeding a foot in length. The late Dr. Elisha Sterling, of Cleveland, Ohio, once sent me a plaster cast of one not more than eight inches in length, with the ovaries exposed, showing the ripe ova. It is not of much importance as a game-fish or as a food-fish. It spawns in early spring, and feeds on small fish, frogs, and tadpoles. It may be fished for in the same way, and with the same tackle as recommended for crappies on a previous page.

THE BANDED PICKEREL

(*Esox americanus*)

The banded pickerel, Long Island pickerel, or brook pickerel, as it is variously known, was one of the first of its family to be recognized. It was described by Gmelin, in 1788, from Long Island, New York. He named it *americanus*, or " American pike," as a variety of the European *Esox lucius.*

It is found only east of the Alleghanies in coastwise streams from Massachusetts to Florida. It is almost a duplicate of the little western pickerel in its general form, and represents that species in eastern waters. The characteristics of fin rays, scales, and squamation of cheeks and gill-covers apply equally to both species.

The ground color is dark green; belly white; sides with about twenty distinct, blackish, curved, vertical bars, often obscurely marked, but not distinctly reticulated. There is a black vertical bar below the eye, and a horizontal band extending from the snout, through the eye, to the gill-cover. The lower fins are often quite red. I have collected it on the east coast of Florida of a beautiful emerald-green coloration, without distinct dark markings, and with orange-colored lower fins — a most beautiful fish.

Although an interesting little fish, it is of no importance to anglers and is merely mentioned here, with the little western pickerel, to enable the reader to identify the different members of the pike family. It spawns early in the spring. It seldom grows beyond a foot in length, and is usually much smaller. Fishing for it is on the same plane with sunfishing, and the lightest tackle should be employed.

CHAPTER V

THE PERCH FAMILY

(*Percidæ*)

MOST of the species belonging to this family are the dwarf perches, the beautiful little darters of the clear streams. The only genera of importance as game-fishes are *Stizostedion*, the pike-perches, and *Perca*, the yellow-perch. They are characterized by an elongate, nearly round body; small, rough, and adherent scales; rather large mouth with sharp teeth; spines on opercle, and preopercle serrate; branchiostegals six or seven; two dorsal fins, the first composed of spines, the second of soft rays; the anal fin with two spines.

GENUS STIZOSTEDION

Stizostedion vitreum. The Pike-perch. Body elongate; back somewhat elevated; head 4; depth 5; eye 4; D. XIV–20; A. II, 12; scales 10–125–25; head and cheeks sparsely scaled; canine teeth on jaws and palatines; opercle with small spines; pyloric cœca 3.

Stizostedion canadense. The Sauger. Body elongate and spindle-shaped; head 3½; depth 4½; eye 5; D. XIII–18; A. II, 12;

scales 9–100–27; head and cheeks scaly; spines on opercle; head depressed and pointed; pyloric cœca 5 to 7.

GENUS PERCA

Perca flavescens. The Yellow-perch. Body oblong, somewhat compressed, the back elevated; head 3¼; depth 3¼; eye 5; D. XIV–15; A. II, 7; scales 6–75–17; top of head rough; profile convex from dorsal to occiput, thence concave to snout, which projects; cheeks scaly; opercles nearly naked; preopercle and shoulder girdle serrated; teeth in villiform bands; branchiostegals 7; scales strongly ctenoid.

THE PIKE–PERCH

(Stizostedion vitreum)

The pike-perch or wall-eye was first described by Dr. Mitchill in 1818, from Cayuga Lake, New York. He named it *vitrea* in allusion to its large vitreous or glassy eye. It would have been indeed fortunate if the name glass-eye or wall-eye, with or without the suffix perch, had been adopted; for this fine fish is a true perch, with nothing "pike-like" in form or habits, except its large mouth and canine teeth, and nothing "salmon-like" except its trimly-shaped body. But these fancied resemblances have caused it to be called in various localities wall-eyed pike, yellow pike, blue pike, glass-eyed pike, salmon, and jack salmon. It is also known in Canada as dorè and okow, and among the commercial fishermen as "pick-

erel." However, the names pike-perch and wall-
eyed pike have been rather universally adopted,
and it will probably be always known by these
names. Pike-perch is the Anglicized form of
Lucioperca, the Latin name of the genus in
Europe.

It is abundant in Canada and the Great Lake
region, and fairly abundant in the upper Mississippi River and its tributaries, and especially in
Lake Pepin. It is found also in the lake region
of northern Minnesota, and in the lakes and
streams of Wisconsin and Iowa. It is not uncommon in the upper Ohio River and tributaries,
south to Tennessee. On the Atlantic slope it is
more rarely found from Pennsylvania to Georgia,
where it often exists in brackish water. I have
taken it in my boyhood days at Ferry Bar, a
point on the Patapsco River, near Baltimore,
Maryland. Its range is being constantly extended by transplantation. The pike-perch is a
very trimly-built and shapely fish. Its body is
rather slender, not much compressed. The head
is well shaped, neither too large nor too small,
with a large mouth well filled with teeth, some
quite long and sharp. The eye is very large and
glassy. Like all the perches it has two dorsal

fins, well separated; the caudal fin is forked. The scales are small and rough. The edge of the cheek-bone is toothed or serrated, and the edge of the gill-cover has one or more small spines. The color varies considerably in different localities, and even in the same waters. The usual color is olive, or greenish brown, mottled with brassy or yellowish blotches forming oblique but indistinct lines, or vermicular markings. The head is similarly colored and marked; the lower jaw is reddish; the belly and lower fins pinkish or yellowish; the first dorsal fin is not much marked, but has a large black blotch on its posterior border; the second dorsal fin is mottled with olive, brown, and yellow; the caudal fin is likewise mottled, with the tip of the lower lobe white or light colored.

The pike-perch frequents waters of good depth, only entering the shallow portions of streams and lakes at spawning time, and at night when feeding. It prefers a bottom of rock or gravel in clear and cool water, and loves to lie in the deep pools at the foot of riffles, or at the entrance of streams; or where the current is strong and deep near mill-dams and under sunken logs, or shelving rocks and banks, and about the timbers of bridges in deep water. It is nocturnal in its habits, for which it is well fitted by its large and prominent eye, and seeks its prey, which consists mostly of small fishes, in shallow water.

It spawns in the spring, and in lakes usually resorts to its spawning grounds in the winter, where it is caught through the ice in large numbers in certain localities, notably in Put-in-Bay on Lake Erie, and in Lake Pepin and other northern lakes. It spawns in sand or gravel in shallow water. Its eggs are small, twelve to an inch, and average fifty thousand to a female. After spawning it retires to deeper water, and in summer locates in the deepest pools. During the spring freshets it sometimes ascends smaller streams in its search for food. Its usual weight does not exceed three or four pounds, though it often grows much larger, from ten to twenty pounds. I have seen preserved heads of fish that must have weighed thirty or forty pounds, which had been caught in Kentucky —in Tygert Creek and Kentucky River. It is highly prized as a food-fish, its flesh being white, firm, and flaky, and of an excellent flavor. It is a commercial fish of much importance, especially on Lake Erie, from whence it is shipped in large numbers to the city markets, where it always commands a ready sale, being in great demand during the Lenten season.

The pike-perch is a good game-fish, taking live bait eagerly, and rising pretty well to the fly. When hooked it is a vigorous fighter, pulling strongly and lustily. It does not exhibit much dash or take line rapidly, but swims away rather slowly, but at the same time is constantly tugging and jerking on the line in such a manner as to require careful handling with light tackle. Ordinary black-bass rods and tackle are well suited for the pike-perch up to six or eight pounds, either for bait-fishing or fly-fishing. Where they are found in considerable numbers, and especially on lakes where pickerel or pike abound, gimp snells should be used instead of gut snells to withstand their sharp teeth; otherwise the tackle may be the same as recommended for black-bass fishing. The best bait is a live minnow, though crawfish are successfully used. On lakes it should be fished for in comparatively deep water, over pebbly or rocky bottom. On streams the likely places are in deep and swift water, at the foot of rapids, or on a rocky lee shore with a brisk wind, where it congregates in search of minnows that are rendered almost helpless by the churning water.

Owing to its nocturnal habits, the hours from about sunset until dark are the most favorable. Night fishing is also quite successful should any one care for it. As a matter of experiment I fished Pewaukee Lake, in Wisconsin, one moonlit evening in summer, many years ago, in company with three other anglers, there being two to a boat. In a few hours twenty-two were landed to each boat, weighing from three to four pounds each. This was my only experience in fishing for pike-perch at night, but I have known many others to practise it very successfully.

Fly-fishing is most successful from about sundown until dark, or later, and on cloudy days also during the afternoon. Two flies on a four-foot leader may be used, one of which should be a light-colored one, as the coachman, or white miller; the other may be any of the hackles or the stone fly, oriole, gray drake, polka, professor, or Montreal. The same instructions concerning fly-fishing for black-bass may be profitably followed for the pike-perch, allowing the flies to sink two or three feet after each cast, though it is a more uncertain fish to locate, being much given to roaming in its search for food at different seasons.

Years ago I had fine sport on several occasions, about sundown, fly-fishing for pike-perch from the bridge over Neenah channel, the outlet of Lake Winnebago, in Wisconsin. It was really the best fishing I have ever had for this fish. All the conditions seemed to be just right, and they responded eagerly to the coachman and oriole at first, but at the approach of dusk they preferred the dusty miller and gray hackle. The fish averaged three pounds, and in the swift water were quite gamy. I have been very successful, on many occasions, fly-fishing on the Muskingum River, in Ohio, fishing just below the dams late in the afternoon; and also about the rocky tow-heads on the upper Ohio River,— the fish, however, averaging only about a pound. But taking everything into consideration, the character of the stream and its surroundings, I think I have had the most enjoyable experience with the pike-perch, both in fly-fishing and bait-fishing, on Rock River, Wisconsin, in the southern part of the state. It is a beautiful, rocky river in places, an ideal stream for wading. The fish also were of good size, running up to five or six pounds.

In fishing for pike-perch in different parts of

the country I have noticed its variableness of coloration, which might be inferred from some of its names, as gray pike, yellow pike, blue pike, white salmon, etc. As I remember them, those caught in brackish water in Maryland were quite greenish, with silvery reflections and with dark markings. On Lake Erie the coloration varies somewhat with age, the younger ones being known as blue pike, the mature fish as yellow pike, and the oldest and largest as gray pike. On the rivers of the Middle West that are subject to periods of high and muddy water they are much paler. On the many pine-fringed lakes in northern Wisconsin and Minnesota the variation in color is quite apparent, both as to the ground color and markings. The older fish are very dark and dull on the back, and the younger ones much brighter.

THE SAUGER

(Stizostedion canadense)

The sauger was first described by C. H. Smith, in 1834, who named it *canadensis*, from having collected his type specimens in Canada.

It is also known as jack, sand-pike, gray-pike, and rattlesnake pike. It is closely related to the pike-perch, though smaller and more slender, with a more pointed head and smaller eye. It is distributed through the Great Lake region and in the upper portions of the Missouri, Mississippi, and Ohio rivers. It grows to a length of twelve to fifteen inches. Its color is paler than the pike-perch, grayish above, with brassy sides, which are marked by several blackish blotches or patches, hence "rattlesnake pike."

It is not nearly so good a food-fish as the pike-perch, and is not of much importance as a game-fish. It may be fished for with the same tackle as that recommended for the calico-bass or crappie, in the same situations mentioned for the pike-perch. I have taken it with a gaudy fly on the Ohio and Muskingum rivers, in Ohio, and in the Big Sandy and Tygert Creek, in Kentucky; also by still-fishing and trolling on Lake Erie about the Bass Islands. The meaning or etymology of the name "sauger" is unknown.

THE YELLOW-PERCH

(*Perca flavescens*)

The yellow-perch was first described by Dr. Mitchill in 1814, from the vicinity of New York. He named it *flavescens*, "yellowish," owing to its coloration. It is closely allied to the perch of

Europe. It is commonly known as perch or yellow-perch, also as ringed-perch and raccoon-perch. It is abundant in the Great Lake region and in coastwise streams of the Atlantic slope from Nova Scotia to North Carolina. It is also common in some of the tributaries of the upper Mississippi River and in certain lakes in northern Indiana. It is a handsome fish, well proportioned, and of a lively disposition. It has a shapely body, with a depth of about one-third of its length, somewhat compressed, and with an arching back. The mouth is moderate in size, with bands of small, bristlelike teeth, but no canines, and has a projecting snout. The head is not quite one-third of the length of the body. Its back is dark olive, sides bright golden yellow, belly pale or pinkish, with half a dozen or more broad, dark, vertical bars. The lower fins are bright red or orange. While the coloration varies somewhat in different situations it is always brilliant, rendering it one of the handsomest fishes among the fresh-water species.

The yellow-perch is gregarious, always in schools, and the fish of a school will be about of a uniform size, be that great or small. It frequents waters of a moderate depth in streams or lakes or ponds. In streams, early in the spring, it frequently resorts to the edge or foot of riffles, when feeding, but later prefers the deeper water under mill-dams and about the submerged timbers of bridges, and the still water under hollow banks, or in the eddies of old logs, rocks, etc. It is averse to a muddy bottom in fresh water, but along the eastern coast it is often found on the weedy shoals of shallow bays in brackish water. In my boyhood days it was a prime favorite with myself and companions. We sought it on the mud-flats, among the water-plants, of the Patapsco River, near Baltimore. It was there known as "yellow Ned," and was considered a good pan-fish.

In Lake Michigan, after leaving its winter quarters in the spring, it fairly swarms about the piers and wharves of Chicago and other towns, where it is caught by thousands by men, women, and children with hand-lines, rods, and dip-nets. It is a very predaceous fish and feeds principally on small minnows and the young of other fishes, also on crawfish, tadpoles, small frogs, insects, etc. In large waters it grows to a pound or two in weight, sometimes more. Usually it is much smaller, a half-pound perch being a good-sized fish in most localities. In midsummer, in weedy ponds, it is not good; but at other seasons, or in clear, cold water, it is an excellent pan-fish, firm and flaky. In brackish water it is good at all seasons. Whenever it has a muddy taste, it should be skinned, by which the objectionable flavor is removed almost entirely, and owing to its adherent scales it is the best plan for dressing it. It spawns early in the spring, in March and April, though in very cold waters not until May. The eggs are about twelve to the inch, and are held together by a glutinous substance in long, ribbonlike masses from two to six feet in length, and from an inch to three or four inches wide.

Light trout tackle, either for bait-fishing or fly-fishing, is suitable for the yellow-perch for those anglers who can appreciate the pleasure to be derived only by the use of appropriate and elegant tackle for any kind of fishing, and a pound perch is well worthy of such implements. With a fly-rod of a few ounces, a light click reel, an enamelled silk line, and a small leader and flies on hooks No. 7, the yellow-perch will not disappoint the most exacting angler who has a true love for the sport. Under such circumstances it is a good game-fish, eager to rise, bold to a degree, and fights to a finish.

Most of the flies used for black-bass, as coach-man, polka, oriole, professor, Abbey, etc., are successful, as well as the hackles of various shades, and occasionally red ibis and stone fly. The late afternoon hours are to be preferred for fly-fishing. The flies should be allowed to sink with each cast, after being fluttered on the surface a few seconds.

In the absence of a more suitable rod, a light one of native cane, nine or ten feet long, will do good service without a reel. The line should be the smallest " sea-grass," or twisted silk. Hooks Nos. 5 or 6, on gut snells, with a small brass box-swivel for connecting snell and line, make up the rest of the tackle.

The most taking bait is a small minnow, but grasshoppers, crickets, white grubs, or earth-worms are good. In tidal waters the shrimp is preferred. But in the absence of any of these baits, cut-bait, either fish or flesh, may be used with good results, for the yellow-perch is not very particular or fastidious. Large perch are also easily taken by trolling with the minnow, or a very small spoon on lakes or ponds. If the spoon is employed, but a single hook should be used, and that not too large. I am not an advocate, however, for trolling for so small a fish, and merely mention it as one of the ways and means that may be followed. There are men who never rise above this method for any game-fish, but they are more to be pitied than blamed. They either lack the skill to practise more approved methods, or are too indolent to learn them.

The yellow-perch has been introduced into some waters west of the Rockies. A few weighing about a pound were sent to me from a lake about forty miles west of Spokane, which were of exceptionally bright coloration and good flavor. In the same box were two pike of about four pounds each, and a large-mouth black-bass of eight pounds, dressed, and very fat, plump, and delicious. These fish were the result of a single plant by the United States Fish Commission some years ago. On the Missouri River, a few miles above the Great Falls, a large lake has been formed by an expansion of the river, caused by building a dam for an electric light plant. Several years ago some yellow-perch were placed in this lake, or in the river just above it, but by whom I have not been able to ascertain. At all events, the lake now swarms with perch, strings of one hundred or more not being an uncommon catch in a single day, as I am credibly informed. As the water above the forks of the Missouri River is too cold for the perch, and the water of the lake too warm for trout or grayling, there seems to be no probability of any harm resulting from the introduction of the yellow-perch, though it was not a wise thing to do. About the only fish in that portion of the Missouri, before the perch were planted just above the Great Falls, were ling, suckers, and catfish.

In the many small lakes near Oconomowoc, Wisconsin, the yellow-perch thrives well. It is caught in the summer by men, women, and children with almost any kind of bait, and often with the rudest tackle. To the summer visitors it is a source of perennial delight, and an unfailing means of enjoyment to the juvenile anglers In my day, Genesee Lake, a few miles from Oconomowoc, contained some of the largest perch of all the numerous lakes and lakelets. In this lake only the small-mouth bass and yellow-perch were found, no large-mouth bass or pike, and the bass and perch were of about the same size — two pounds. This uniformity of weight did not obtain in any of the other lakes. A basket of perch from Genesee Lake was a handsome sight, and the fish were unusually sweet and savory. During the winter the residents catch yellow-perch through holes cut in the ice in great numbers, in all of the lakes mentioned. It was here that I devised my "Oconomowoc" bass fly with creamy yellow body, hackle of hairs of deer's tail, cinnamon (woodcock) wings, and tail of ginger; but for the perch of Genesee I found that with a tail of scarlet wool it was more effective. Many a two-pound perch responded to that lure, in days long gone, and as Thoreau says, "It is a true fish, such as the angler loves to put into his basket or hang on top of his willow twig on shady afternoons."

CHAPTER VI

THE GRAYLING FAMILY

(*Thymallidæ*)

Thymallus signifer. Head 5½; depth 4⅔; eye 3; D. 24; A. 11; scales 8–88 to 90–11; cœca 18; body elongate, compressed, highest under the anterior portion of the dorsal; head rather short, subconic, compressed, its upper outline continuous with anterior curve of the back; mouth moderate, the maxillary extending to below the middle of the eye; maxillary 6 (?) in head; jaws about equal; tongue, in the young, with teeth, which are usually absent in the adult; eye quite large, rather longer than snout; scales moderate; lateral line nearly straight; a small bare space behind isthmus; dorsal fin long and high, about 3½ in length of body; adipose fin small; anal fin small; gill-rakers short and slender, about 12 below the angle.

Thymallus tricolor. Head 5, depth 5½, eye 4, D. 21 or 22; A. 10; scales 93 to 98; gill-rakers 7 + 12; maxillary 2½ in head; dorsal fin 5½ in length of body. Otherwise much as *T. signifer.*

Thymallus montanus. Head 5; depth 4½; eye 3½; D. 18 to 21; A. 10 or 11; scales 8–82 to 85–10; gill-rakers 5 + 12; maxillary 3 in head; dorsal fin 4½ in length of body. Other features much resembling *T. signifer* and *T. tricolor.*

OWING to the restricted area of its distribution, the "graceful, gliding grayling" is known to but comparatively few anglers in America. He who has been so fortunate as to have this beautiful fish respond to his deftly cast flies, will bear me out in the assertion that for courage, finesse, and all the qualities that constitute a true game-fish, the grayling is the equal of its congener, the trout.

In France it is known as ombre, in Germany as asche, and in Norway as harren. Among all English-speaking people it is the grayling, though occasionally it is called umber in parts of England. All of these names are somewhat descriptive of its grayish, ashy, or bluish coloration. Gliding along in clear, swift water it seems, indeed, a gray shadow; but fresh out of its native element it becomes a creature of mother-of-pearl, so beautiful and varied are its tints.

The graceful outlines and beautifully-moulded proportions of the grayling, together with the satiny sheen and delicate coloration of her adornment, have always impressed me as essentially feminine. The evanescent play of prismatic hues on her shapely and rounded sides, when fresh from the pure and crystal stream she loves so well, reminds one of changeable silk shot with all the colors of the rainbow. Her tall dorsal fin, with its rose-colored spots, she waves as

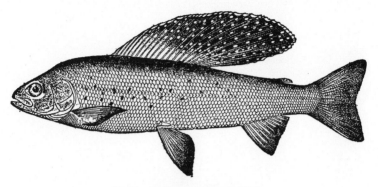

THE ARCTIC GRAYLING
Thymallus signifer

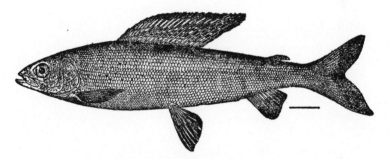

THE MICHIGAN GRAYLING
Thymallus tricolor

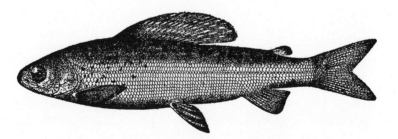

THE MONTANA GRAYLING
Thymallus montanus

gracefully and effectually as the nodding plume of a duchess.

The grayling was named by the ancients *Thymallus*, owing to a smell of thyme that was said to emanate from the fish when freshly caught. However that may have been in days of old, it is not so now, though an odor of cucumbers is sometimes perceptible when it is just out of the water. But the name, if not the odor, has endured to the present day, for *Thymallus* is still its generic appellation. The graylings were formerly included in the salmon family, and are still so considered by European ichthyologists, who include them in the genus *Salmo*. Dr. Theodore Gill, however, has formed them into a separate family (*Thymallidæ*), owing to the peculiar structure of the skull, whereby the parietal bones meet at the median line, excluding the frontal bones from the supra-occipital; whereas in the other salmonids the parietals are separated by the intervention of the supra-occipital bone, which connects with the frontals.

There are three species in America: one in the Arctic regions, one in Michigan, and one in Montana. To the untrained eye no great difference is apparent between these various species as to form and coloration,[1] and their habits are similar, all loving clear, cold, and swift water, with gravelly or sandy bottom. They feed on insects and their larvæ, small minnows, crustaceans, and such small organisms. They spawn in the spring. The eggs are smaller than trout eggs, running seven to the inch. They hatch in from ten days to two weeks, according to temperature of the water.

THE ARCTIC GRAYLING

(*Thymallus signifer*)

The Arctic grayling was first described by Sir John Richardson, in 1823, from specimens

[1] SPECIFIC CHARACTERIZATIONS OF THE GRAYLINGS

	T. signifer	*T. tricolor*	*T. montanus*
Head in length	5½	5	5
Depth in length	4⅔	5½	4¼
Eye in head	3	4	3¼
Maxillary in head	6 (?)	2½	3
Scales	8–88 to 90–11	93–98	8–82 to 85–10
Gill-rakers	12 below the angle	7 + 12	5 + 12
Dorsal rays	20–24	21–22	18–21
Height of dorsal fin	3½ in length	5½ in length	4½ in length

collected at Winter Lake, near Fort Enterprise, in British America. He named it *signifer*, or "standard-bearer," in allusion to its tall, waving, gayly-colored dorsal fin. It is presumably the oldest and original species, and it is not unlikely that it was transported to Michigan and Montana on an ice-field during the glacial period. It is often called Bach's grayling, in honor of an officer of that name who took the first one on the fly, when with the Arctic expedition of Sir John Franklin, in 1819. It abounds in clear, cold streams of the Mackenzie and Yukon provinces in British America, and in Alaska up to the Arctic Ocean. This boreal grayling has a somewhat smaller head than the other species, its upper outline being continuous with the curve of the back. The mouth is small, extending to below the middle of the eye, which latter is larger than in the other graylings, while its dorsal fin is both longer and higher, and contains a few more rays. The sides are purplish gray, darker on the back; head brownish, a blue mark on each side of the lower jaw; the dorsal fins dark gray, splashed with a lighter shade, with rows of deep blue spots edged with red; ventral fins with red and white stripes. Along

the sides are scattered a few irregularly-shaped
black spots.

A friend of mine, an ardent angler, returned
recently from Cape Nome and the Yukon, in
Alaska, where he resided for several years. He
informed me that the grayling is very abundant
in the streams of that region, and that he had
taken thousands on the fly; but not knowing
that they differed from the Montana grayling, he
did not examine them closely.

THE MICHIGAN GRAYLING
(*Thymallus tricolor*)

The Michigan grayling was first described by
Professor E. D. Cope, in 1865, from specimens
from the Au Sable River. He named it *tricolor*,
on account of its handsomely-decorated fins and
body. At that time it was abundant in the Au
Sable, Manistee, Marquette, Jordan, Pigeon, and
other rivers in the northern part of the lower peninsula of Michigan, and in Otter Creek, near
Keweenah, in the upper peninsula. It has a somewhat larger head than the Arctic form, its length
being about one-fifth of the length of the body;
the outline of the latter does not differ except
in not being so prominent over the shoulder.

The coloration is purplish gray with silvery reflections, darker on the back, belly white and iridescent; sides of head with bright bluish and bronze lustre; sides of the body with small, black, irregular spots; ventral fins with oblique, rose-colored lines; dorsal with alternate dusky and rose-colored lines below, and alternate rows of dusky green and roseate spots above; caudal fin dusky with a middle roseate stripe.

In 1870–1876 I visited most of the grayling streams in Michigan, and found it abundant, affording fine fishing. At that time it was also in the Boyne, and in Pine Lake and River. I also took it in Lake Michigan while fishing for cisco from the pier at Charlevoix. Fish running from a pound to a pound and a half were common, and occasionally one of two pounds was taken.

It is sad to contemplate the gradual disappearance of this fish from the once densely populated streams of Michigan. At the present day the angler is fortunate, indeed, who succeeds in taking a brace of grayling where a few years ago his basket was soon filled. This deplorable state of affairs has been brought about by the axe of the lumberman, whose logs, descending the small streams on the spring rise, plough up the spawning beds, smothering the eggs and killing the helpless fry. As brook-trout spawn in the fall they escape this calamity, the fry being old enough in April to take pretty good care of themselves. The decrease of both trout and grayling is commonly attributed to over-fishing; but while this may have its influence to a limited extent in lessening the numbers for a season, other causes must be looked for to account for the permanent depletion of certain waters.

A stream or pond will support but a limited number of fish, the number depending on the supply of natural food for both young and mature. By the supply of food on one hand, and the natural enemies of the fish on the other, a certain balance is maintained which if disturbed by, say, overfishing one season, will be restored by natural laws the next. And this state of affairs will continue so long as the natural conditions of the waters remain un-disturbed.

By cutting down the pine trees at the sources of the streams and along the small tributaries, which are the spawning grounds of both trout and grayling, the natural conditions are changed. The scorching rays of the summer sun are admitted where once mosses and ferns and the trailing arbutus luxuriated in the shade of a dense growth of pines and hemlocks and firs. The soil becomes dry, the carpet of green shrivels and dies, and the myriads of insects that once bred and multiplied in the cool and grateful shade, and whose larvæ furnish the food for the baby fish, disappear. The brooks and rivulets diminish and vanish. A page has been torn from the book of nature, and the place that trout and grayling knew so well is known no more forever.

THE MONTANA GRAYLING

(*Thymallus montanus*)

The Montana grayling was collected by Professor James W. Milner, of the United States Fish Commission, in 1872, from a tributary of the Missouri River, at Camp Baker, in Montana. He named it *montanus*, from the name of the state. Lewis and Clark, however, during their wonderful journey that blazed the western course of empire, described, but did not name it, seventy years before, from fish taken near the head waters of the Jefferson River.   A few years ago (1898) it was my good fortune to be the first to call attention to this prior description.   Knowing that Lewis and Clark ascended the Jefferson nearly to its source in the Rocky Mountains, in 1805, I thought it extremely probable that those remarkably close observers had mentioned the existence of this beautiful and well-marked species.   Upon investigation I found my surmise to be correct. On page 545 of Dr. Elliott Coues's edition (1893) of " The Lewis and Clark Expedition," I found the following : —

" Toward evening we formed a drag of bushes, and in about two hours caught 528 very good fish, most of them large trout.   Among them we observed for the first time ten or twelve trout of a white or silvery color, except on the back and head, where they are of a bluish cast; in appearance and shape they resemble exactly the speckled trout, except they are not so large, though the scales are much larger ; the flavor is equally good."   (In a foot-note Dr. Coues stated that this fish remained unidentified.)

The locality where these fish were taken was near the head waters of the Jefferson River, where Lewis and Clark abandoned their canoes and crossed the Continental Divide on horses purchased from the Indians. At this point the grayling is abundant to-day, as I know from personal observation, and coexists with the red-throat trout almost to the exclusion of all other species.

Lewis and Clark were both remarkable for clear and correct descriptions of the animals and plants met with during their journey, many of which were new to science; but as they neglected to give them scientific names, others have reaped the honors of many of their discoveries. I published my identification of the fish in question as being undoubtedly the grayling, and soon afterward received a letter from Dr. Coues, congratulating me and indorsing my opinion, which he said was certainly correct.

The Montana grayling is found only in the tributaries of the Missouri River above the Great Falls. In Sheep and Tenderfoot creeks, tributaries of Smith River, in the Little Belt Mountains, it is fairly abundant, as it is likewise in the three forks of the Missouri, — the Gallatin, Madison, and Jefferson rivers. Its ideal home is in several tributaries at the head of Red Rock Lake, swift gravelly streams, and especially in the upper reaches of the Madison above the upper cañon, where the water is rapid, though unbroken, the bottom being dark obsidian sand, with a succession of pools and shallows. I have taken fish weighing two pounds in Beaver Creek, in the upper cañon, which is also an ideal stream. Such situations are peculiarly adapted to the grayling, being preferred to the broken water of rocky streams so much favored by trout.

The Montana grayling is a trimmer-built fish than its Michigan cousin, being not quite so deep, proportionally, and with larger scales. Its dorsal fin is about the same height, but with one or two less rays.

Its back is gray, with purplish reflections; sides lighter, with lilac, pink, and silvery reflections; belly pearly white. It has a few irregularly-shaped black spots on the anterior part of the body, but none posteriorly as sometimes on the Michigan grayling. It has two oblong dark blotches in the cleft of the lower jaw, and a heavy dark line running from the ventrals to the pectoral fin; these markings are more pronounced in the male, being quite faint or wanting in the female. The dorsal fin has a rosy-red border, six or seven rows of roseate, roundish spots, ocellated with white, and gray blotches form lines between the

rows of red spots; in the upper, posterior angle
of the dorsal fin are several larger oblong rosy
spots; the ventral fins have three rose-colored
stripes along the rays; the pectoral and anal fins
are plain; the caudal fin is forked.

As a game-fish the grayling is fully the equal
of the trout, though its way of taking the artificial
fly is quite different, and the old hand at trout
fishing must pay court to "the lady of the
streams" with the greatest assiduity before he is
successful in winning her attention to his lures.
And even then he must become fully conversant
with her coy and coquettish way of accepting his
offer, though it be cast never so deftly. There
is a rush and snap and vim in the rise of a trout
to the fly that is lacking with the grayling. The
trout often leaps above the water to seize the fly,
while it is taken more quietly and deliberately,
though just as eagerly, by the grayling from
below. In other words, it is "sucked in," as
English anglers term it, though that hardly ex-
presses it, as the act is not so tame as might be
inferred. On the contrary, the grayling rises
from the bottom of a pool and darts upward like
an arrow to seize the fly, though as a rule it does
not break water, and is not so demonstrative as

the trout; but it seldom misses the mark, if the fly is small enough, which the trout often does.

Sometimes the grayling will rise a dozen times to a fly, and for some reason refuse it, but will take it at the very next cast. Just why this is so is one of the unanswerable problems that often vexes or confounds the angler. Presumably the fly is too large, or is not presented in just the right way to please her ladyship. But the angler should not despair under such circumstances, but remember the old couplet, " If at first you don't succeed, try, try again." Moreover, he must remember that he is fishing for grayling, not for trout. He must not cast on a riffle, or at its head, but below, in the eddy or still water, where it is deepest. There lie the large fish, though small ones may be in the shallower water, and it is the latter that perplex one by their antics, oftentimes leaping over one's flies in play.

Trout generally lie in ambush beneath the bank, shelving rocks, or roots, usually in shallow water, from whence they rush with tigerlike feroc- ity upon the fly, often leaping over it in their eagerness for the fancied prey. On the contrary, grayling lie on the bottom of pools, in swift water, entirely in the open. They are also gregarious, assembling in schools, while the trout is a lone watcher from his hidden lair.

Some dry fly-fishers of England, echoing the opinion of Charles Cotton, term the grayling a "dead-hearted fish" that must be taken with a wet or sunken fly. This idea of its lack of gameness is implied in Tennyson's lines: —

> "Here and there a lusty trout,
> And here and there a grayling."

As the English grayling grows only to half of the weight of the trout, it suffers by comparison when killed on the heavy rods of our English brothers. Their assertion, also, that the grayling has a tender mouth, and must be handled gingerly, is another fallacy, inasmuch as it has as tough lips as the trout, but the smaller hooks of grayling flies do not hold so firmly as the larger and stronger hooks of trout flies.

It must not be supposed that the grayling is not a leaping fish because it takes the fly from beneath the surface of the water. On the contrary, in its playful moods it may be seen leaping above the surface the same as a trout, and moreover it breaks water repeatedly after being hooked,

which the trout seldom does.   It puts up a stiff
fight also beneath the surface, being much aided
in its resistance by its tall dorsal fin.   It is no
disparagement, then, to the gamesome trout, to
declare the grayling its equal when of similar
size and weight.

Grayling fishing has been practised in England
for centuries.   In addition to fly-fishing, swimming the maggot, where a tiny float is used, is
a common method.   An artificial bait, called the
grasshopper, is likewise employed.   While grayling are taken during the trout season, in spring
and summer, the most successful season seems to
be from September to December, when they are
at their best, both as to gameness and condition.

With English anglers the universal practice is
to fish up-stream, as the fish are not so apt to see
the angler, and that plan undoubtedly has its
advantages in the clear and shallow streams of
England.   In fishing for grayling, however, it is
advised by some of their best anglers to cast
across the stream, instead of above, and allow the
flies to float down.   No reason is given for this
deviation from the generally accepted method
with trout; but I imagine that as grayling lie on
the bottom of deep pools, it has been found by

experience that they are not so apt to see the angler as other species in mid-water or near the surface, especially in the clear chalk streams.

In America, the streams being deeper, the necessity for fishing up-stream is not so apparent. Fishing down-stream is by far the best plan, for obvious reasons, if the angler wades slowly and cautiously, so as not to roil the water. The principal reason is that one's line is always straight and taut in swift water, and the flies can be more easily controlled and floated down over the fish, which always heads up-stream. Upon hooking the fish it can be drawn to one side, whereby the other fish in the pool are not much more alarmed than in the case of casting up or across. Casting across seems to be really a concession to the advantage of fishing down-stream.

The fly-rod, reel, line, and leader ordinarily employed for trout-fishing may be used also for grayling, though I would advise some modifications. While a first-class split-bamboo rod of three and a half or four ounces may be advantageously used by an angler who knows how to handle a very light rod, I prefer one of five or six ounces. Such a rod is certainly light enough to be used all day without fatigue, and it is well to have the

resourceful reserve of an ounce or two for emergencies. In any case it should not exceed ten
and one-half feet in length, if built on the modern
plan, where most of the pliancy is in its upper
two-thirds, the lower third being stiffish and
springy, constituting its backbone. A very good
rod can be constructed with ash butt, and lancewood, greenheart, or bethabara upper pieces, and
one that will be almost as light as split-bamboo,
and certainly more serviceable in the long run.
I would also advise flush, non-dowelled joints,
and reel-bands instead of a solid reel-seat, the latter being of no advantage and only adding to the
weight of the rod; moreover, it is now put on
the cheapest rods to make them sell. A plain
groove for the reel, with bands, is very much better.

As a matter of course the line should be of
braided silk, enamelled, and suited to the weight
of the rod, as small as size G, but not larger than
size E. It may be level, but a tapered line is
better for casting, and is also better adapted for
the delicate leader that must be employed.

A tapered leader six feet long is best, but
should not be shorter than four feet. It must be
made of the very best silkworm gut fibre, round,
clear, and unstained. The distal end should be

made of the finest drawn gut, known as gossamer, and taper to the larger or proximal end, which should be the smallest undrawn gut.

In England the most delicate leaders and extremely small flies are employed for grayling. The flies are usually tied on Pennell hooks, turndown eye, sizes o, oo, ooo, Kendal scale, which are smaller than No. 12, Redditch scale, the latter being the smallest size commonly used in America. The favorite flies in England have yellowish — lemon to orange — bodies, and bodies of peacock harl, either green or bronze. Flies with purplish, black, or slate-colored bodies are more sparingly employed. They are either hackles or split-winged flies. The formulas for some of the favorites are as follows:—

Red Tag. Body bright green harl from the " moon " of a peacock's feather; hackle, bright red cock's hackle; tag, bright red wool; hook, No. o, Kendal scale.

Orange Bumble. Body, orange floss silk, ribbed with a strand of peacock's sword feather and fine flat gold tinsel; hackle, honey dun cock, wrapped all down the body; hook No. o, Kendal scale.

Green Insect. Body, bright green peacock's harl; hackled with a soft silver-gray hen's feather; hook No. o, Kendal scale.

Bradshaw's Fancy. Body, copper-colored peacock's harl; hackled with a feather from the neck of a Norwegian crow; tag, bright crimson wool or silk, with a couple of turns of the same at the head; tying silk, dark purple; hook No. o, Kendal scale.

Claret Bumble.   Body, claret floss silk, ribbed with a strand of pea-
    cock's sword feather; medium blue dun cock's hackle; hook,
    No. o, Kendal scale.

Most of the foregoing are fancy flies, but are
considered the best killers on English waters.   In
this country it has been demonstrated, also, that
flies with bodies of peacock harl, or with yellowish bodies, have been more uniformly successful
than others.   From this it would appear that the
predilection of grayling for certain colors in artificial flies is much the same both in this country
and England.   From my own experience I can
recommend the following well-known flies, adding,
however, that their construction should be a little
different from the conventional trout flies of these
names in having a red tag or tail of scarlet
wool, instead of the usual tail, and in having narrow split wings instead of the regular style of
full wings: —

Yellowish-bodied flies: professor, queen of the
water, Oconomowoc, Lord Baltimore.   Green-
bodied flies: coachman, Henshall, and grizzly king.
Other useful flies are black gnat, cinnamon, iron-
blue dun, oriole, red ant, gray hackle, and black
hackle.   They should all be tied on Sproat or
O'Shaughnessy hooks, No. 12, Redditch or com-

mon scale. Two flies only should be used in a cast, and of different colors.

Bearing in mind that the portions of a stream mostly used by grayling are the sandy and gravelly pools in swift, smooth water, they are fished for in much the same way as trout, except that the flies are allowed to sink below the surface, very much as in black-bass fishing. It is very important that the line and leader are always taut, inasmuch as the rise of the fish is not always seen, except as a quick flash or shadow beneath the surface. With a tight line the fish will be more apt to hook itself. With the small hooks of grayling flies, it is not wise for the angler to attempt to "strike," as in trout or black-bass fishing.

Upon hooking the fish it should be led sidewise from the pool, if possible, so as not to disturb or frighten the others of the school; and for the same reason it should be kept near the surface until taken into the landing-net.

Either a light trout bait-rod or the fly-rod may be employed for bait-fishing for grayling, with fine silk line, leader, and hooks Nos. 6 to 8 with a split-shot sinker a foot above the hook. English-anglers use a small float, but in fishing downstream it is not advisable, as the current prevents

o

the bait from touching the bottom, and renders the use of a float for this purpose unnecessary. The bait should be kept from six inches to a foot above the bottom. The best bait is the larva of the caddis-fly, a small worm or caterpillar encased in a bag or covering composed of bits of bark, sticks, etc.; it is known in the Rocky Mountain region as the "rockworm." Earthworms, small grasshoppers, crickets, and grubs of various kinds are also useful.

When it became known to fishculturists, about 1874, that the grayling existed in Michigan, attempts were made to propagate it artificially, but without success, as the same lines were pursued as with the brook-trout. It remained for the United States Fish Commission to successfully cope with the problem in Montana, under my supervision. Beginning with 1898, we have hatched millions at Bozeman Station and the auxiliary station near Red Rock Lake, at the head of the Jefferson River. We have also shipped millions of eggs to different parts of the Union, as far east as Maine, New Hampshire, and Vermont, mostly to United States Fish Commission stations, where they were hatched and planted in suitable streams. It is to be hoped that some of these plants will result in the permanent establishment of this beautiful and desirable fish in eastern waters.

The eggs of the grayling are smaller than those of the trout, being but one-seventh of an inch in diameter. When first extruded they are amber-colored, owing to a large oil-drop, which renders them lighter than trout eggs, almost semi-buoyant, and for this reason are best hatched, or at least "eyed," in hatching jars. My plan is to keep them in the hatching jars until the eye-spots show, when they are removed to hatching-trays until incubation is complete.

In a few days after extrusion the eggs become crystal-like or hyaline in color, when the embryo can be seen in motion. The period of incubation is from ten days to two weeks. The fry when hatched are very small, about the size of mosquito "wigglers" (larvæ). Their umbilical yolk-sac is absorbed in a few days, when it becomes impera-tive to supply them with stream water, which contains the small organisms (*Entomostraca*) on which they feed at first. Afterward they can be fed artificially the same as trout fry, which they soon outgrow.

There is an erroneous opinion that has gained

considerable currency among anglers to the effect that grayling and trout are antagonistic, and that to this cause is to be attributed the decrease of grayling in the waters of Michigan. My observations have led me to the conclusion that this opinion is not supported by any evidence whatever. When I fished the streams of that state, years ago, both trout and grayling were plentiful in the same waters, and were living in harmony as they had done from time immemorial. Their habits and choice of locality being different, the trout hiding under cover and the grayling lying in exposed pools, their struggle for existence or supremacy does not bring them much in opposition, or cause them to prey on each other or on their eggs or fry in an unusual degree, or to such an extent as to effect the marked decrease of either species. Honors are even. It is the same in Montana. In that state the red-throat trout and grayling seek out such portions of the streams as are best suited to them; but very often they are found together on neutral ground, where they live peaceably and not at variance with each other. As no disturbing element has yet been introduced, their numbers still bear the same relative proportion that has existed since the days of yore.

Likewise in England, in such historic waters as the Wye, the Derwent, the Wharfe, or the Dove, hallowed by "meek Walton's heavenly memory," the grayling and trout still coexist in about the same relative proportion that has been maintained since and before the days of Dame Juliana Berners, Izaak Walton, and Charles Cotton in the fifteenth century. On those quiet streams no cause has ever been allowed to militate against the well-being of either species, or to disturb the natural conditions to any considerable extent.

In a recent number of the *London Fishing Gazette* is one of the best articles on the English grayling that I have ever seen. It is written by Mr. E. F. Goodwin, who is undoubtedly fully conversant with his theme and well acquainted with the habits of that fish. Among other things he says: —

"When in season I maintain that the grayling will give excellent sport on suitable tackle, is splendid eating, and is as handsome a fish as any angler need wish to gaze upon. What more can one want? How Charles Cotton could have written in such terms of condemnation of the sporting qualities of this fish as to call him 'one of the deadest-hearted fishes in the world, and the bigger he is the more easily taken,' passes my understanding, although we must remember that this remark was passed to ' Viator ' on his catching a grayling in the early part of March, when the fish would be out of condition in all probability. I confess to a feeling of disappointment at the summary way in which Walton dismisses the grayling, showing that he did not think very highly of him either from an edible or sporting point of view.

"Grayling will rise readily to the artificial fly, and although they will come again time after time if missed (or perhaps I should say if they miss the fly, which is more usual), they require the neatest and finest tackle and the most delicate handling to secure them; and as Francis Francis truly says, 'when you have hooked a grayling, your next job is to land him.' . . . There is a lot of difference between the way a well-conditioned trout and grayling fight after being hooked, and this may account for some of the condemnation heaped upon the latter as to its non-sportive character; for although not so lively as the trout with its mad rushes for liberty, yet the kind of resistance is more dangerous to the hold you have on him, for the grayling tries the hold of the hook in every possible way, and from every possible point of that hold. To my mind a grayling is much more difficult to land than a trout, and the more I fish for grayling the more convinced I am of his game-ness and sporting qualities. Certainly there are a great many more grayling lost after being hooked than trout, and this is accounted for prin-cipally not so much from the reputed tenderness of the mouth as from the fact of the fish not being so firmly hooked as the trout usually is.

"The ideas of grayling not heading up-stream and of being deleterious to the trout have been perpetuated by author after author, just copying one another without really ascertaining the facts. . . . As regards the advisability of introducing grayling into a trout stream, that depends en-tirely upon the nature of the river. As far as my experience and observation go, grayling only become detrimental to the trout in that, being active and voracious feeders, they consume the food that otherwise would have belonged to and been partaken of by the trout. It is certain that these fish live together in general amity. The grayling is but seldom a fish eater, and therefore any accusation as to its being destructive to the fry of trout is untenable. That it, in the trout-spawning season, may help itself to what it can find of the superfluous ova which float down the stream no one can object to, but as to its burrowing in the redds and disturbing the hatching ova, I very much doubt it. Both the late Dr. Brunton and Dr. Hamilton were very strong in their assertion that this was a matter of impossibility with the grayling, and yet we are assured by Dr. James A. Henshall that the fry of grayling are as much addicted to cannibalism as the pike-perch fry."

After giving a brief space to natural bait-fishing, he goes on to say: " But after all there is only one way in which this fish should be caught, and that is with the fly. This ground has been gone over so many times that it only remains for me to say that, the grayling being a bold and daring riser, never be discouraged if you fail to hook him, even if he rise at your fly time after time. He lies very low in the river when watching for his prey, and therefore is not so easily disturbed; and if you remain quite still when he has risen and missed the fly and gone down to his lair, he will surely rise again. His rise, too, is different to a trout. A trout, from lying close to the surface when feeding, takes without effort the flies floating over him, and also is easily scared. A grayling, from lying deep in the water, quite close to the bottom, comes up with great rapidity, and seldom takes the fly until it has passed him; and should he miss it, which often happens, disappears so quickly that he may well be compared to a shadow — hence the name of 'umber,' from *umbra*, a shadow. Should you hook him, up goes his great dorsal fin and down goes his head in his determination to get to his hiding-place, and it depends on his size and gameness, as well as the skill of the angler, whether he succeeds or not. I have often heard anglers complain that grayling are more difficult to hook than trout. Experienced anglers are all aware that grayling are not so easily hooked on the rise as trout, but he offers the best compensation in his power by consenting to rise over and over again until if you do not hook him the fault is yours, not his. When he rises at a passing fly he must ascend at lightning speed in order to cover the distance in time to catch it; having done so, he turns instantly head down and descends at the same speed. This is really the 'somersault' so well known to grayling fishers. With a long line it is next to impossible to strike a grayling on the instant, and a taut line in this fishing is of even greater importance than in trout-fishing."

I have given the above liberal quotations because the article agrees so well with my own practice in grayling fishing, and accords with the habits of the American graylings as I have observed them.

THE MORE SPORTSMANLY WAY OF CATCHING
MASCALONGE

CHAPTER VII

THE SALMON FAMILY
(*Salmonidæ*)

THIS is quite an extensive family, embracing the salmons, trouts, and whitefishes, and is characterized principally by an adipose fin and small, smooth scales. It is my province to consider only the Rocky Mountain whitefish and the cisco, as the salmons and trouts are described in another volume of this series. There are a number of whitefishes, but none of them can be considered game-fishes except the one about to be described, as they rarely or never take the fly or bait.

Coregonus williamsoni. Rocky Mountain Whitefish. Head $4\frac{1}{2}$ to 5; depth 4 to 5; eye $4\frac{2}{3}$; D. 11 to 14; A. 11 to 13; scales 8 to 10–83 to 87–7 to 10; body oblong, little compressed; head short, conic, the profile rather abruptly decurved; snout compressed and somewhat pointed at tip, which is below the level of the eye; preorbital broad, $\frac{2}{3}$ the width of the eye; maxillary short and very broad, reaching to the anterior margin of eye, and is contained 4 times in length of head; mandible 3 times; gill-rakers short and thick, $9 + 15$; pectoral fin $1\frac{1}{4}$ in head; ventral $1\frac{2}{3}$; adipose fin large, extending behind the anal fin.

Coregonus williamsoni cis-montanus. Montana Whitefish. Head 5; depth 5 to 5^1; pectoral fin 1^1 in head; ventral 1$\frac{4}{5}$; scales 90. Otherwise like the typical form.

Argyrosomus artedi sisco. Cisco. Head 4 to 5; depth 4 to 4$\frac{1}{2}$; eye 4 to 5; D. 10; A. 12; scales 8–65 to 80–8; body long, slender and somewhat compressed; head long, pointed and compressed; mouth large, lower jaw somewhat projecting, maxillary reaching to pupil; mandible 2$\frac{1}{8}$ in head; dorsal fin high, its rays rapidly shortened; caudal fin forked.

THE ROCKY MOUNTAIN WHITEFISH

(*Coregonus williamsoni*)

This fine fish was first described from the Des Chutes River in Oregon by Dr. Charles Girard in 1856, who described most of the fishes collected during the Pacific Railroad Survey, and named the one under consideration in honor of Lieutenant R. S. Williamson, who had charge of one of the divisions of the Survey.

Its general form is not unlike that of the grayling, which has led to the absurd opinion, held by some, that the grayling is a hybrid, or cross, between this whitefish and the red-throat trout, its body being rather long, nearly elliptical in outline, and somewhat compressed. It is found in the clear streams on both slopes of the Rocky Mountains, and on both sides of the Cascade Range. In the tributaries of the Missouri River in Montana it differs slightly from the typical form, and is

known as the variety *cis-montanus*. It is bluish
or greenish on the back, sides silvery, belly white.
All of the fins are tipped with black; caudal and
adipose fins are steel-blue.

I know this fish only from the streams of Montana, where it coexists with the red-throat trout and
grayling. It spawns in the fall. It feeds on insects and their larvæ, small crustaceans, and the
eggs of other fishes. It grows to about a foot in
length, usually, and to a pound in weight, though
I have taken much larger specimens. It is a
very fair food-fish, — as good, I think, as the
red-throat trout, as its flesh is firmer and flaky,
and devoid of any muddy or musky flavor.

It rises to the artificial fly as readily as the
trout or grayling, and to the same flies, though a
little more partial to small, dark, or grayish ones,
as black, brown, and gray hackles, black gnat,
oriole, gray drake, etc. When the streams are
higher and not so clear, lighter-colored flies are
useful, as professor, coachman, Henshall, miller,
etc. Light trout fly-rods and tackle are used
both for fly- and bait-fishing by Rocky Mountain
anglers, — the bait, when used, being the larva of
the caddis-fly, and known as "rockworm." Grasshoppers are employed in the late summer and

fall. Fly-fishing, however, is the most successful method.

Large baskets of whitefish are made in the three forks of the Missouri River, especially in the lower Gallatin River, where it is taken with the grayling, the red-throat trout not being so plentiful in that part of the stream. The tributaries of this river are also well supplied with whitefish. Bridger Creek, one of the tributaries of East Gallatin River, has some large whitefish. I have taken them in that stream up to two pounds; for gameness they were equal to trout of the same weight, and just as good for the table. They are at their best in the early fall months, before spawning, when they are fat and in fine fettle. At this season they must be looked for in deep holes, especially in August and September, when they are gregarious, and one's basket may be filled from a single hole when of considerable extent. Later they depart for the shallows and pair off for spawning, when they seldom rise to the fly.

There is a sentiment among trout fishers, and among people generally in a trout region, that no other fish is quite so good to eat, or possessed of as much gameness, as the trout. While

I concede beauty of form and coloration to the trout, far excelling all other fresh-water fishes, there are others equally as good for the table, or even better. When camping by mountain streams, freshly-caught trout, fried to crispness in bacon fat, has a happy combined trout-bacon flavor that is certainly delicious, especially when one has the sauce of a camping appetite to favor it; but under similar conditions the mountain whitefish, in my opinion, is fully as good. Nine out of ten persons who are prejudiced in favor of the trout will declare that it has no scales, thus showing a lack of comparison and observation. In the Rocky Mountain region, where there are so few species of fish for the angler, usually only trout, grayling, and whitefish, the latter should be better appreciated.

THE CISCO

(*Argyrosomus artedi sisco*)

The cisco, or so-called "lake-herring," was first described by the French ichthyologist, Le Sueur, in 1818, from Lake Erie and the Niagara River. He named it in honor of Petrus Artedi, the associate of Linnæus, and the "Father of Ichthyology." The variety *sisco* was described and named by Dr. David Starr Jordan, in 1875, from Lake Tippecanoe, Indiana. It was for a long time supposed to exist only in Lake Geneva, Wisconsin, except in the Great Lakes, and an absurd opinion was prevalent that there was an underground communication between that lake and Lake Superior by which the cisco entered it. Soon after Dr. Jordan had discovered it in Tippecanoe Lake I found it in several lakes in Wisconsin, as La Belle, Oconomowoc, and Okauchee. The cisco is somewhat smaller than the lake-herring, but otherwise it is about the same. It is almost elliptical in outline, the body being compressed. The mouth is rather large, with the jaws more projecting than in the lake white-fishes. The coloration is bluish or greenish on the back, with silvery sides and white belly. The scales are sprinkled with black specks. It is a very pretty fish, is gregarious, swimming in large schools, and feeds on the minute organisms found in lakes of good depth. It remains in deep water most of the year, but resorts to shallower water in the summer, preparatory to spawning. From the last of May to June, when the May-fly appears in vast swarms on the western lakes, the cisco approaches the surface to feed on them. It is at this time that they take an artificial fly of a grayish hue. It grows to a length of ten or twelve inches, and is highly esteemed as a food-fish.

At Lake Geneva, when the May-fly appears, crowds of anglers assemble to cast the artificial fly and the natural "cisco-fly," as the May-fly is called. A very light trout fly-rod with corresponding tackle can be utilized for cisco, with gray hackle, gray drake, or green drake, on hooks Nos. 8 to 10. The fishing is done from boats or the shore. In using the natural fly the same sized hooks mentioned will answer. As the May-fly alights on every object, the boat and clothing of the angler as well, the supply of bait is constant and convenient.

The cisco can be caught in winter, through the ice, in water from fifty to seventy-five feet deep, and many are taken in this way from the lakes near Oconomowoc, Wisconsin. A small white or bright object is used as a decoy to attract the fish, which is kept in motion near the baited hook, and on a separate line. The bait may be a very small bit of white bacon or ham fat, or fish flesh, though insect larva is better.

When the talismanic words, " The cisco is running," are pronounced, crowds of anglers from Chicago, Milwaukee, and all intermediate points, with a unanimity of purpose, rush as one man to the common centre of Lake Geneva, in eager anticipation of the brief but happy season of "ciscoing." Anglers of every degree — armed with implements of every description, from the artistic split-bamboo rod of four ounces to the plebeian cane pole or bucolic sapling of slender proportions, and with lines of enamelled silk, linen, or wrapping cord — vie with one another in good-natured rivalry in the capture of the silvery cisco. Very little skill is required to fill the creel, as the schools are on the surface of the water in myriads, and the most bungling cast may hook a fish. Though the etymology of the cisco is unknown, it is a veritable entity, whose name is legion during the month of June at Lake Geneva.

The cisco is a localized variety of the so-called lake-herring of the Great Lakes, and holds the same relation to it that the landlocked salmon does to the Atlantic salmon. Being confined to small lakes, the cisco does not grow so large as the lake herring. Before the Chicago and Milwaukee railway was built, in Wisconsin, there was a plank road extending from Milwaukee to

Watertown, and thirty miles west of Milwaukee this road crossed the outlet of Oconomowoc Lake. Within fifty yards or so of the bridge there stood a roadside tavern where the freight wagons stopped at noon on their way from Lake Michigan to Watertown. I have been informed by old residents of that section that in the fall of the year, about the spawning period of the cisco, boxes of fresh fish were frequently carried by these wagons, some of which were cleaned and dressed for dinner on the bank of the outlet of the lake, and the offal thrown into the stream. It is not unlikely, inasmuch as the fish were so recently caught, that the eggs and milt of the cisco thus became commingled, fertilizing the eggs, which were subsequently hatched. This opinion is supported by the fact that the cisco is found in that locality only in the chain of lakes composed of Oconomowoc, Okauchee, and La Belle lakes, all of which are connected by Oconomowoc River. It is possible that Lake Geneva was stocked in a similar manner from Racine or Kenosha. If it is objected that eggs from dead fish would not be fertilized, there is still a tenable theory: When the fish are taken from the nets alive, many of them are so ripe that the eggs and milt ooze from them. Under these circumstances some of the eggs would become fertilized without a doubt, and by adhering to the fish when placed in the boxes for transportation, they might be carried to the place mentioned, and there deposited in the stream in the manner related.

CHAPTER VIII

THE DRUM FAMILY
(*Sciænidæ*)

THE drumfish or croaker family is quite a large one, comprising nearly one hundred and fifty species, inhabiting the sandy shores of the seas or the brackish water of the bays and estuaries, sometimes ascending tributary rivers to fresh water; the fresh-water drum, hereafter to be described, however, is the only species permanently residing in fresh water. The members of this family have usually an elongate body, with rough-edged (ctenoid) scales; the dorsal fin is deeply notched, or in some species separated into two fins, with the soft-rayed portion, or the second dorsal, composed of many rays, while the spiny-rayed portion has but few; some have barbels, but all have large ear-bones; the air-bladder is usually large and complicated, and is supposed to be the source of the drumming, croaking, or grunting sounds common to most of the species.

Cynoscion regalis. The Weakfish. Body elongate, somewhat compressed; head $3\frac{1}{8}$; depth $4\frac{1}{4}$; eye 6; D. X–I, 27; A. II, 12;
scales 6–56–11; mouth large, maxillary reaching beyond pupil;
teeth sharp, in narrow bands, canines large; soft dorsal and
anal fins scaly, the scales caducous; gill-rakers long and slender,
$x + 11$.

Cynoscion nothus. The Bastard Weakfish. Body elongate, slightly
compressed; head $3\frac{1}{2}$; depth $3\frac{3}{4}$; eye 4; D. X–I, 27; A. II, 9
or 10; scales 6–60–7; mouth moderate, maxillary reaching posterior margin of pupil; snout short; body rather deep and
more compressed than above species; back somewhat elevated;
caudal fin weakly double concave; gill-rakers long and slender,
$4 + 9$.

Menticirrhus saxatilis. The Kingfish. Body elongate, but little
compressed; head 4; depth $4\frac{1}{2}$; eye small 7; D. X–I, 26; A.
I, 8; scales 7–53–9; mouth large, maxillary reaching middle of
eye; spinous dorsal elevated; pectoral fins long; teeth villiform; snout long and bluntish; scales all ctenoid.

Micropogon undulatus. The Croaker. Body rather robust, the
back somewhat elevated and compressed; head 3; depth $3\frac{1}{3}$;
eye 5; D. X–I, 28; A. II, 7; scales 9–54–12; mouth rather
large, maxillary reaching front of eye; profile rounded; snout
convex, prominent; preopercle strongly serrate; anal under
middle of soft dorsal; caudal fin double truncate; gill-rakers
very short and slender, $7 + 16$.

Leiostomus xanthurus. The Lafayette. Body oblong, ovate, the
back compressed; head $3\frac{1}{2}$; depth 3; eye $3\frac{1}{2}$; D. X–I, 31; A.
II, 12; back in front of dorsal high, convex and compressed to
a sharp edge; profile steep and convex, depressed over the eyes;
mouth small and inferior, maxillary reaching to below pupil;
snout blunt; pharyngeals with three series of molars posteriorly;
teeth in upper jaw minute, none in lower jaw in adult; gill-rakers
short and slender, $8 + 22$; caudal long and forked.

THE WEAKFISH

(Cynoscion regalis)

The weakfish, or squeteague, was first described by Bloch and Schneider, in 1801, from the vicinity of New York. They named it *regalis*, or "royal." In the Southern states it is called gray-trout and sea-trout. The name weakfish is doubtless derived from the Dutch, and is said to have originally meant a soft fish. Jacob Steendam, in a poem in " Praise of New Netherland," in 1661, has

" Weekvis, en Schol, en Carper, Bot, en Snoek,"

meaning weakfish, plaice, carp, turbot, and pike. The name squeteague is of Indian origin.

The natural habitat of the weakfish is along the Atlantic coast south of Cape Cod, occasionally straying to the Gulf of Mexico. It is most abundant between Buzzards Bay and Chesapeake Bay. It is a handsome, shapely fish, resembling somewhat the salmon in outline. It has a robust body, with a depth of about one-fourth of its length. It has a long, pointed head, nearly as long as the depth of the body. The mouth is large, with projecting lower jaw. The teeth are sharp, in narrow bands, with several fanglike canines in front of the upper jaw. The dorsal fins are but slightly separated, and the caudal fin is almost square.

The color of the back and top of the head is bluish or bluish gray, with silvery sides and white belly, and with purple and golden iridescence. A series of dark, diffused spots or blotches form transverse or oblique streaks, more pronounced on the upper part of the body, from whence they run downward and forward. The cheeks and gill-covers are silvery and chin yellowish; the ventral and anal fins are orange; dorsal fin dusky; pectoral fins yellowish; caudal fin with upper part dark and lower part yellowish.

The weakfish is a warm-water fish, visiting the coast and bays during the spring, summer, and fall, though more abundant in the summer. They are surface feeders, and swim in large schools in quest of menhaden, scup, and other small fishes. They are more numerous some seasons than others, probably owing to certain conditions affecting their food, temperature of water, and the abundance or scarcity of their enemy, the bluefish. They seldom, if ever, ascend the streams to fresh water, but remain about the outer beaches, entering the inlets and estuaries on the flood tide in pursuit of their prey, and go out again with the ebb; at least this is the habit of the largest fish, known as "tide-runners." Smaller fish probably remain in the bays and bayous, resorting to deep holes at low water.

Its breeding habits are not well understood, though it spawns in the bays in early summer, about May or June. The eggs are quite small, about thirty to the inch, are buoyant or floating, and hatch in a few days, usually in two. I have taken many hundreds in Chesapeake Bay in August, but do not remember ever catching one containing roe during that month. It is an excellent food-fish if perfectly fresh, but soon deteriorates, becoming quite soft and losing its characteristic flavor when out of the water a few hours. It is quite an important commercial fish during summer in the eastern markets. Small ones, below a pound in weight, are delicious pan-fish; larger ones should be baked. Its usual weight is two or three pounds, and its maximum ten or twelve; occasionally they are taken still heavier — twenty or twenty-five pounds.

Being a surface feeder it is a good game-fish on light tackle, taking bait or an artificial fly with a rush and snap that reminds one of a trout, and for a short time it resists capture bravely. Its first spurt, when hooked, is a grand one, and when checked darts in various directions, making for the weeds if any are near, or toward the bottom, or rushing to the surface leaps out, shaking itself madly to dislodge the hook. It must be handled carefully and gingerly, for it has a tender mouth from which the hook is apt to be torn if too much strain is exerted at first.

A very light striped-bass rod may be utilized, but the most suitable is the "Little Giant" rod of seven and one-half feet and eight ounces in ash and lancewood. A good multiplying reel with fifty yards of braided linen line, size G, a three-foot leader, and snelled hooks, Sproat the best, Nos. 1–0 to 3–0 for the tide-runners, and Nos. 1 or 2 for school fish, together with a landing-net, constitute the rest of the tackle.

The most satisfactory mode of fishing for weakfish is from a boat anchored near the channel, or tied to a pier or wharf in a tideway. The time for fishing is on the flood tide, from half flood to half ebb, as the tide-runners are going in or out in large schools. As little noise as possible should be made by any necessary movements in the boat, as the fish are easily frightened. Long casts should be made toward the advancing or retreating fish, and the bait kept in motion by being reeled in. No sinker or float is required, as the bait must be kept near the surface. Menhaden or minnows, shedder-crab, lobster, bloodworms, clam, and shrimp are all good natural baits. A small spinner, or a small mother-of-pearl squid, if reeled in rapidly, often proves very taking; also a large, gaudy fly, as the red ibis, soldier, silver doctor, Jock Scott, royal coachman, etc., can be used with good effect when the fish are running strongly and in goodly numbers.

Still-fishing, with a float, and a sinker adapted to the strength of the tidal current, can be practised in the eddies of the tide, or at slack water near deep holes, using the natural baits mentioned. Another method is casting with heavy hand-line in the surf from the outside beaches, using block tin or bone squids, and hauling the fish in, when hooked, by main strength. The largest fish are taken in this way; but while it is in a degree exciting, it can only be said to be fishing, not angling. Many anglers, however, prefer it to any other mode of fishing. Another favorite method, but a tame one, is drifting with the wind and tide, following a school of fish and taking them by trolling with hand-line. If suitable rods and tackle were used, it would not be objectionable.

Next to the striped-bass the weakfish is the most important game-fish of the East Coast, and to judge from the greater number of anglers who pursue "weakfishing," it is far and away the favorite with the majority. The estuaries and bays of the Jersey coast, Long Island, and Staten Island, and along the Sound, afford good fishing in the season and at favorable stages of the tide. These localities are more frequented by anglers than any other section of the East Coast. While ideal angling can only be found on inland waters in casting the fly for salmon, black-bass, or trout, amidst the rural and pastoral scenes of hill and hollow, with the birds and sweet-scented blossoms ever near the rippling streams — a full measure of enjoyment is vouchsafed to the salt-water angler in the exhilarating sail to the fishing-banks, the sunlit crests of the incoming tide, and the health-giving ozone of the chlorinated breeze. Then follows the ready response of the gamy weak-fish to the angler's lure, the brave fight and happy landing of the prize. This is surely sport galore, and not to be gainsaid by the most prejudiced.

THE BASTARD WEAKFISH

(Cynoscion nothus)

The bastard weakfish was first described by Dr. Holbrook, in 1860, from the coast of South Carolina. He named it *nothus*, meaning " bastard," in contradistinction to the well-known weakfish just described. It is a rare fish of the South Atlantic coast, preferring deep water, but otherwise of similar habits, and of the same general form as the weakfish of the northern waters. It differs from it in coloration, and has somewhat smaller scales, a smaller mouth, and more compressed body, which is also a little deeper and more elevated. Its color is grayish-silvery, thickly sprinkled with small, dark specks on the upper half of the body, and silvery below, a row of dark spots marking the division. There is another species inhabiting the Gulf coast which will be noticed later. Whenever met with they can be taken by the same methods and with the same tackle as recommended for the northern weakfish.

THE KINGFISH

(Menticirrhus saxatilis)

The kingfish is also known as barb and sea mink in the North, and in the South as whiting.

It was first described by Bloch and Schneider, in 1801, from the vicinity of New York. They named it *saxatilis*, meaning "living among rocks," which by the way it does not do, as it prefers hard, sandy shoals. Its range extends along the Atlantic coast south of Buzzards Bay, occasionally straying to the Gulf of Mexico. It is most abundant, however, between Montauk Point and Cape Hatteras.

It has a long, rather round body, not much compressed, its depth being nearly a fourth of its length. The head is long, with a blunt snout projecting beyond the mouth, which is small, with tough, leathery lips, and with a single barbel on the chin. Both jaws have bands of small, brushlike teeth, the outer ones in the upper jaw somewhat longer. The upper angle of the caudal fin is sharp, the lower angle rounded.

Its color is gray with steely lustre on the back, fading gradually to the belly, which is bluish white. There are several dark, oblique bands, running from the back downward and forward, and one extending from the nape downward, forming a broad " V " with the one next to it; along the border of the belly is a horizontal dark streak running from the middle of the body to the tail.

The kingfish is a bottom feeder, and as might be inferred from the character of the teeth is partial to crabs, shrimps, young lobsters, and mussels, but does not object to the sand-lance and other small fishes, and sandworms, and is found on the hard, sandy shoals where such organisms abound. It visits the shores from spring until November, but is more abundant in the summer, when it enters the bays and rivers. It is usually found in deep water, feeding along the channels. Although it seems to consort a good deal with the weakfish, its habits of feeding are quite different from that fish. It spawns in the summer, earlier or later, according to the temperature of the water, though but little is known of its breeding habits.

Its flesh is flaky, of firm texture, and has a delicious flavor when perfectly fresh, which, however, is lost when out of the water a short time. It is of small size, usually weighing from a half pound to two pounds, though occasionally reaching five or six pounds. But although so small it is justly esteemed and in great demand, the smaller ones as pan-fishes, for breakfast, and the larger ones for chowders, for which it is unexcelled by any other fish.

For its size, the kingfish is considered the gamest of all salt-water fishes. It bites savagely, suddenly, and with a vim and purpose that are sometimes startling to the unwary angler. And when he takes the proffered bait he stands not upon the order of going, but goes at once, and with a dash that is remarkable for its length in so small a fish. When checked, he darts from side to side with amazing quickness, or makes straight for the surface, when the angler is surprised to find him of so small a size. He is *multum in parvo*, — a large soul in a small body.

In sheltered estuaries and bays where the tide does not run strongly or swiftly, or during the stages of slack water, the most suitable tackle consists of a black-bass bait-rod and reel, one hundred yards of fine braided linen line, a three-foot leader, and Sproat hooks, Nos. 1 or 1–0, on stout gut snells, the leader being connected with the line by a brass box-swivel or swivel-sinker of small size. Where the rush of the tide is greater, a natural bamboo chum rod or the Little Giant rod is appropriate, as a heavy sinker must be used to keep the bait near the bottom. To meet the varying conditions of the tide, sinkers of different weights are needed, and a landing-net should not be forgotten when the rod is a light one.

The fishing is done from a boat anchored near the edge of the channels or in the vicinity of hard shoals of sand, ledges of rocks, or near oyster bars, in water of pretty good depth. The bait may be shedder-crab, clam, blood-worm, or shrimp. All are good, but crab is, perhaps, the best, and should be kept in motion.

The northern kingfish must not be confounded with the kingfish of the Florida Keys, which is a fish of the mackerel tribe, akin to the Spanish mackerel, a game-fish of high order, growing to a weight of forty pounds. I was amused several years ago when a correspondent applied to the angling editor of one of the sportsman's journals for information concerning the kingfish of Florida. The editor, not knowing any better, confounded it with the northern kingfish, and recommended the usual means of capture for that fish. I wondered, at the time, how the inquiring angler succeeded with the nimble acrobat of the coral reefs, still-fishing, with such tackle.

There are two closely allied species — the Carolina whiting (*Menticirrhus americanus*) and the surf or silver whiting (*Menticirrhus littoralis*), —

Q

which differ somewhat in coloration and in some
unimportant structural differences; otherwise they
are very similar to the kingfish. The former inhabits the deeper water, while the latter frequents
the shallow sandy shores of the southern coast
from Carolina to Texas. Their feeding habits
are similar to those of the kingfish, and in their
season they can be captured in the same way.

THE CROAKER

(*Micropogon undulatus*)

The croaker was described by Linnæus, in
1766, from South Carolina. He named it *undulatus*, "undulating or wavy," owing to the undulating character of the markings on the body and
fins. Its range extends along the Atlantic coast
and Gulf of Mexico from the Middle states to
Texas, though it is more abundant from the
Chesapeake Bay to Florida. The outline of the
body is somewhat elliptical and compressed, not
much elevated on the back, but with rather a
regular curve from the snout to the tail; its depth
is less than a third of its length. The head is
about as long as the depth of the body, with a
prominent, somewhat blunt snout, and a rather
large mouth, with small barbels beneath the lower

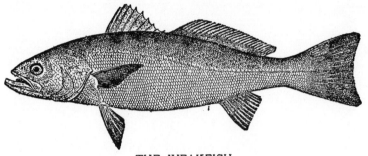

THE WEAKFISH
Cynoscion regalis

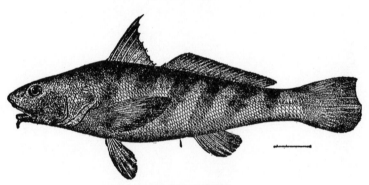

THE KINGFISH
Menticirrhus saxatilis

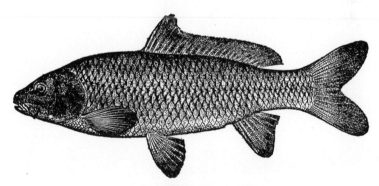

THE GERMAN CARP
Cyprinus carpio

jaw. The border of the cheek-bones is strongly toothed. The teeth of the jaws are in brushlike bands, with somewhat longer ones in the upper jaw. There are two dorsal fins, slightly connected; the caudal fin is double concave or trifurcate. The back is dusky gray with silvery lustre, sides silvery or brassy, belly white and iridescent. There are a number of dusky or cloudy vertical or oblique bands, and the upper part of the body is profusely sprinkled with numerous dark spots, irregularly placed, in undulating lines. A dusky spot is at the base of the pectoral fin; the dorsal fins are marked with dark spots, which form lines along the soft dorsal fin.

The croaker frequents grassy situations in the brackish water of bays and bayous, feeding on crabs, shrimps, and other crustaceans, and small fishes. It grows to a length of ten or twelve inches, and is a good pan-fish when perfectly fresh. It spawns in the autumn.

On the grassy flats of the Patapsco and other tributaries of the Chesapeake Bay I have caught countless numbers of the "crocus," as we boys called it. Just under the gill-cover, nearly always, we found a parasitic crustacean or sea-louse, a half inch in length, resembling the land

crustacean known as the wood-louse, or sow-bug,
— probably an isopod.

A very light rod, a fine linen line, snelled
hooks Nos. 1 to 3, and a small sinker or brass
swivel for connecting line and snell are all that
are needed for the croaker, as a reel is not necessary. The boat is anchored on grassy flats in
water from six to twelve feet in depth. Shrimp
is the best bait, though cut-bait of clam or fish
is good. A float may be used to keep the bait
from the bottom in still water. While this fish
and the next, the spot or Lafayette, are usually
classed as small fry, and particularly suited to
boy anglers, they are such good pan-fish that
many "grown-ups" are quite enthusiastic in their
capture. They hold about the same relation
to the more important game-fishes of the coast
that the sunfishes do to the black-bass, trout,
pike, etc., of inland waters. When no better fishing offers they will fill the void very satisfactorily
when light and suitable tackle is employed.

THE LAFAYETTE

(*Leiostomus xanthurus*)

The Lafayette, spot, or goody, as it is variously
called, was described by Lacépède, in 1802, from

South Carolina. He named it *xanthurus*, meaning "yellow tail," under the impression that its
caudal fin was yellow, — which, however, it is not.
Its range extends from Cape Cod to Texas,
though it is most abundant from New Jersey to
Florida. It is found throughout its range in
brackish-water bays and bayous, and is somewhat similar in appearance to the croaker. It
has a short, deep body; the back in front of
the dorsal fin is compressed to a sharp edge or
"razor-back"; the outline of the back is arched,
highest over the shoulder, with a steep profile
from thence to the snout; the depth of the body
is more than a third of its length. The head is
not so long as the depth of the body; the snout is
blunt and prominent; the mouth is small. There
are few or no teeth in the lower jaw, while those
in the upper jaw are quite small. The throat is
well armed with molars and brushlike teeth.
There are two dorsal fins, slightly connected; the
caudal fin is forked. It is bluish or dusky above,
with silvery sides and white belly; when fresh
from the water it is very iridescent. It has
about fifteen narrow, dark, wavy bands extending
obliquely downward and forward, from the back
to below the lateral line; the fins are olivaceous

and plain; it has a very prominent and distinct round black spot just above the base of the pectoral fin, which has given rise to the name spot in some localities.

Like the croaker, the Lafayette resorts to grassy and weedy situations in the brackish-water bays, estuaries, and tributaries. In Florida it is present all the year, but does not enter northern waters until summer and autumn, when it is often found in company with the croaker or white-perch. It feeds on shrimps and other small crustaceans and small mollusks. It spawns in southern waters in the fall. Although but a small fish, growing to eight or ten inches in length, and usually to but six inches, it is a great favorite as a pan-fish, as when perfectly fresh it is a delicious tidbit or *bonne-bouche* of most excellent flavor.

The same tackle recommended for the croaker is well adapted for the spot, though the hooks should be smaller, Nos. 4 to 6. It is found in the same situations as the croaker, and often in shallow water, or about the piling of bridges and wharves, wherever shrimps abound. My method, many years ago, was to use a light cane rod, ten or twelve feet in length, and a fine line of about the same length, very small hooks, about No. 8, with bait of shrimp, cut clam, oyster, sandworm, or earthworm. I used no float, but held the rod elevated sufficiently to keep the bait from touching the bottom, thus maintaining a taut line, so that the slightest nibble of the fish could be felt, when I would endeavor to hook it at once, for it is as well versed in bait-stealing as the cunner.

It is only necessary to refer to the many names by which this little fish is known in various sections of the country to prove its popularity. Some of these are the spot, goody, Cape May goody, and Lafayette of northern waters, the roach and chub of Carolina, and the chopa blanca (white bream) and besugo (sea-bream) of the Portuguese and Spanish fishermen of Florida. It appeared in unusually large numbers in northern waters about the time that Lafayette visited this country in 1834, hence one of its numerous names.

Years ago I have seen crowds of men, women, and boys occupying front seats on the wood-wharves of Baltimore harbor engaged in fishing for spots and croakers, on Saturday afternoons, and many a boy was tardy at Sunday-school the next morning through picking out the bones from his Sunday breakfast.

CHAPTER IX

THE DRUM FAMILY (*CONTINUED*)
(*Sciænidæ*)

THE most conspicuous and characteristic features by which the members of this family may be known were given in the preceding chapter, where the brackish-water and salt-water species were described. There is but one species found in fresh water, a description of which follows.

Aplodinotus grunniens. The Fresh-water Drum. Body oblong, much elevated, and compressed; profile long and steep; snout blunt; head $3\frac{1}{8}$; depth $2\frac{3}{4}$; eye moderate; D. X, 30; A. II, 7; scales 9–55–13; mouth small, low, and horizontal, lower jaw included; teeth in villiform bands, pharyngeals with coarse, blunt, paved teeth; preopercle slightly serrate; the dorsal fins somewhat connected; scaly sheaths at base of spiny portion of dorsal and anal fins; second anal spine very large; gill-rakers short, 6 + 14; pyloric cœca 7; caudal fin double truncate.

THE FRESH-WATER DRUMFISH
(*Aplodinotus grunniens*)

This well-known fish of the Middle West is also known as lake-sheepshead on the Great Lakes, white-perch on the Ohio River, gaspergou in Louisiana, and as bubbler, croaker, thunder-pumper, and other names in various sections of the country. It was first described by Rafinesque, in 1819, from the Ohio River. He named it *grunniens*, meaning "grunting," from the grunting sound it makes, in common with other members of the drum family, when taken from the water. It inhabits the Great Lakes and other smaller lakes in the vicinity, extending along the Mississippi Valley to Louisiana, Texas, and Mexico.

The fresh-water drum is somewhat elliptical in outline, with quite a hump over the shoulders, with a depth of about one-third of its length, while its head constitutes more than a fourth of the length of the body. The single dorsal fin has the appearance of two. The ear-bones (otoliths) are quite large and resemble porcelain in their peculiar whiteness, and have a semblance of the letter " L " seemingly cut on them. From this circumstance they are known as "lucky-stones," and are often carried by boys as pocket-pieces.

It is of a grayish silvery hue, dark on the back, fading to white on the belly. In the lakes of the North it has several oblique dusky streaks or bands, resembling in a minor degree those of the sheepshead of the coastwise streams and bays. In southern waters the streaks are not so apparent, and it is called white-perch, owing to its silvery appearance. It is a bottom fish, feeding mostly on mollusks, which it crushes with the blunt teeth of the throat. It also feeds on small fishes, crawfish, and other small organisms. Its spawning habits are unknown, but it probably spawns in the spring and summer.

On the Great Lakes it grows to an enormous size, occasionally reaching fifty or sixty pounds, though as usually taken by anglers it is from three to ten pounds in weight. It is of no value as a food-fish in that region, being seldom eaten and heartily despised. On the Ohio and lower Mississippi rivers its weight is much less, from one to six pounds, and it is there considered a good pan-fish, selling readily in the markets. There is no doubt but that it is of better flavor in southern waters when of small size.

As a commercial fish it is taken in nets in the North, and in fyke-nets in the southern extent of its range. On northern lakes it is often taken by anglers when fishing for black-bass, and being a strong, vigorous fish with the family habit of

boring toward the bottom when hooked, it furnishes fair sport, and with considerable jeopardy
to light tackle, when of large size. The angler
is at first elated with what he imagines to be
a fine bass until its identity is established, when
his enthusiasm gives place to infinite disgust.
And this is one reason why it is despised in
northern waters, and very unjustly, too, for it is
game enough, so far as resistance is concerned,
and is entitled to that much credit. In southern
waters it bites freely at small minnows, crawfish,
or mussels, and is there better appreciated and
has a fair reputation as a game-fish. I have
enjoyed fishing for it with light tackle on White
and St. Francis rivers in Arkansas, and some
of the streams in Mississippi. Light black-bass
tackle is quite suitable for it.

CHAPTER X

THE MINNOW FAMILY
(*Cyprinidæ*)

THIS family of fresh-water fishes numbers probably a thousand species, mostly of small size in America and known universally as "minnows." In the eastern hemisphere the species grow larger, and of these, two have been introduced into America, — the German carp and the goldfish.

Cyprinus carpio. The German Carp. Body robust, compressed, heavy anteriorly; head 4½; depth 3½; scales (normally) 5-38-5; mouth moderate, with four long barbels; teeth molar, 1, 1, 3-3, 1, 1; dorsal fin elongate, dorsal and anal fins each preceded by a serrated spine. D. III, 20; A. III, 5.

THE GERMAN CARP
(*Cyprinus carpio*)

The carp was described and named by Linnæus in 1758. Its original home was in China, and from thence it was introduced into Europe, and from there to America.

Since the introduction of the carp into the United States, some thirty years ago, it may now be said to inhabit every state in the Union, having escaped from the ponds in which it was placed at first, into almost every stream, especially in the Mississippi Valley.

The dorsal fin is single, extending from the middle of the back nearly to the tail, highest in front. In the typical scale-carp the scales are large, there being about thirty-eight along the lateral line, with five rows above it and five rows below. But domestication has greatly altered the squamation; thus in the leather-carp the body is naked, with the exception of a few very large ones on the back; in the mirror-carp there are a few rows of very large scales. The coloration is as variable as its scales. It is usually of some shade of olive or brown, with golden lustre, darkest on the back, with the belly whitish or yellowish.

In Europe the carp hibernates, or remains dormant during the winter, burying itself in the mud of the bottom with its tail only exposed. In America it seems to have abandoned this habit almost entirely, especially in the more southern waters. It is not strictly, if at all, a herbivorous fish as has been alleged, but stirs up the bottom of ponds in search of minute animal organisms, rendering the water foul and muddy.

It also devours the spawn of other fishes, though some persons contend that it does not, which is absurd, when it is considered that almost all fishes are addicted to this natural vice. I know from my own observation that the carp is not exempt from the habit. It grows to a length of two feet under favorable conditions. One of twenty-four inches will weigh about ten pounds. As a food-fish it ranks below the buffalo or sucker. It sells readily, however, to negroes, Chinese, and Polish Jews of the cities.

I have no love for the German carp, but as it is now so plentiful in most waters, especially in the Mississippi Valley, and is constantly increasing in numbers, it may be well enough to devote a small space to it as a game-fish. It is a very poor fish at best, and as the poor we have always with us, we will never be rid of it. In England, where it has existed for centuries, it is considered a very shy and uncertain fish to catch; and the larger the fish, the more difficult to circumvent. The best success, and the best is very poor, is met with on small, stagnant ponds, with comparatively small fish. English anglers use a small quill float and split-shot sinker, allowing the bait to just touch the bottom. They then stick the butt of the rod in the ground and retire out of sight of the fish, watching the float meanwhile. They use for bait, worms, maggots, and pastes of various kinds, and usually ground-bait the " swims " to be fished, a day in advance.

Where the carp are large, five or six pounds, the rod, reel, and line recommended for black-bass fishing will subserve a good purpose. A leader three feet long, stained mud color, must be used, with small hooks, Nos. 7 or 8, tied on gut snells. One of the best baits is a red earthworm.

I think the hook can hardly be too small; Nos. 10 or 12 would probably be more successful than larger ones, as the fish is apt to eject the bait at once upon feeling the hook concealed in it. And this is especially important if such baits as bread paste, hard-boiled potato, or boiled grain are employed.

The carp has a peculiar mouth, and feeds much like the sucker. It draws in mud and water and food together, strains the water through the gills, expelling it by the gill-openings, and probably macerates the residue by means of the tongue and the cushiony lining of the buccal cavity before swallowing it. During this process of mouthing the bait the fish is very likely to discover the hook, if large, and eject it.

When once hooked, the fish is not to be lightly esteemed. The angler will have all he can attend to with a light rod in a weedy pond, or even in clear water if the fish is of large size. As most other game-fishes may in time disappear before the Asiatic carp, the analogue of the Mongolian boxer, it may be well and prudent to learn some of the ways to outwit him. In China and Japan the carp is considered before any other fish for food, and is emblematic of strength, vigor, and other good qualities. It is a custom in Japanese households, upon the birth of a male child, to hoist a flag representing a carp, in order that he may grow in strength and all manly attributes. In England the carp is not much liked. On the continent of Europe it is considered a good food-fish, but it is confined in clear running water to deprive it of its earthy flavor before it is marketed or eaten. It is likewise kept within proper bounds, although it has been cultivated for centuries. In the United States, however, it has spread over the Mississippi Valley and elsewhere from overflowed ponds until it bids fair to become a nuisance, inasmuch as our waters seem to be particularly suited to it. As there are so many better species of food-fishes in this country, both in fresh and salt water, there was no excuse or necessity for its introduction, which I consider as great a calamity as that of the English sparrow or the Shanghai chicken, and adding a third foreign evil that we will never be rid of.

I have experimented with carp fishing, but I think the results were never twice alike. A great deal depends on the condition of the water. In ponds that are kept constantly muddy by the rooting of the carp, it is difficult for them to see the bait, and they must then depend on the olfactory sense to find it. This may take a longer time than the patience of the angler will admit. When the water is clear, as on a stream, the carp is too apt to see the angler, and being naturally a shy fish will not go near the bait under these circumstances. There is then nothing to do but to fix the rod in the bank and lie down beside it, or behind a bush or screen, until the moving of the float announces the hooking of the fish. By using a small float, fine line, and very small hooks, and a variety of baits, as earthworms, boiled grain or vegetables, pastes of various kinds, and

a good stock of patience, one may eventually succeed in taking a few fish; but the game is hardly
worth the candle.

As the fish has its advocates, however, I add
the following account of angling for carp in
England, where it has been acclimated for
several centuries. The directions given are
abridged from Cornwall Simeon, a writer on
natural history and angling:—

" The tackle required will simply be a long rod,
a reel containing not less than fifty yards of
fineish line, a fine but sound casting-line nearly
as long as the rod, hooks of about No. 9 size tied
on gut to match, and a small, unpretending float,
besides a good lump of the crumb of new bread,
and a landing-net. Select a quiet, shallow part
of the pond, especially if the weather be hot, and
near its edge stick a few small bushes as a screen.
Then plumb the depth of the water, and cover
the whole of your hook, leaving not the slightest
part visible, with a piece of bread kneaded into
paste, and setting the float two or three feet
farther from the bait than the depth of the water,
throw it well out, drawing in afterward all the
slack of your line. You may then rest your rod
on a forked stick, and sitting down, smoke your

pipe if you like, and proceed to ground-bait the place by filliping in bread pills all round your bait and pretty wide of it. The two great objects should be not to alarm the carp and to get them to feed. They are very timid, and if they once take fright at anything and leave a place in consequence, it will generally be a good while before they will return to it. For this reason I prefer not to throw in any ground-bait when fishing for them until all my preparations are made and the actual bait is in the water. When they begin to come to the bread, if the bottom is at all muddy and the water not too deep, you will see lines of mud stirred up by them as they come on, nuzzling in it like so many pigs. You have then only to keep quiet and bide your time. The float will give you sufficient warning when to strike, and you should only do so when the carp is going well and steadily away with it. If your tackle is sound, and you are not in too great a hurry, you may make pretty sure of landing him."

CHAPTER XI

THE CATFISH FAMILY
(*Siluridæ*)

THE catfish family is represented by many species in the United States. They have the body entirely naked, barbels about the mouth, and an adipose fin, after the fashion of the fishes of the salmon family. They vary greatly in size, from the little stone-cat of three inches to the immense Mississippi-cat of nearly two hundred pounds. But one species will be noticed.

Ictalurus punctatus. The Channel-catfish. Body elongate, slender, compressed posteriorly; head 4; depth 5; eye large; D. I, 6; A. 25 to 30; head slender and conical; mouth small, upper jaw longest; barbels long, the longest reaching considerably beyond the gill opening; humeral process long and slender; caudal fin long and deeply forked.

THE CHANNEL-CATFISH
(*Ictalurus punctatus*)

The channel-cat was first described by Rafinesque, in 1820, from the Ohio River. He named it *punctatus*, or " spotted," owing to the black

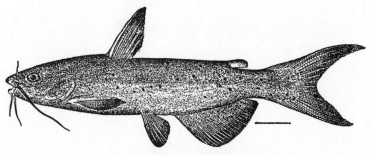

THE CHANNEL–CATFISH
Ictalurus punctatus

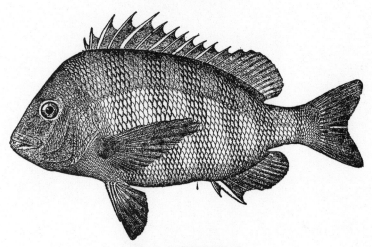

THE SHEEPSHEAD
Archosargus probatocephalus

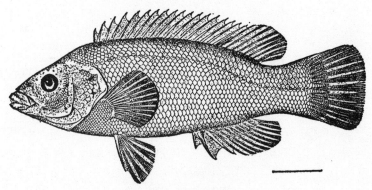

THE CUNNER
Tautogolabrus adspersus

spots on its sides. It is also known as white-cat and blue-cat in various parts of its range. It is found in rivers of the Great Lake region and Mississippi Valley, and in the streams tributary to the Gulf of Mexico.

It is the most trimly-built of all the catfishes, with a long, slender body and small head. It is olivaceous or slate color above, sides pale and silvery, with small, round, dark spots; belly white; fins usually with dark edgings.

Unlike most of the catfishes the channel-cat is found only in clear or swift streams, never in still, muddy situations. It is a clean, wholesome fish, and feeds mostly on minnows and crawfish. It is a good food-fish, the flesh being white and firm and of a rich flavor. It grows to a weight of twenty pounds, occasionally, though usually to five or six pounds.

The channel-cat is a very fine game-fish. It takes the live minnow readily, also shedder craw-fish, and will not refuse earthworms, cut butcher meat or liver. When hooked it is second to no other fish of its size as a bold, strong fighter be-neath the surface. The angler who has "tackled," in a literal sense, a channel-cat of five pounds, on a light rod, can vouch for its gameness.

As it coexists with the black-bass in streams in the Mississippi Valley, and is usually taken by the angler when angling for that fish, the rod, reel, line, and hook recommended for the black-bass will be found eminently serviceable for the channel-cat. It is fond of the deep pools below mill-dams, and in the channels of streams off gravelly or rocky shoals, and near shelving banks and rocks. The method of casting the minnow for black-bass answers well for the channel-cat, though the casts should not be so frequently made, and more time should be allowed for the display of the minnow in mid-water.

Still-fishing with a small, live minnow for bait is the plan generally followed; and as the bait should be left to its own devices for several minutes at a time, a light float is sometimes useful for keeping it off the bottom. When crawfish, cut-bait, or worms are used, the float must always be employed for the same reason. The fish should be given several seconds to gorge the bait, and then hooked by an upward, short, and quick movement of the tip of the rod. When hooked it should feel constantly the strain of the bent rod, and no more line given than is actually necessary; otherwise the struggle will last a long time. No half-hearted measures will answer for the channel-cat, which has a wonderful amount of vitality. He must be subdued by the determined opposition of a good rod and a strong arm.

There are a number of other catfishes that are taken by angling, but none are worthy of the name of game-fishes, though as food they are nearly all to be commended. There are two other species of channel-cats, though neither is quite so good either as game-fishes or for food. They are the blue-cat, also known as chuckle-head cat (*Ictalurus furcatus*), which may be known by its more extensive anal fin, which has from thirty to thirty-five rays, and its bluish silvery color, and with but few if any spots. The other is the willow-cat, or eel-cat (*Ictalurus anguilla*), of a pale yellowish or olivaceous color, without spots. Both of these fishes are found in southern waters from Ohio to Louisiana. The channel-cats are often called forked-tail cats, as they are the only catfishes that have the caudal fin deeply forked.

I think no one appreciates the gameness of the channel-catfish, or has such a just estimation of its toothsomeness, as the Kentucky darky. He will sit all day long, a monument of patience, on a log or rock at the edge of a "cat-hole" of the stream, with hickory pole, strong line and hook, and a bottle cork for a float. He baits his hook with a piece of liver or a shedder crawfish — "soft craw," he calls it, and only uses minnows when the other baits fail. Apropos of this love for the channel-cat may be related the true incident of the "corn-field" darky who, while fishing for cats, had the luck to hook a fine black-bass, which was landed after a "strenuous" struggle, to the envy of his companions. After surveying it with evident admiration awhile, he unhooked it, and with a profound sigh he deliberately threw it back into the stream to the amazement and disgust of the others. "Good Lawd, Jeff," exclaimed one, "w'at yo' done do dat fur? dat sholy wa' a good bass; must a weighed more'n a couple o' poun's!" He surveyed the group with supreme contempt for a moment before he replied, "W'en I go a-cattin', I go a-cattin'." What greater tribute to the channel-cat than this!

On the other hand I was once fly-fishing on a black-bass stream in Kentucky, with a friend from Ohio who was casting the minnow. Having each made a good basket we were ready to quit, as the evening shadows were lengthening and the air was becoming decidedly cool. I was taking my rod apart, but my friend wanted to make "just one more cast," which happened to be on an inviting-looking "cat-hole." As I was tying the strings of my rod case I heard him exclaim joyfully, "I've got the boss bass of the season!" Turning, I perceived him wildly dancing on the edge of the pool, his rod bent to an alarming curve, and the strain on his line evidently near the danger point. I watched in vain for the leap of the bass, and then concluded he had business on hand for an uncertain period, for I felt sure that he had hooked a channel-cat of considerable avoirdupois. The fight was well sustained, and a gallant one on both sides; but it seemed impossible for the light rod to bring the fish near enough to slip the landing-net under it. Finally he backed away from the stream, drawing the fish close to the shore, where I netted it — a channel-cat of five pounds. When my friend saw what it was, he was the most disappointed and disgusted man in Kentucky. "Great Scott!" he yelled, "I nearly ruined my rod for a confounded catfish." — "Well," said I, "you had your fun; he

put up a good fight; what more do you want?"
— "Want! want!" he angrily cried, "I want to
stamp the life out of the horrid brute; and I'll do
it, too!" But I unhooked the fish and strung it
on a willow branch. I had it stuffed and baked
for our dinner next day, when he acknowledged
that it was the best fish he ever ate, and was
entirely consoled for the strain to his rod, to say
nothing of his temper, and ever after had a better
opinion of the channel-cat.

FISHING FOR CUNNERS

CHAPTER XII

THE SHEEPSHEAD FAMILY

(*Sparidæ*)

THIS family embraces the sheepshead, porgies, and sea-breams. It is characterized principally by a heavy, compressed body, strong jaws and teeth, the front ones incisor-like and broad, and flat, grinding teeth or molars in the back of the mouth, like a pavement of small, rounded pebbles, for crushing the shells of mollusks.

Archosargus probatocephalus. The Sheepshead. Body short, deep, and compressed, with large scales; head $3\frac{1}{2}$; depth 2 to $2\frac{1}{2}$; eye 4; D. XII, 10 or 12; A. III, 10 or 11; scales 8–48–15; mouth large, nearly horizontal, maxillary $2\frac{2}{3}$ in head; incisors $\frac{3}{4}$, entire in adult; molars in 3 series above and 2 below; gill-rakers about 3 + 6; dorsal and anal spines notably heteracanthous; frontal bone between the eyes convex and honeycombed; occipital crest broad and honeycombed.

Stenotomus chrysops. The Scup. Body ovate-elliptical; head $3\frac{1}{2}$; depth 2; eye 4; D. XII, 12; A. III, 11; scales 8–50–16; profile steep; nape convex; a strong depression in front of the eye; snout short; temporal crest obsolete; incisor teeth narrow; molars in 2 rows above; gill-rakers small, about 6 + 10; caudal fin forked; top of head, snout, orbitals, and chin naked; a scaly sheath at base of soft dorsal and anal fins; scales on cheeks.

THE SHEEPSHEAD

(*Archosargus probatocephalus*)

In his account of the fishes in the vicinity of New York, in 1788, Schöpf, a surgeon in the British army, placed the sheepshead in the European genus *Sparus*, but gave it no specific name. From his description the ichthyologist Walbaum, in 1792, named it *probatocephalus*, which being translated means "sheep head." This fish inhabits the Atlantic and Gulf coasts from Cape Cod to Texas, where it is common during the summer months, but it is especially abundant in the bays of Florida during the entire year. Its body is nearly half as deep as long, is much compressed, and elevated and arched over the shoulder. The head is large, about a third of the length of the body, with a steep profile, rounded in front of the eyes, which with its incisor teeth bears a slight resemblance to the profile of a sheep. The mouth is large, with strong incisor teeth in front, and several series of molar teeth in both jaws. The general tint is dusky gray, with silvery lustre, paling to the belly; about half a dozen broad, black bars cross the body, from above downward, very distinct in the young, but becoming fainter with age.

As might be inferred from the character of its teeth, the sheepshead resorts to mussel shoals, oyster bars, bridge piers, and old wrecks, where mussels and barnacles abound, and on which it feeds, pinching them from their beds with its strong incisor teeth and crushing them with its molars. It is gregarious, feeding in schools, especially in southern waters, several hundred having been taken on a single tide at places in Florida. It appears in northern waters in June and disappears in the fall, probably wintering at great depths of the sea contiguous to the coast. Its usual maximum weight in northern waters is from three to six pounds, though occasionally reaching ten, fifteen, or even twenty pounds, though these heavy fish are exceedingly rare. Its average size in Florida is less than in the North.

It is highly esteemed on the East Coast as a dinner fish, baked or boiled, and owing to its fine flavor has been called the turbot of America, though it is really much superior, in northern waters, to that vaunted aldermanic delicacy. In Florida, however, it is very lightly esteemed as a food-fish, and is seldom eaten where other and better fishes are available. Perhaps its abundance has something to do with its depreciation, though I am convinced, from numerous trials and tests, that it is not so good a fish in southern waters as in the North, having a sharp, saline taste that is not agreeable to most palates. While confined to salt and brackish waters in the North, it often ascends the rivers of Florida to fresh water.   I have seen it in the large springs, the head waters of several rivers on the Gulf coast, its barred sides being plainly discernible on the bottom at a depth of fifty or seventy-five feet, in the clear and crystal-like water.

The difference in flavor between the sheepshead of the North and South may perhaps be due to the character of their food.   It is especially noticeable that fishes of the salt water that pass the winter season in the deep sea, as the salmon, shad, etc., possess a more superior flavor than those that feed constantly and during the entire year along the shores.   While nothing is really known concerning the spawning habits of the sheepshead in northern waters, it probably spawns in early summer.   From my own knowledge I can say that it spawns in Florida, on the Gulf coast, during March and April.   Its eggs are very small, about thirty to the inch, are buoyant or floating, and hatch in two days.

A good rod for sheepshead fishing is the natural bamboo rod, known as the striped-bass chum rod. It is light, and strong enough to withstand the vicious tugs, spurts, and especially the propensity of boring toward the bottom, that is characteristic of this fish. A rod of steel, or lancewood, or ash and greenheart, or bethabara, though heavier, is better and stronger. It should be about eight feet in length, with double guides. A multiplying reel carrying sixty yards of braided linen line, size E or F, Sproat hooks, Nos. 1–o to 3–o on gimp snells, with sinkers, and a wide-mouthed landing-net, make up the rest of the tackle. The short barb, with cutting edges, of the Sproat hook renders it superior to the Virginia, Chestertown, or blackfish hooks formerly so much in vogue for the sheepshead. A brass box-swivel is necessary for connecting the line with the snell of the hook.

While the sheepshead often bites at all stages of the tide, the most favorable time is about slack water; from that stage, to half flood or half ebb, good success may usually be expected. The largest fish are taken from a boat anchored over or near mussel shoals or oyster beds. Smaller ones can be caught from old wharves or bridges whose piling is studded with barnacles and mussels, and about which shrimp abound. During slack water a light sinker is sufficient; but when the tide runs strongly, heavier ones must be used, as it is imperative to keep the bait near the bottom, especially if fishing from a boat. If fishing from a wharf, it does not matter so much, provided the bait is deep enough to prevent the fish from seeing the angler. While this is a precaution that must be observed with all fishes, I do not think the sheepshead is so shy a fish as some maintain; at least I have never found it so.

The best bait is shedder-crab, fiddlers, or hermit crabs. Clam bait, though, is cheaper and more universally used in the North. In Florida the fiddlers can be scooped up by the peck on the inside beaches of the bays, and contiguous to good sheepshead fishing. If the clam is large, the meat should be cut up for bait; but if quite small, or if mussels are used, the shells may be merely cracked or smashed, and put on the hook entire. The latter is the mode where the fish are scarce or shy, but I prefer to use the meat only, discarding the shells; in the case of fiddlers, when very small, they should be used *au naturel*, or whole.

The bait should be cast and allowed to sink, and the line reeled enough to keep the bait off the bottom, but close to it. A taut line should be maintained always, so as to feel the slightest nibble. If crab bait, or cut clam, is used, the fish should be hooked, if possible, at the first bite, however slight, by a quick and somewhat vigorous upward jerk of the tip, otherwise the sheepshead is apt to nip off the bait; or if sufficient force is not used, the hook fails to enter the well-armed mouth. One or other of these contingencies is almost sure to follow, if the fish be not hooked. A small sheepshead is a more adroit stealer of bait than the cunner. It has a way of deftly pinching the bait from the hook without much, if any, disturbance. When small clams or mussels are used in the cracked shells, it is thought best by some anglers to give the fish a little time to " shuck " the bait before jerking on the rod. But my advice is to yank him just as quickly as if crab bait were employed. To hesitate is to be defrauded of either the fish or the bait.

When the fish is hooked he should be kept from the bottom by the spring of the rod, and brought as near the surface as possible. When line is given during his frantic rushes, the spring and resistance of the rod should never be lessened. Once on the surface he is easily kept there until conquered; but if allowed to descend to the bottom, he is pretty hard to manage, as his resistance then is very much greater, and he endeavors to tear out the hook by forcing his jaws among the rocks and débris or weeds. He should always be taken into the landing-net, and care must be observed to avoid his strong and sharp fins when removing the hook.

In Florida the sheepshead is almost gregarious, congregating about oyster bars, old wharves, and near inlets in great numbers. At Colonel Summerlin's wharf, at Punta Rassa, I knew of a man, fishing for market, I presume, who took several hundred on a single tide. The wharf just across the bay at Sanibel Island is also a famous locality for sheepshead. The largest I ever caught in that state was just inside of Little Gasparilla inlet, near a steep bank on the north side. The settlers of Florida take them in cast-nets, and the commercial fishermen in haul seines; the latter either ship them on ice, or salt them along with mullet, as they take salt well. With the exception of the mullet, the sheepshead is the most abundant fish of both the east and west coasts of Florida, but it is seldom found in the dense salt water along the keys at the southern end of the peninsula, as it is essentially a brackish-water fish. The angler need never repine for a lack of sport in the " flowery state " if he is fond of " sheepsheading," and he will have no difficulty in securing bait, for the fiddlers are to be found in myriads convenient to good fishing grounds.

THE SCUP

(*Stenotomus chrysops*)

Another fish of the *Sparidæ* family is the scup, or porgy, which was first described by Linnæus, in 1766, from specimens sent to him from South Carolina by Dr. Garden. He named it *chrysops*, or " golden eye." The names scup and porgy are derived from the Indian name scuppaug. The porgy is mentioned, like the cunner, in deference to the ladies and the rising generation of anglers, to whom it is fair game on the summer excursions to the seashore. It is confined to the Atlantic coast from Cape Cod to South Carolina, being especially abundant in northern waters. A kindred species, the fair maid (*Stenotomus aculeatus*), is common from Cape Hatteras south-

ward, there taking the place of the northern
scup.

The porgy is a short, deep, and compressed
fish, rather elliptical in outline, its depth being
nearly half of its length, and with the back
elevated over the nape. Its head is of moderate
size, with a steep profile, depressed in front of
the small eye. The mouth is rather small and
the snout short. Its incisor teeth are very narrow and rather conical or pointed, resembling
canines; there are two rows of molar teeth in
the upper jaw. The color is brownish on the
top of the head and back with greenish and
golden reflections, and bright and silvery below;
the dorsal, anal, and caudal fins are dusky or
mottled, and the pectoral fin yellowish.

The scup appears along the shores of the East
Coast about the first of May, sometimes earlier,
and continues until late in the fall, when it retires
to its winter quarters in the depths of the sea. It
is a bottom fish, feeding on crustaceans and small
mollusks, and is found wherever they abound on
the outer shoals. It usually spawns in June; the
eggs are quite small, measuring about twenty-five
to the inch; they are buoyant or floating, and
hatch in four or five days. When perfectly

fresh it is an excellent pan-fish, its flesh being firm, white, flaky, and of a fine, sweet flavor, but owing to its abundance is not properly appreciated. It grows to a foot or more in length, weighing a pound or two, though its usual maximum length is ten inches, and weight half a pound. Very rarely the oldest fish sometimes reach a length of fifteen to eighteen inches, weighing from two to four pounds.

The scup is usually taken by hand-line and clam bait on the fishing banks from the excursion steamers; but fishing from small boats anchored over the shoals, with suitable tackle, is more sportsmanlike. It is a very free-biting fish, but is not possessed of much gameness, though the pleasure of angling for it is much enhanced by the employment of light tackle.

A trout bait-rod is quite in order for the scup, though a light natural cane rod about ten feet long, fitted with reel seat and guides, will answer a good purpose. A small multiplying reel is not essential, though it is an advantage in accommodating the line to different depths; and then a larger fish than the scup may be hooked. The line should be of small size, Sproat hooks Nos. 6 to 8 on gut snells, with leader three feet long, connected to the line by a swivel-sinker, and of a weight adapted to the strength of the tide. A float may be used in shallow water to keep the bait from the bottom when clam or shrimp is used. In localities where tautog, sea-bass, or weakfish are likely to be met with, a heavier rod, like the Little Giant, or a light striped-bass rod, may be of an advantage to one not accustomed to lighter rods, and the hook may be a trifle larger.

CHAPTER XIII

CUNNER, FLOUNDER, SMELT

Tautogolabrus adspersus. The Cunner. Family *Labridæ*, the Wrasse fishes. Body oblong, not elevated, slender and compressed, with cycloid scales; lateral line well developed; mouth moderate, terminal; premaxillaries protractile; maxillaries without supplemental bone, slipping under edge of preorbital; head pointed; snout moderate; maxillary reaching front of eye; preopercle serrate; opercles scaly; interopercle naked; head $3\frac{1}{4}$; depth $3\frac{1}{4}$; D. XVIII, 10; A. III, 9; scales 6–46–12; 5 canines in front of upper jaw, about 4 in the lower; bands of small concave teeth behind canines; preopercle with 5 rows of small scales; opercle with 4 rows, rest of head naked; gill-rakers very short, about 6 + 11.

Pseudopleuronectes americanus. The Flatfish or Flounder. Family *Pleuronectidæ*, the Flatfishes. Head 4; depth $2\frac{1}{4}$; D. 65; A. 48; scales 83; body elliptical, an angle above the eye; head covered above with imbricated ctenoid scales, blind side of head nearly naked; body dextral; teeth compressed, incisor-like, widened toward tips, closely set, forming a continuous cutting edge; right side of each jaw toothless; highest dorsal rays less than length of pectorals, and more than half the length of head; anal spines present.

Osmerus mordax. The Smelt. The American smelt belongs to the family *Argentinidæ*. The body is long and slender; head 4; depth $6\frac{1}{2}$; eye 4; D. 10; A. 15; P. 13; scales 68; head and mouth large; small teeth along the edge of the maxillary; strong, fanglike teeth on tongue and front of vomer; cardiform teeth on palatines, pterygoids, and hyoid bone; mandible with moderate teeth, its tip projecting; maxillary reaching middle of eye; scales deciduous; dorsal fin rather posterior, the ventrals under its front.

THE CUNNER

(*Tautogolabrus adspersus*)

THE cunner was named *adspersus*, meaning " besprinkled," by Walbaum, in 1792, from the description of Schöpf, who simply gave its common name, burgall, in his " History of New York Fishes," in 1788. Its specific name is in allusion to the fancied mottled markings. It belongs to the *Labridæ* family. Its habitat is the North Atlantic coast from Labrador to Sandy Hook, not appearing much farther south.

The cunner is known by various other names, as burgall, chogset, blue-perch, etc. It has an oblong and rather robust body, its depth being about a third of its length. Its head is about as long as the depth of the body and pointed, with a mouth of moderate size, well filled with unequal, conical, and sharp teeth, in several series.

The coloration is variable, though usually bluish, more or less mixed with bronze or brown, with brassy sides and pale belly; sometimes brassy spots on the head and back; young examples

THE FLOUNDER
Pseudopleuronectes americanus

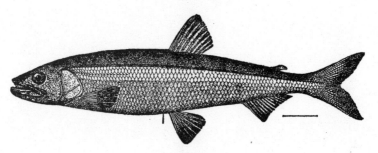

THE SMELT
Osmerus mordax

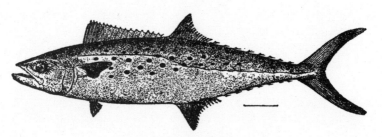

THE SPANISH MACKEREL
Scomberomorus maculatus

exhibit dark blotches and markings. It resorts to the same feeding grounds as the tautog, and about old wharves and bridges where shrimp and barnacles abound, and in such situations is always abundant. It spawns in the early summer, about June. Its eggs are small, about twenty-five to the inch, and hatch in four or five days. It grows to about a pound in weight, though it usually does not exceed half that amount.

While it is generally considered worthless, or at best a poor food-fish, it is really a pretty fair pan-fish, and if it were not so common would be found oftener on the table of fish lovers. As a game-fish it is anathema with most anglers. It is despised because it responds so readily to the angler's lures, taking the bait intended for larger and more desirable fish. But on this very account it is ever dear to the heart of the juvenile fisherman, who glories in his string of cunners with as much pride and enthusiasm as his larger brothers with their tautog, sea-bass, or striped-bass.

It can be caught with almost any kind of tackle or bait. The cunner has no particular vanity in the way of either. A piece of liver on an ungainly hook and twine string is as welcome as the choicest shrimp on one of Harrison's best Sproat hooks on a snell of the finest silkworm fibre. My heart goes out to the boy angler with his cane pole and cut-bait, fishing for cunners. And should he in time become the most finished salmon fisher, he will look back to his cunner days as conducive of more real pleasure than any he may have found since. The cunner is here recorded for the urchin with the cane pole.

THE FLOUNDER
(*Pseudopleuronectes americanus*)

There are quite a number of flounders, or flat-fishes, on the East Coast, but the one best known to juvenile anglers is the one with the long name recorded above. It belongs to the flatfish family *Pleuronectidæ*, and was noticed by Schöpf as early as 1788, and from his description was named by Walbaum *Pleuronectes americanus*, which means, literally, "the American side-swimmer." It inhabits the North Atlantic coast from Labrador to the Chesapeake Bay, and is abundant in all the bays and estuaries of the Middle states, where it is variously known as flatfish, flounder, winter flounder, mud-dab, etc.

Its body is elliptical in outline, about twice as

long as broad, and very much compressed or flat. The head is small, less than a fourth of the length of the body, with a small mouth containing closely set, incisor-like teeth. As usual with all of the flatfishes, the dorsal and anal fins are very long, horizontally, the color on the exposed or right side is rusty brown, obscurely mottled, with the under or left side white.

The flounder is partial to sheltered coves and quiet bays, preferring bottoms of sand or mud, though sometimes it is found in rocky situations. It is sedentary in its habits, partially burying itself in the sand or mud, where it remains during the entire year, feeding on minute shells, crustaceans, worms, etc.

It spawns in the spring, during March and April. The eggs are very small, about thirty to the inch; and unlike those of most marine fishes they do not float, but are heavy enough to sink, forming bunches or clusters on the bottom, adhering to the weeds, etc., where they hatch in from two to three weeks. The fry swim upright, like other fishes, with an eye on each side of the head, but as they grow older they incline to one side, the under eye moving gradually to the upper side, so that at the age of three or four months both eyes are on the upper side, as the result of a twisting of the bones of the head. The right side, being constantly exposed to the light, becomes darker or colored, while the left side, being deprived of light, becomes pure white.

It is an excellent food-fish, its flesh being firm, white, and of good flavor; and as it is easily procured in winter when other fishes are comparatively scarce, it is a favorite at that season. It rarely grows to more than a foot in length or a pound in weight. As it can be caught in early spring, late fall, and winter, when other fishes are absent or not inclined to bite, the angler with light tackle may obtain considerable sport with this fish, as it will eagerly take almost any kind of natural bait. A bait-rod used for trout or black-bass or a light cane rod can be utilized, with very fine linen line, a three-foot leader, and hooks Nos. 7 or 8, on gut snells; a reel is not necessary, but is convenient. Using as light a sinker as possible, with clam or sandworm bait, the angler may be assured of success. The fishing may be done from a boat anchored at low tide on muddy or grassy flats, or from wharves or piers favorably located.

THE SMELT

(*Osmerus mordax*)

The smelts were formerly classed with the salmon family, but are now placed in a separate one, *Argentinidæ*, in which are included a number of allied species. To all external appearances the smelt is a true salmonid, and differs from the trouts and salmon chiefly in the form of the stomach and its appendages. The American or Atlantic smelt was first described by Dr. Mitchill, in 1815, from the vicinity of New York; he named it *mordax*, or "biting." Its habitat is along the Atlantic coast from the Gulf of St. Lawrence to Virginia, but it is most abundant northward. It is landlocked in a number of northern lakes.

The smelt is a very pretty, graceful fish, with a long, slender body, long, pointed head, and large mouth, with a somewhat projecting lower jaw. The small adipose fin, which is peculiar to all of the salmonids, is situated far back, opposite the end of the anal fin; the caudal fin is deeply forked. Its color is pale olive-green above, silvery below, translucent, with an obscure, longitudinal, broad, satin-like band along the sides. The fins are greenish, with a few punctulations.

The smelt enters the tidal rivers and brackish bays in the fall and winter in countless myriads, preparatory to spawning. It feeds principally on the small fry of other fishes, mostly at night, and along the shores in shallow water. It spawns in March, in both fresh and brackish water. The eggs are small, about twenty to the inch, and are adhesive. A medium-sized fish yields fifty thousand eggs, which hatch in two or three weeks, according to the temperature of the water, though usually in from sixteen to eighteen days. Though small, it is highly prized as a food-fish, having a delicate and delicious flavor. When fresh it emits an odor resembling that of cucumbers. Its usual size is from five to nine inches and weighing from two to four ounces, though occasionally reaching a foot or more in length. The smaller fish are more prized, the largest having a rank oily flavor. It is caught in large seines by fishermen and shipped fresh to the markets, and in winter is taken in great numbers with hook and line through the ice.

Smelt fishing is a very popular pastime along the East Coast in the fall and winter, as it is at a time when not many other fishes are to be caught. In the inland lakes it is, as has just been men-

tioned, caught with hook and line through holes
cut in the ice; but this is tame sport compared
with fishing in open water with very light tackle.
The angler can utilize his trout fly- or bait-rod, or
if he prefers, a very light natural cane rod eight
or ten feet long. A reel is not necessary. The
line should be of the smallest size, linen or silk,
though silk lines soon rot in salt water. A fine
leader three or four feet long, with hooks Nos. 3
to 6, on single gut snells, are next in order.
When the fish are swimming in schools near the
surface, especially at night, a sinker need not be
used; under other circumstances, and when the
tide is strong, one of suitable weight should be
added. The fishing is usually best on the flood
tide, and almost any kind of bait will answer; but
shrimp is best, though sandworms, very small minnows, or even earthworms are useful. Given the
proper time and place, and with tackle and bait
in readiness, it only remains to cast the baited
hook, retrieve the fish, and so on *ad infinitum*.

CHAPTER XIV

THE MACKEREL FAMILY

(*Scombridæ*)

THE fishes of this family are all pelagic, and most of them are highly valued for food. They are characterized by an elongate body, more or less compressed; pointed head; large mouth; sharp teeth; two dorsal fins; the anal and second dorsal fins are similar in shape and size, and both are followed by detached finlets; the caudal fin is widely forked or falcate, its pedicle very slender and with a sharp keel; scales small and smooth.

Scomberomorus maculatus. The Spanish Mackerel. Body elongate, covered with rudimentary scales, which do not form a distinct corselet; head pointed, short and small; mouth wide; strong teeth in jaws, knife-shaped; sandlike teeth on vomer and palatines; gill-rakers 2 + 11; caudal peduncle with a single keel; head 4½; depth 4½; D. XVII–18–IX; A. II–17–IX; eye 4¾; soft dorsal inserted in advance of anal, somewhat; lateral line undulating, with about 175 pores; spots bronze.

Scomberomorus regalis. The Cero. Body rather elongate, its dorsal and ventral curves about equal; mouth large, maxillary reaching to below the eye; angle of preopercle produced backward; pectorals scaly; caudal less widely forked than *maculatus*; teeth triangular, compressed, about 40 in each jaw; pectorals scaly; spots and stripes brownish; head 4¼; depth 4½; D. XVII–I, 15–VIII; A. II, 14–VIII.

Sarda sarda. The Bonito. Body elongate, moderately compressed, robust; head 3¾; depth 4; D. XXI–I, 13–VIII; A. I, 13–VII; P. 10; scales small, those of the pectoral region forming a distinct corselet; teeth moderate, slightly compressed, about 40 in each jaw; mouth large, maxillary reaching beyond orbit; lateral line slightly undulating, with nowhere a decided curve.

THE SPANISH MACKEREL

(*Scomberomorus maculatus*)

The Spanish mackerel was first described by Dr. Mitchill, in 1815, from the vicinity of New York. He named it *maculatus*, or "spotted," owing to the large bronze spots on its sides.

It is common to the southern portions of the Atlantic and Pacific coasts and the Gulf of Mexico, ranging in summer as far north as Cape Cod, and is one of the trimmest and most graceful fishes known, as well as one of the most beautiful both in form and coloration. It is especially adapted for rapid and sustained motion. Its long, graceful, and elliptical body is four times its depth. The head is as long as the depth of the body, with a large mouth, and sharp, lancet-shaped teeth in both jaws. It has two dorsal fins; the second dorsal and anal fins are nearly opposite each other, are similar in outline, and are each followed by nine detached finlets; the caudal fin is widely forked, the lobes being long and pointed or crescent-shaped. Its color is silvery, bluish or greenish above, paling to white on the belly, with iridescent reflections; the sides are dotted with some thirty bronze or golden spots, a fourth of an inch or more in diameter; the first dorsal fin is dark in front, whitish behind; the second dorsal is yellowish; the anal fin is pale; the pectoral fin is yellow, bordered with black; the caudal fin is dusky.

The Spanish mackerel is gregarious and migratory, swimming in large schools, and feeding at the surface on pilchards, anchovies, and sardines in Florida, and on silversides and menhaden in northern waters. When feeding, the schools are constantly leaping above the surface, and the flashing of their silvery forms in the bright sunlight is a beautiful and inspiriting sight, enhanced by the flocks of gulls and terns whirling and darting above the schools, eager for such stray morsels and fragments as they are able to seize. In the Gulf of Mexico it often feeds in company with the salt-water trout, and in northern waters with the bluefish and weakfish.

It is a fish of the warm seas, approaching the shores for spawning and feeding when the temperature becomes suitable. It appears on the Gulf coast of Florida in March and April, though I have observed it as early as January in forward seasons. Its advent on the Atlantic coast is later, progressing gradually northward, reaching the vicinity of New York in July and August, and disappearing in October or November. Its breeding season in the Gulf of Mexico is in the early spring, and as late as August or September at the northern extent of its range. Its spawning may cover a period of many weeks, as the fish do not all mature at one and the same time. The eggs are quite small, about twenty-five to the inch, float at the surface, and hatch in a single day. The newly hatched fry are very small, about the tenth of an inch long, but in a year will have attained a length of six inches. The average weight of a mature fish is from two to four pounds, rarely exceeding six or eight pounds.

The Spanish mackerel is held in the highest esteem as a food-fish, being considered one of the very best, second only to the pompano of the Gulf or the whitefish of the Great Lakes. It has a mackerel flavor, but one peculiarly its own for richness and sapidity of savor. It is a game-fish of high degree, and worthy of the angler's highest regard. Its manner of fighting, when hooked, is mostly on the surface of the water, darting here and there with dazzling rapidity, in straight and curving lines, leaping into air, and bounding over the water with a velocity and nimbleness that is difficult to follow with the eye in the bright sunlight.

In northern waters it is usually taken by trolling with a small mother-of-pearl squid, or one of block tin, using a long hand-line, as the fish is rather shy and difficult to approach with a boat. In Florida, however, great sport can be had with a light rod, both in fly-fishing and bait-fishing, from the sand-spits at the entrance to deep inlets, and from the long piers and wharves that extend to deep water. The angling is done in March and April, when the fish are running into the bays in great schools on the flood tide, often in company with the salt-water trout.

A black-bass or trout fly-rod of seven or eight ounces is very suitable for fly-fishing, with a click reel and a braided linen line of pretty large size, say D or E, in order to give weight enough for casting. The enamelled silk line is, of course, better, but it does not last long in salt water. Any bright or gaudy fly will answer, on hooks Nos. 1 to 3, though yellowish or grayish flies are perhaps more attractive. A single fly only should be used, with a three or four foot leader. Black-bass rods and tackle are just right for bait-fishing for the Spanish mackerel, except that a braided linen line, and not a silk line, should be used for reasons just given. The best bait is a small, bright fish, three or four inches long, either mullet or anchovy, hooked through the lips. A small pearl squid, or a very small trolling-spoon or spinner, may be used instead, but the minnow is far and away the most attractive lure.

The bait is cast as far as possible toward the school as it is running past the point of an inlet or the end of a pier, and reeled in slowly, but rapidly enough to keep the bait on or near the surface, no sinker being employed. If the fishing is done from a pier, a very long-handled landing-net must be provided. The best plan is to fish from a small boat moored to the pier, as the angler is not so likely to be seen by the fish, and they are more easily landed. The same method is pursued in fly-fishing in the general features,

except that the fly is allowed to sink after fluttering it awhile on the surface; no other special
suggestions are needed. I have found the following flies useful: gray drake, green drake, red
ibis, oriole, professor, and silver doctor, in black-
bass patterns, on hooks Nos. 1 to 3.

THE CERO

(Scomberomorus regalis)

The cero, or sierra, was described by Bloch, in
1795, from a drawing of a specimen from the
West Indies, by Plumier. He named it *regalis*,
meaning "royal" or "regal." It belongs to the
West Indian fauna of fishes, and is common from
Florida to Brazil. Occasionally it strays in the
summer as far north as Massachusetts. It is
closely allied to the Spanish mackerel, and resembles it in form, but differs very much in coloration and size, being more sombre and much
larger. Its color is brownish on the back, with
silvery sides and belly; it is marked with two
dusky longitudinal stripes, and several rows of
dark spots, not bronze or golden as in the Spanish
mackerel.

I have met with the cero only along the Florida
reefs and keys. It does not swim in such large

schools as the Spanish mackerel, and does not accompany it in its wanderings into the bays or along the shores, but seeks the same localities, and is of similar habits, as the kingfish-mackerel. It feeds entirely on fishes. Its breeding habits have not been studied, though they are doubtless not unlike those of the Spanish mackerel, except as to the locality and season of depositing its eggs. Its usual weight is five or six pounds, though it sometimes grows to five feet in length and twenty pounds or more in weight.

I have taken it with bone and block-tin squids, trolling from a yacht, and also from an anchored boat with rod and line, by casting mullet or sardines for bait. A striped-bass rod and tackle are suitable, as it is a strong and powerful fish, making extraordinary leaps when hooked. For its weight I know of no gamer fish, but my experience in rod-fishing has been somewhat limited, being confined to the capture of half a dozen fish.

I was once yachting along the Florida keys, and while anchored near Bahia Honda I put off in the dinghy to cast mullet bait for cero and kingfish (*Scomberomorus cavalla*). The latter is a near relative of the cero, and they resemble each other so closely that it is often difficult to distinguish between them. The king-fish is rather more slender, the adult fish being of a uniform slaty hue, usually without spots or markings of any kind, and grows to a larger size, often to fifty pounds or more. It is fully described in another volume of this series.

On the occasion referred to I captured a number of kingfish and two ceros of about the same relative weight, from eight to ten pounds. The conditions were quite favorable to compare their gameness, but I was unable to perceive any difference in this respect. Both fish took the bait with a rush, and when hooked exhibited game qualities of the highest order, leaping continuously and to a height of five or six feet. Their swift rushes, as they cut through the water with incredible swiftness, and for which they are especially built, were very trying to my light striped-bass rod. I lost a number of fish that shook out the hook when leaping. I used the Sproat bend, No. 7–o, but 5–o would be large enough for the average-sized cero. My line was a braided linen, size E, to which the snelled hook was attached by a small brass box-swivel; but knobbed hooks, if they can be obtained of suitable size, are to be preferred.

THE BONITO
Sarda sarda

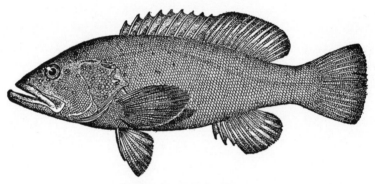

THE NIGGER–FISH
Bodianus fulvus

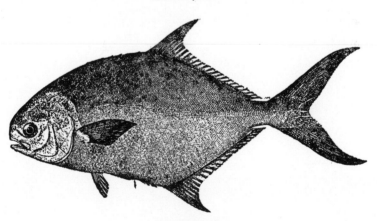

THE POMPANO
Trachinotus carolinus

The market fishermen of Key West troll for kingfish and cero in their schooner smacks, using coarse hand-laid cotton lines, and codfish or other large hooks as mentioned. The bait is usually a piece of white bacon-rind, cut in an elliptical shape to resemble a fish, and strung along the shank of the hook, and fastened at the top by a piece of fine copper wire. This rude device is very successful, as they take hundreds of fish in a few days, of a size running from ten to fifty pounds. The cero and the kingfish are favorite food-fishes in Key West, where large quantities are consumed; and years ago many were carried to Havana by the smacks, until a prohibitive duty was imposed by the Spanish governor-general, in order to favor Spanish fishermen. Under the changed conditions that now exist in Cuba this trade will doubtless be resumed. Both the cero and kingfish are excellent food-fishes, with a flavor much like that of the Spanish mackerel, but more pronounced, — that is, not so delicate and delicious, but more pungent.

Northern anglers who go to Florida in quest of the tarpon will find in the cero and kingfish game-fishes of great merit on light tackle.

THE BONITO

(Sarda sarda)

The bonito is a very handsome and gamy fish belonging to the mackerel family. It was named *sarda* by Bloch, in 1793, from its being taken in the vicinity of Sardinia. It inhabits both coasts of the Atlantic Ocean, and the Mediterranean Sea. It is not uncommon from the region of Cape Cod southward to Florida and the West Indies, where it is more abundant.

It has a long, graceful body, nearly round, its depth a fourth of its length. It is elliptical in outline, tapering to a very slender caudal pedicle, which is strongly keeled. The mouth is large, with strong, conical teeth. The caudal fin is deeply forked, or swallow-like. Its color is dark steel-blue above, silvery below, with white belly. There are numerous dark oblique stripes running from the back downward and forward, by which it is easily recognized. The ventral fins are whitish, the other fins are bluish black.

The bonito is a pelagic fish, approaching the shores in search of food, which consists of small fishes almost entirely. It grows to a length of three or four feet, though it is usually taken of ten or twelve pounds in weight. It does not rank high as a food-fish, having rather dark flesh of a strong mackerel flavor, rather too pungent to be agreeable, but it is liked generally by sailors. There is another fish of the Atlantic coast (*Gymnosarda pelamis*), of the mackerel family, that is known as the oceanic bonito. It may be distinguished by its stripes being horizontal, instead of oblique; it is rather rare.

The bonito is taken only by trolling with a small fish for bait, or a block-tin, bone, or shell squid, from a sailing vessel, and with bluefish tackle. It is frequently caught by the Key West fishermen when trolling for kingfish with a bait of bacon-rind. It is a powerful fish, and withal a very game one, being a swift swimmer, and must be handled very carefully when hooked. The line should be a heavy one of braided linen or cotton, and a foot or two of brass or copper wire should be used as a snell to withstand its sharp and numerous teeth. A Sproat or O'Shaughnessy hook, No. 7–0, is about right when bait is used, and one of similar size with artificial squids, or spinners.

I was once trolling in the vicinity of the Dry Tortugas, and in a short time took four bonitos of about twelve pounds each. As the yacht was going at a spanking rate with a beam wind, the strain on the line was tremendous, and in each case the vessel had to be luffed up into the wind to enable me to land them. As one fish was more than enough for the crew, and as I had occasion to land at Fort Jefferson, on Garden Key, I resolved to donate the others to the garrison of the fortress. On going ashore I found the "garrison" to consist of one man, the corporal in charge of the property. He said he did not think he alone could get away with the fish, but as the lighthouse keeper of the fort would return from Loggerhead Key in the afternoon, he thought that they, together with his dog, might manage to dispose of them. Afterward he informed me that he and the light-keeper had finished one bonito, and the dog, whose name was Bonaparte, had made way with the others, or as he expressed it: "Bone eet two," and said this without any intent to pun on bon-i-to; he thought that I was amused at the capacity of Bonaparte as an ichthyophagist, being unconscious of his play on the words which caused my merriment.

CHAPTER XV

THE GROUPER FAMILY

(*Serranidæ*)

THE fishes of this family are characterized by an oblong body, more or less compressed, covered with adherent scales of moderate or small size, which are usually ctenoid; the dorsal and ventral outlines do not usually correspond; premaxillaries protractile; teeth all conical or pointed, in bands, present on jaws, vomer, and palatines; pseudobranchiæ large; gill-membranes separate, free from isthmus; cheeks and opercles scaly; preopercle usually serrate; opercle ending in one or two flat spines; lateral line not extending on the caudal fin; lower pharyngeals narrow, with pointed teeth; gill-rakers armed with teeth.

Mycteroperca microlepis. The Gag. Body comparatively elongate and compressed; head 2½; depth 3½; eye 6; D. XI, 16 to 19; A. III, 11; scales 24–140–50; pores about 90; dorsal fin single, its spines slender and weak; head long and pointed; mouth large, the maxillary reaching beyond the eye; teeth in narrow bands, each jaw with two canines; gill-rakers few, 12 on lower part of anterior arch; scales very small, chiefly cycloid; pre-

opercle with a shallow emargination above the angle, with radiating serræ; caudal lunate; lower jaw projecting.

Mycteroperca falcata phenax. The Scamp. Body elongate; head
3; depth 3½; D. XI, 18; A. III, 11; eye 5; scales 24-135-43;
dorsal fin single, the spines slender and weak; head pointed;
mouth large, the maxillary reaching posterior border of the eye;
teeth in narrow bands, each jaw with two strong canines, nearly
vertical; preopercle finely serrate, a notch above the angle; scales
mostly cycloid; outer rays of caudal produced.

Mycteroperca venenosa. The Yellow-finned Grouper. Body elongate; head 3; depth 3¼; eye 7; scales 24-125-*x*; D. XI, 16;
A. III, 11; head rather blunt; mouth large, the maxillary reaching much beyond the eye; teeth in narrow bands, each jaw
with two strong canines, not directed forward; preopercle without salient angle, its emargination slight; dorsal fin single, its
spines not very weak; caudal fin lunate; anal rounded.

Epinephelus adscensionis. The Rock Hind. Body robust, little
compressed; head 2½; depth 3; eye 6; scales 12-100-40; D. XI,
17; A. III, 7; head subconic, acute; anterior profile straight;
mouth large, the maxillary reaching beyond the eye; lower jaw
strongly projecting; teeth in broad bands, the canines short and
stout, those of the lower jaw the largest; preopercle finely serrate, convex, with but slight emargination; scales strongly
ctenoid; dorsal fin single, its spines strong; caudal fin slightly
rounded; gill-rakers short and thick.

Epinephelus guttatus. The Red Hind. Body rather slender, moderately compressed, the back somewhat elevated; head 2½;
depth 3⅛; eye 4⅓; scales 19-100-*x*; D. XI, 16; A. III, 8; head
long and pointed; mouth moderate, the maxillary reaching below posterior margin of eye; lower jaw rather weak, its tip little
projecting; teeth rather strong, in moderate bands, both jaws
with two curved canines, those in upper jaw largest; preopercle
weakly serrate, with a salient angle, which is armed with
stronger teeth; caudal fin rounded.

Petrometopon cruentatus. The Coney. Body oblong, rather deep
and compressed; head 2½; depth 2¾; eye 5; scales 8-90-30;
D. IX, 14; A. III, 8; head moderate, a little acute anteriorly,
profile nearly straight; mouth large, the maxillary reaching

beyond the eye; lower jaw not strongly projecting; teeth in narrow bands, the depressible teeth of the inner series very long and slender, those of the lower jaw and front of upper especially enlarged, longer than the small, subequal canines; preopercle convex, very weakly serrate, its posterior angle obliquely subtruncate, without salient angle or distinct emargination; opercle with three distinct spines; scales rather large, and mostly strongly ctenoid; dorsal fin single, its spines rather slender and pungent; anal fin rounded; pectorals long; caudal fin very convex.

Bodianus fulvus. The Yellow-fish. Body oblong, moderately compressed; head $2\frac{2}{3}$; depth 3; eye 5; scales 9-100-33; D. IX, 14 to 16; A. III, 8 or 9; head rather pointed, with curved profile; mouth moderate, the maxillary reaching beyond the eye; lower jaw strongly projecting; teeth in narrow bands, rather large, the depressible teeth rather small, canines small, subequal; preopercle with weak serrations, its outline convex, with a shallow emargination; opercle with three distinct spines; dorsal fin single, with slender and pungent spines; scales rather large, mostly strongly ctenoid; caudal fin truncate, its angles slightly rounded; pectorals long; ventrals short.

Diplectrum formosum. The Sand-fish. Body elongate, the profile strongly arched above the eyes; head 3; depth $3\frac{1}{2}$; eye 5; scales 9-85-22; mouth large, maxillary reaching middle of eye; lower jaw slightly projecting; canine teeth small; preopercle finely serrate at upper margin; preopercle with two clusters of divergent spines; opercular flap short and sharp; top of cranium smooth and very convex; 11 rows of scales on cheeks; fins, except caudal, scaleless; 15 scales before dorsal; dorsal fin single, with low spines, the first three graduated; caudal deeply lunate, the upper lobe the longest, sometimes ending in a long filament.

THE GAG

(*Mycteroperca microlepis*)

The gag is one of the series of fishes known as groupers in Florida, of which there are quite

a number. It was first described by Goode and
Bean, in 1879, from West Florida; they named
it *microlepis*, or "small scale," as its scales are
of less size than the other species of the same
genus. It is known only from the South
Atlantic coast and the Gulf of Mexico, from
North Carolina south to Pensacola.

It has a rather long, shapely body, with pointed
head and an evenly curved profile. Its mouth
is large, with projecting lower jaw. Both jaws
are armed with narrow bands of sharp teeth and
two canines, the upper ones directed forward.
The predominating hue of the gag is brownish
or brownish gray, with lighter sides, in deep-
water specimens; those of shallow water, especially in grassy situations, are greenish or olivaceous, mottled with a darker shade, and more or
less clouded. Very small and indistinct dusky
spots sometimes cover the entire body, and a
faint mustache is usually present. The dorsal
fin is olive; the top of the soft dorsal fin rays
is darker, with white edge; the caudal fin is
bluish black, with white edge. It is a voracious
fish, feeding on small fishes and crustaceans, and
grows to a large size; twenty or thirty, or even
fifty, pounds in weight is not uncommon, though

usually taken of from six to ten pounds. It resorts, when large, to the banks and rocky reefs in deep water. Those of less size frequent the inshore waters. It is a fine food-fish, and a very game one on the rod.

A light striped-bass rod, or the natural bamboo chum rod, with good multiplying reel and fifty yards of braided linen line, size E, and Sproat or O'Shaughnessy hooks, Nos. 3–0 or 4–0, on gimp snells, with a brass box-swivel for connecting snell and line, and a sinker adapted to the strength of the tide, make up the tackle for the gag. A large landing-net or a gaff-hook should not be forgotten.

Rod fishing is done in comparatively deep water on the rocky reefs or shelly banks along the keys, from an anchored boat. Any natural bait, as a small fish, crab, crawfish, or conch, will answer, though a small fish, as the mullet, sardine, or anchovy, is the best. When of large size the gag is a very gamy fish, and must be handled very carefully to preserve one's tackle intact.

It is taken more frequently by trolling with a strong hand-line from a sailing yacht, in the same way as trolling for bluefish. A small

silvery fish is the best lure, though a strong
spinner or a shell or block-tin squid answers well.
Even a piece of bacon-rind cut in the semblance
of a fish proves very attractive, in the manner
commonly used by the fishermen of Key West in
trolling for the kingfish.

The largest groupers can be taken on rocky
bottom in the deep holes about the inlets. On
the southeast coast, Indian River Inlet, under
the mangroves, and Jupiter Inlet, both afford
good grouper fishing. Farther south, at Hillsboro and New River inlets, and in the deep
holes about the passes between the Florida Keys,
from Cape Florida to Key West, groupers are
more or less abundant. The first gag I ever
caught was in the winter of 1877, while trolling
off Cape Florida; it was a big one, too, weighing about fifty pounds. "What is it?" asked a
Kentucky boy who was with me. I was com-
pelled to look it up in my books before replying
that I thought it was a "scamp," as it agreed
pretty well with the description of that grouper,
though I was not fully satisfied that my identification was correct, and less so, when in about
an hour we caught a real scamp. This was
some two years before the gag was described as

a new species by Drs. Goode and Bean, from Pensacola. As I had no means of preserving the fish, it was baked for our dinner, and proved to be very good indeed.

In fishing for groupers the angler must keep them well in hand so as to prevent their getting into the holes and crevices of the rocks, as they are sure to do if given the chance, and from where it is almost impossible to dislodge them. They should be brought to the surface, or near it, as soon as possible after hooking them, and kept there until ready for the landing-net or gaff-hook. Most people in Florida fish for groupers with hand-lines, but with the tackle recommended the fish will be more easily subdued and landed, and the pleasure much enhanced, to say nothing of the question of sportsmanship as between the two methods.

THE SCAMP

(*Mycteroperca falcata phenax*)

The scamp is a grouper that resembles very much the gag. It was first described by the Cuban ichthyologist Poey, in 1860, from Cuban waters. He named it *falcata*, or "scythe-shaped," from the curving of the caudal fin. The form common to Florida is a variety or subspecies, that differs principally in the angle of the canine teeth and to some extent in coloration. The variety was first described by Jordan and Swain, in 1884, who named it *phenax*, meaning "deceptive," and equivalent to "scamp." It is abundant along the Florida Keys and the offshore "snapper banks," from Key West to Pensacola; those of smaller size frequent inshore waters.

It resembles the gag very much in its general appearance and in the shape of its body, with a somewhat larger mouth and more projecting lower jaw, also a larger caudal fin, which is more crescentic or scythe-shaped. The depth of its body is about a third of its length. The teeth are in narrow bands, with two canines in each jaw, but these are not so strong as in the Cuban form, and those in the upper jaw are not directed so much forward, nor the lower ones so much backward. The caudal fin is concave or crescentic, and the scales are larger than those of the gag. The color is pinkish gray above, paler purplish gray below; the upper part of the body and head is covered with small, rounded, irregular dark brown spots; the sides and caudal fin with larger and longer pale brownish blotches, somewhat reticulate; fins dusky, some edged with white. Its habits are similar to those of the gag, just described, in whose company it is found. It grows to a length of two feet or more, and to ten pounds or more in weight. The remarks concerning the tackle and fishing for the gag apply equally as well for the scamp.

This fish, with the gag, is sometimes taken on the snapper banks by the red-snapper fishermen, though it is not shipped to the northern markets as it does not bear transportation so well as the red-snapper, and is sold for home consumption or eaten by the crews. I first saw this fish as has just been related, in 1877, when it was caught by a Kentucky friend, and it had very much the same appearance as the gag. We then decided that both fish were scamps, my friend remarking that " The only difference is that this fellow seems to be more of a scamp than the other one," an opinion I fully indorsed. The scamp does not stray so far north as the gag, being confined to subtropical regions. It is regularly taken to the Key West market by the commercial fisherman, where it commands a ready sale, being well esteemed as a food-fish. The first specimens I afterward preserved were secured from this source.

THE YELLOW-FINNED GROUPER

(Mycteroperca venenosa)

This grouper was first noticed by Catesby, in
1743, from the Bahamas, and was named by
Linnæus, in 1758, who bestowed the specific title
venenosa, or " venomous," as its flesh was said by
Catesby to be poisonous at certain times. It is
common at the Bahamas, and from the Florida
Keys southward to the West Indies, and perhaps
to South America. Its form is very similar to
the gag and scamp; its depth is a third of its
length. Its head is as long as the depth of the
body, and rather blunt, with the profile somewhat
uneven, but curved; the mouth is large, with
narrow bands of teeth, and two canines in each
jaw which are not directed forward.

Not much is known concerning this fish, as its
flesh is reputed to be poisonous at times, and it
is seldom eaten.

Its coloration is quite varied and beautiful; it
is olive-green on the back, pearly bluish below,
breast rosy. The upper parts are marked with
broad reticulations and curved blotches of bright
light green, which are especially distinct on the
top of the head; the entire body and head are

covered with orange-brown spots of various sizes with dark centres; the iris of eye is orange, as is the inside of the mouth; the dorsal fin is olive-brown, with whitish blotches and a few dark spots; the pectoral fin is yellow, and all other fins have black edges. Its habits are similar to those of the other groupers. It grows to three feet in length, and frequents rocky situations.

THE ROCK HIND

(*Epinephelus adscensionis*)

This grouper is one of the most bizarre and gayly colored in the family *Serranidæ*. It was first accurately described by Osbeck, in 1757, from Ascension Island, which accounts for its specific name, *adscensionis*, as bestowed by him.

It is very widely distributed over both hemispheres, being known from Ascension and St. Helena Islands, Cape of Good Hope, and is abundant from the Florida Keys to Brazil. In outline it resembles the other groupers, having a robust body, but little compressed; its depth is a third of its length, its head is as long as the depth of the body, is pointed, with a profile straight from the snout to the nape, thence curved regularly to the tail. The mouth is large, with the lower jaw more prominent or projecting than in any of the other groupers; the teeth are in broad bands, with short and stout canines.

Its ground color is olivaceous gray, with darker clouds; the head and entire body are profusely covered with red or orange spots of varying size, those on the lower part of the body the largest, nearly as large as the pupil of the eye; parts of the body and fins have irregularly-shaped, whitish spots or blotches; there are several ill-defined, clouded, blackish, vertical, or oblique blotches across the body, some of them extending upward on to the dorsal fin, with the interspaces lighter; the fins are likewise spotted with red and white.

The groupers known as "hinds," as the red, rock, brown, speckled, spotted, or John Paw hinds, are so named from being spotted, and resembling somewhat in this way the hind or female red deer. They are all good food-fishes, and are found regularly in the Key West market, though not so plentiful as the snappers, grunts, etc., but bringing a better price. The rock hind, as might be inferred from its name, frequents rocky situations about the channels between the keys, feeding mostly on small fishes and marine invertebrates. It grows to a length of eighteen inches. Its spawning habits have not been studied, though it probably spawns in the spring.

A light bait-rod, similar to a black-bass rod, with corresponding tackle, with hooks Nos. 2–0 to 3–0, on gimp snells, will answer for this fish, using sardines or anchovies, which are abundant along the shores, for bait.

THE RED HIND

(*Epinephelus guttatus*)

This beautiful grouper rivals the rock hind in its gay and varied coloration. There is some uncertainty about the correct specific name of this well-marked species. The last name to be adopted is *guttatus*, meaning "spotted," conferred by Linnæus in 1758, based on the early and vague descriptions of Marcgrave and others on specimens from Brazil and the West Indies. It belongs to the West Indian fauna, its range extending from the Florida Keys to South America; it occasionally strays north in the summer to the Carolina coast.

It resembles the other groupers in its general form, but is more slender, has a larger eye, and its lower jaw does not project so much. The depth of its body is a little more than a third of its length. Its head is long and pointed, considerably longer than the depth of its body, with a mouth of moderate size, and a weak lower jaw, which projects but slightly; the eye is very large; the teeth are in bands, with two curved canines in each.

The pattern of the coloration and the markings are similar to those of the rock hind, but differ in color. The upper part of the body is grayish or yellowish olive, the belly reddish; the entire head and body are profusely covered with scarlet spots of nearly uniform size, except those on the breast and belly, which are a little larger; there are a few spots, both red and whitish, on the bases of the fins; there are three broad, oblique, obscure bands running upward and backward on the sides, extending on to the dorsal fin; the upper fins are edged with black; the pectoral fin is reddish yellow.

The red hind, like the rock hind, frequents rocky places and feeds mostly on small fishes. It grows to a length of about eighteen inches, and is an excellent food-fish. Not much is known concerning its breeding habits, though it probably spawns in the spring. The same tackle recommended for the rock hind, and the same baits, will do as well for the red hind, as they are found together.

THE CONEY

(*Petrometopon cruentatus*)

This beautiful fish is allied to the groupers, and belongs to the family *Serranidæ*, previously described. It was described and named by Lacépède from a drawing by Plumier, made from a specimen from Martinique. Lacépède recorded it in his "Natural History of Fishes," 1803, conferring on it the name *cruentatus*, meaning "dyed with blood," in allusion to its red spots. It belongs to the West Indian fauna, with a range extending from the Florida Keys to Brazil; it is quite common about Key West, being seen in the markets every day.

The body has the somewhat elliptical outline of the other groupers, but is more oblong and deeper, its depth being more than a third of its length. The head is moderate in size, rather pointed, its length less than the depth of the body; the mouth is large, with the lower jaw projecting but slightly; the teeth are in narrow bands, the inner series long, slender, and depressible; the canines small. Its ground color is reddish gray, a little paler below; the head and body are covered with bright vermilion spots, larger and brighter anteriorly.

It frequents rocky situations, like the coney of Holy Writ. It is highly esteemed as a food-fish, but is of smaller size than the groupers previously described, seldom growing beyond a foot in length or a pound in weight. It probably spawns in the spring. It is quite a gamy fish for its size on light tackle.

It is usually taken by the market fishermen on the same tackle as the grunts, snappers, porgies, etc., among the rocks of the channels, in rather deep water, with fish bait. It is well worth catching, if only to admire its graceful shape and brilliant coloration.

For the coney, black-bass rods, braided linen line, size F, with Sproat hooks, No. 2–0 or 3–0, on gimp snells, and sinker adapted to the strength of the tide, with the smallest fish for bait, will answer admirably. The little whirligig mullet, or spiny crawfish, or even cut-fish bait, are all good baits to use as occasion may demand.

CATCHING SPANISH MACKEREL ON THE EDGE OF THE
GULF STREAM

THE YELLOW-FISH

(Bodianus fulvus)

The yellow-fish differs from the other groupers in the less number of spiny rays in the dorsal fin; otherwise it is much the same. It was described by Linnæus, in 1758, from the account of the "yellow-fish" by Catesby, in 1743, from the Bahamas. Linnæus named it *fulvus,* or "tawny," from its coloration. This is also a fish belonging to the West Indian fauna, its range extending from the Bahamas and the Florida Keys to South America.

The outline of body of the yellow-fish is similar to that of the hinds, being nearly elliptical, and with a depth of a third of its length, and moderately compressed. The head is long and pointed, longer than the depth of the body, with an evenly curved profile from the snout to the dorsal fin; the lower jaw projects very much; the mouth is large, with narrow bands of teeth, and small canines. Its general color is yellow, darker or orange-red on the back, with two black spots on the tail; there are a few violet spots about the eye, and some blue spots on the head and anterior half of the body, those on the head with dark margins; the head, and pectoral and dorsal fins, are reddish.

The yellow-fish is found in the deeper channels in rocky situations. It feeds on small fishes principally. It is not very common, and is much prized as a food-fish by the people of Key West. The common varieties are the red and brown yellow-fishes, which differ only in coloration from the yellow ones. It is taken with the other channel fishes, and with the same baits and similar tackle, by the market fishermen; but the angler should utilize his black-bass rod, with braided linen line, size F, and hooks No. 2–0 on gimp snells. As it is a bottom feeder a sinker must be used to keep the bait at the proper depth. For baits, any small fish or sea-crawfish or prawns or shrimps will answer.

THE SAND-FISH

(Diplectrum formosum)

The sand-fish, or, as it is sometimes called, the squirrel-fish, also belongs to the family *Serranidæ*. It was first described by Linnæus, in 1766, from Dr. Garden's specimens from South Carolina; he named it *formosa*, or "handsome," from its pretty form and coloration. It inhabits the Atlantic coast from South Carolina to South America, and is common to both coasts of Florida, and

especially about the keys. It has a rather elliptical body in outline; its depth is less than a third
of its length, being elongate and rather slender
as compared with other allied species. The
head is as long as the depth of the body, with an
arched profile above the eyes; the mouth is large,
the lower jaw projecting a little; the upper border
of the cheek-bone is serrated, with two clusters
of small, sharp spines; the teeth are in narrow
bands; the canine teeth are small.

Its color is light brown above, silvery white
below; there are several dark and broad vertical bars across the body, and a dark blotch
at the base of the caudal fin; the body has
eight narrow bright blue longitudinal stripes,
which are more distinct above, and paler below;
the head is yellow, with several wavy blue stripes
below the eye and several between the eyes;
the upper fins have blue and yellow stripes, and
the caudal fin has yellow spots surrounded by
bluish markings.

It frequents sandy shoals, and also rocky
shores, feeding on small fishes and crustaceans.
It is a good pan-fish, growing to about a foot
in length, but usually to six or eight inches.
The same tackle and baits used for the hinds,

coney, and yellow-fish will also answer well for the sand-fish, which consists of black-bass rod, braided linen line, size F, hooks No. 1 or 1–0, and suitable sinker and swivel. It is a good game-fish for its size on the light tackle just mentioned, and is well worth a trial on account of its beauty, and excellence for the table, even if its gameness is not considered.

While engaged in a scientific expedition to Florida many years ago, my vessel ran aground one afternoon in Barnes Sound, southwest of Biscayne Bay. The bottom was a sandy marl and quite soft, so that we were unable to use the setting poles to any advantage in moving the boat. I observed quite a school of fish surround-ing the vessel, which proved to be sand-fish. I put out a stake to mark the stage of the tide, and while waiting for the flood tide I put in the time fishing, and soon had enough sand-fish for supper and breakfast. This was rather fortunate, as we were still aground the next morning, for strange to say the depth of the water had neither in-creased nor diminished for sixteen hours; there was no tide in that remote corner of the universe. We then took out the ballast of about a ton of pig-iron and put it in the dory we had in tow.

This lightened up the vessel enough to enable us to shove her off into deeper water. I think we never enjoyed any fish quite so much as those delicious little sand-fish, and it has ever since been one of my favorite fishes.

CHAPTER XVI

THE CAVALLI FAMILY

(Carangidæ)

THE members of this family differ from the true mackerels by a less number of spines in the first dorsal fin, and in having but two spines in the anal fin, and no detached finlets; also in having smaller teeth. Some of the species are described in another volume of this series, to which the reader is referred.

Carangus chrysos. The Runner. Body oblong, moderately elevated, the dorsal and ventral outlines about equally arched; head 3¾; depth 3¼; eye 3½; lateral line with 50 scutes; D. VIII–I, 24; A. II–I, 19; profile forms a uniform curve; snout rather sharp; mouth moderate, slightly oblique, maxillary reaching middle of orbit; teeth comparatively large; a single series in lower jaw; upper jaw with an inner series of smaller teeth; no canines; teeth on vomer, palatines, and tongue; gill-rakers long and numerous; pectoral fin not longer than head; scales moderate; cheeks and breast scaly; black opercular spot.

Carangus latus. The Horse-eye Jack. Moderately deep; head 3¾; depth 2½; scutes 30; D. VIII–I, 20; A. II–I, 17; head bluntish; profile curved; mouth moderate; lower jaw prominent; villiform teeth on upper jaw, vomer, palatines, and tongue; weak canines in lower jaw; breast scaly; maxillary reaching posterior edge of pupil; pectoral fin about as long as head; cheeks and upper part of opercles scaly; gill-rakers rather long, about 12 below the angle.

Trachinotus carolinus. The Pompano. Body oblong, comparatively robust; head 4; depth 2⅓; eye 4ȥ; scales small and smooth; D. VI–I, 25; A. II–I, 23; profile of head evenly convex; snout bluntly rounded; mouth small, maxillary reaching middle of eye; jaws without teeth in the adult; maxillary without supplemental bone; dorsal and anal fins falcate, anterior rays nearly reaching middle of fins when depressed; dorsal lobe 4½ in body; anal 5½; dorsal lobe pale.

THE RUNNER

(*Carangus chrysos*)

The runner was first described by Dr. S. L. Mitchill, in 1815, from the vicinity of New York. He named it *chrysos*, meaning "gold," from the golden sheen of its sides. It inhabits the Atlantic coast from Cape Cod to Brazil, but is most abundant on southern shores and in the Gulf of Mexico.

It has an oblong body, its depth a little less than a third of its length, with the dorsal and ventral curves about equal. The head is shorter than the depth of the body, with a uniformly curved profile and rather sharp snout. The mouth is moderate in size and low, with a single series of teeth in the lower jaw, and two in the upper one, but no canines; there are also small teeth on the roof of the mouth and tongue. Its

colour is greenish olive on the back, and golden
yellow or silvery below; there is a black blotch
on the border of the gill-cover; the fins are all
plain.

The runner, as its name indicates, is a great
forager, and is the swiftest and most graceful of
all the jacks or cavallies. It ranges farther
northward than the other species of the genus.
It frequents the reefs and the shores of the keys
and mainland of Florida in search of food, which
consists of small fishes, as sardines, anchovies,
mullets, etc., crustaceans, and other small organisms. It is the best of the jacks as a food-fish,
and is in great favor at Key West. For its
size it is also the gamest, but as it rarely exceeds
a foot in length it is not so much sought, generally, as the larger jacks. It is, however, a great
favorite with the juvenile anglers at Key West,
as it can be taken from the wharves with almost
any kind of bait. On account of its activity and
gameness it furnishes fine sport on light tackle,
and under these conditions is worthy the attention of the angler. A light black-bass rod,
braided linen line, size G, hooks No. 1 or 1–0 on
gimp snells, a light multiplying reel and sinker
adapted to the tidal current, comprise a good

outfit for the runner, which is also known as hard-tail and jurel in some localities. About Key West and the neighboring keys the best bait is the little whirligig mullet (*Querimana gyrans*), which whirls on the surface in large schools, or cut bait or shrimps may be used to advantage.

The author of a recently published book on the fishes of Florida makes the following queer statement, "It seems to me the runners are hybrids from the crevalle and bluefish species or families, as they certainly resemble both of those fishes." It would be strange did they not resemble the fishes named, as all are of the mackerel tribe, and all are distinguished by having falcate anal and dorsal fins of about the same relative size, and placed about opposite each other, and also have swallow-shaped caudal fins with slender caudal pedicle; but there the greatest resemblance ends. I have never seen a hybrid among fishes in the natural state. They can be produced by the fishculturist between kindred species, but there is no especial benefit to be derived from such experiments. Hybrids, or so-called mules, are infertile, and incapable of reproducing their kind.

THE HORSE-EYE JACK
(Carangus latus)

The horse-eye jack was first described by Louis Agassiz, in 1829, from Brazil, who named it *latus*, or "broad," owing to its short and deep form. It differs from the runner mostly in being deeper in body, and in its large eye. It has a few less soft rays in the dorsal and anal fins, and but thirty-five bony scutes along the lateral line; otherwise it is very similar. Its color is bluish above and golden or silvery below, and it has a black spot on the margin of the gill-cover, but of less size than that of the runner. While it is similar in habits to the runner, it has a more extended range, inhabiting all warm seas.

The horse-eye jack grows to a larger size than the runner, but is not nearly so good a food-fish, though nearly its equal as a game-fish. Its flesh is reputed to be poisonous at certain seasons in the tropics, and whether true or not, it is not held in much favor, though it is caught by boys at the wharves of Key West, and I presume is eaten. The same tackle and baits recommended for the runner can be utilized for the horse-eye jack.

THE POMPANO

(Trachinotus carolinus)

The pompano was first described by Linnæus, in 1766, from Dr. Garden's specimens from South Carolina, which accounts for its specific name. It is abundant on the South Atlantic and Gulf coasts, to which it is mostly confined, though it occasionally strays north to Cape Cod in summer, and rarely to the West Indies.

It has a short, deep body, being nearly half as deep as long, oblong and robust. Its head is short, about half as long as the depth of the body, with a small, low mouth, and with few or no teeth in the jaws; the snout is blunt, the profile from end of snout to the eye about vertical, and from thence to the dorsal fin is regularly arched. The color is bluish above and golden or silvery below; the pectoral and anal fins are yellow, shaded with blue; caudal fin with bluish reflections.

The pompano frequents the sandy beaches of the keys and islands of the Gulf coast, mostly the outside shores, where it feeds on beach-fleas and the beautiful little mollusks known as " pompano-shells," also on small shrimps and other shore-loving organisms. I consider the pompano to be the best food-fish in either salt or fresh water — the prince of food-fishes, it is incomparable. It is caught principally in haul seines by the fishermen on the flood tide. On the Atlantic coast it is abundant at Jupiter inlet and at Lake Worth, but not so plentiful as about the outside and inside beaches of the islands about Charlotte Harbor on the Gulf coast. In the summer it strays northward to the Carolina coasts. Its usual weight is a pound or two, rarely exceeding eighteen inches in length or four pounds in weight. It is often confounded with several other species, as the permit (*Trachinotus goodei*), which reaches three feet in length and twenty-five or thirty pounds in weight; also with the gaff top-sail pompano (*Trachinotus glaucus*), and the round pompano (*Trachinotus falcatus*), both of which grow larger than the true pompano and are often sold for the genuine article by dealers; but no one who has eaten a true pompano can be deceived by these other species. It spawns in the summer.

It is difficult to take the pompano with the hook except on the flood tide, when it is running in schools, feeding along the shores, though it is occasionally caught by still-fishing in the bays with bait of beach-fleas or cut clam. The tackle should be very light and the hook small, Nos. 6 or 8, on fine gut snells. When hooked it is a game-fish of more than ordinary cunning and cleverness, and one of two pounds will tax the angler's skill on a six-ounce rod. They can be taken in the surf of the outside beaches of the islands, on the flood tide, with beach-flea bait, by casting it into the schools with a fly-rod; and this is the best form of fishing for this grand fish.

The hooked pompano frequently breaks water among its other manœuvres to escape the angler, and as a leaper at other times has quite a reputation. I have often had them leap into my boat, both when anchored and moving, but usually when sailing near a school. The name pompano is probably derived from the Spanish word *pampana*, a "vine leaf," owing to its shape resembling somewhat a leaf of some kind of vine; the books say a "grape leaf," to which the pompano has a remote resemblance if the extended fins are taken into account. There is another Spanish word *pampano*, more nearly resembling pompano in sound and spelling. It means "a young vine branch or tendril," and if the aquatic capers and aerial saltations of the pompano when hooked are to be brought into the comparison, they cannot be exceeded by that most intricate dance, the "grape-vine twist," even when performed by the most agile plantation negro. But seriously, when its size is considered, one would have to go far afield, or rather search the waters under the earth, for a better fish for the angler or the epicure.

I have seen more pompano about the beaches of Big and Little Gasparilla Keys of Charlotte Harbor, on the Gulf coast, than elsewhere in Florida. On their outside beaches, during the flood tide, the beach-fleas and pompano-shells come rolling in on every wave. The little mollusks disappear beneath the sand in the twinkling of an eye, but the crustaceans are again carried out by the receding wave. And this continues during the first half of the flood tide, during which time schools of pompano are feeding on them. On one such occasion myself and a friend were "flea-fishing" for pompano; that is, we were using fly-rods and very small hooks baited with beach-fleas, which we cast in the same manner as artificial flies. My friend, fishing at the water's edge, often forgot in his eagerness to step back to avoid each "ninth wave," which would wet him to his knees. However, in that warm, sunny clime the involuntary bath did him no harm, and he had his compensation in a basket of fine pompano, which were duly planked for dinner and eaten, bones and all, — for their bones are very soft and semi-cartilaginous. The head of a broiled or planked pompano is a *bonne-bouche* that once eaten will ever be held in grateful and gratified remembrance.

CHAPTER XVII

THE CHANNEL FISHES

THE channels among the reefs and keys from Cape Florida to Key West and vicinity abound with a number of percoid, or perchlike, fishes, belonging to several families. They are mostly of small size, comparatively, but afford good bottom fishing. They are all good food-fishes and find a ready sale in the markets of Key West. Most of them are remarkable for their gay and brilliant coloration.

The coralline formation of the keys and reefs renders the use of seines and nets impossible, so that all of the fishing for market is done with hook and line, — usually with sea-crawfish bait, though a few are taken in traps formed of heavy wire. The fishes consist of grunts, snappers, groupers, porgies, etc., and are carried to market alive in the wells of the small vessels known as "smackees."

A fleet of larger vessels, mostly schooner-rigged, troll along the keys and reefs for the larger surface-feeding fishes, as kingfish, cero, Spanish mackerel, bonitos, large groupers and snappers, etc. The troll is usually a piece of bacon-skin cut of an elliptical shape to simulate a fish, and is impaled on a codfish hook with a snell of copper wire, and a laid cotton codfish line of a size nearly as large as a lead-pencil. The hooking and hauling aboard of the fish, while under sail, so disables it that it is killed by a blow on the head and carried to market on ice.

As all of the grunts, snappers, porgies, and other channel fishes grow only to a foot or two in length, the same tackle may answer for all. The fishing is done in water of varying depth, from a few feet to twenty or more, from an anchored boat. The best plan for the angler who is visiting Key West for the first time is to go out with a market fisherman in his boat and learn by ocular evidence the *modus operandi* of channel fishing. After that he will be prepared to follow his own devices and fish in the same or an improved way.

A stiffish black-bass rod, or the Little Giant rod of seven and one-half feet and eight ounces, a modification of the Henshall black-bass rod, are quite suitable, though the market fishermen use hand-lines altogether.   The rest of the tackle needed is a multiplying reel, a braided linen line, size E or F, Sproat or O'Shaughnessy hooks of various sizes, from Nos. 1 to 3–0, according to the size of the mouths of the different fishes, though No. 1–0 will be found to be a good average size.   Sinkers of different weights, from one to six ounces, to meet the strength of the tide, and a strong landing-net must be added. The hooks should be tied on single, strong silk-worm fibre.

The best bait is the sea-crawfish (*Palinurus*), or spiny lobster, which grows to the size of the common lobster, and is found in the crevices of the coral reefs or among the rocks and shells at the bottom, from whence it is taken by the fish spear called "grains."   The flesh is taken from the shell and cut up for bait, and the shell itself is tied to a line and sunk near the bottom to attract the fish.   Shrimps are also good bait, as are any of the small fishes, or conchs cut into suitable sizes.   Any of the various crabs can also be utilized.   The large conchs *Strombus* and *Pyrula* are good, and a large one will furnish bait for a whole day.

BAIT FISHES

For the information of anglers who would like to know something of the small fishes used for bait, their names at least, I think it not out of place to mention them here. The mullet is one of the fishes most frequently utilized. There are several species belonging to the family *Mugilidæ:* the common mullet (*Mugil cephalus*), the white mullet (*Mugil curema*), both of which are abundant in Florida, especially the first named. There is a somewhat rare species along the coasts, but common at Key West, the fantail mullet (*Mugil trichodon*). A very abundant but very small species, and one that makes a capital bait for fishes with small mouths, is the whirligig mullet (*Querimana gyrans*).

There are several species of sardines belonging to the herring family (*Clupeidæ*). They may be found in all bays along the coasts, going in and out of the inlets with the tide. The most common species are the silver sardine (*Sardinella humeralis*), which has a dark spot at the base of the pectoral fin, and the striped sardine (*Sardinella sardina*), which has faint streaks along the sides.

The anchovies belong to the family *Engrauli-*

didæ, and may be distinguished by their very wide mouths, which open back to the gill-cover. The species all look very much alike; the most common ones are the banded anchovy (*Stolephorus perfasciatus*), with narrow silvery longitudinal band, and from two to three inches long; the big anchovy (*Stolephorus brownii*), which is deeper and grows larger, from four to six inches in length; these two species are mostly confined to the south and west coasts. Another species, also abundant on the east coast, is the silver anchovy (*Stolephorus mitchilli*), which is more silvery or translucent in appearance than the others, with yellowish fins and dotted body.

There are a number of crabs that are excellent baits, as the hermit crab (*Eupagurus*), which lives in the cast-off shells of univalve mollusks; fiddler crab (*Gelasimus*), which abounds in myriads on the inside shores of the bays; the spider crab (*Libinia*), which is quite common in shallow water, sometimes covered with bits of weeds, shells, etc.; the common crab (*Cancer*); the lady crab (*Platyonichus*), beautifully spotted; the stone crab (*Menippe*), quite a large crab, with very large claws; the mud crab (*Panopeus*), a small crab and a very good bait. There are a number

of crustaceans, commonly called beach-fleas, that
are good baits for small-mouthed fishes along
the Florida coasts, among which may be mentioned the beach-flea (*Orchestia*); the sand-bug
(*Hippa*); the gribble (*Limnoria*); also the shrimp
(*Gammarus*); and the prawn (*Palæmonetes*).

THE GRUNT FAMILY

(*Hæmulidæ*)

The grunts have an oblong body, more or less
elevated and compressed; head large, its sides
usually scaly; mouth low and horizontal, usually
curved; sharp or pointed teeth; dorsal fin single,
with a marked angle at the junction of the spiny
and soft portions; the dorsal spines ten or twelve;
anal fin with three spines, the second one the
largest; caudal fin concave. The coloration is
bizarre and usually brilliant, with the lips and
inside of the mouth bright red or scarlet. They
are all good pan-fishes, and from their habit of
emitting vocal sounds when caught are called
"grunts." They feed on crustaceans, small fishes,
and the innumerable marine invertebrates that
inhabit the coral reefs and coralline rocks.

Hæmulon plumieri. The Common Grunt. Body moderately elongate; the back elevated and somewhat compressed; head
long, the sharp snout projecting; head 2⅔; depth 2⅔; eye 5;

D. XII, 16; A. III, 8; scales 5–50–17; anterior profile more or less S-shaped; the nape gibbous; mouth very large, the gape curved, maxillary reaching beyond front of eye; lower jaw slightly included; teeth strong, in broad bands, those of the outer series enlarged; antrorse teeth of posterior part of both jaws strong; interorbital space convex; preorbital rather deep; preopercle finely serrate; scales above lateral line much enlarged anteriorly.

Hæmulon sciurus. The Yellow Grunt. Body oblong, the back not much elevated; head 2¾; depth 2⅜; eye 4; scales 7–53–14; D. XII, 16; A. III, 8; interorbital space convex; preopercle finely serrate; profile nearly straight; snout moderately acute; mouth large, the gape curved, the maxillary reaching a little past front of pupil; lower jaw slightly included; teeth strong; upper jaw in front with about 3 strong canines on each side; front teeth of lower jaw rather strong; blue stripes on body.

Hæmulon album. The Margate-fish. Body comparatively deep, the back much elevated and compressed; the anterior profile steep; head 3; depth 2⅔; eye 6; scales 7–46–16; D. XII, 16; A. III, 7; snout pointed; mouth large, the maxillary extending to front of eye; lower jaw included; teeth not very large, in narrow bands; interorbital space strongly convex; preorbital deep; preopercle finely serrate; soft part of anal and dorsal fins covered with thin, translucent scales.

Hæmulon parra. The Sailor's Choice. Body comparatively deep, the back compressed and arched; anterior profile rather steep and convex; head 3; depth 2⅔; eye 4; scales 5–50–14; D. XII, 17; A. III, 7; mouth rather small, the maxillary extending to front of eye; teeth in bands, rather strong, the outer large, antrorse teeth of lower jaw well developed; preopercle finely serrate; lower jaw slightly included; interorbital space convex; preorbital rather deep.

Orthopristis chrysopterus. The Pig-fish. Body ovate-elliptical, somewhat elevated at shoulders, considerably compressed; head 3⅛; depth 2¾; eye 5; scales 10–60–19; D. XII, 16; A. III, 12; snout long and sharp; jaws equal, each with a narrow band of slender teeth, the outer above a little larger; mouth small, the maxillary not reaching to eye; preopercle very slightly

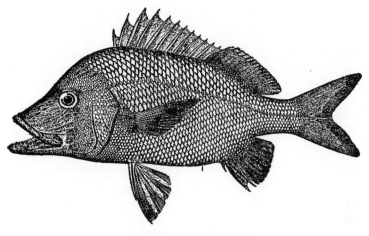

THE BLACK GRUNT

Hæmulon plumieri

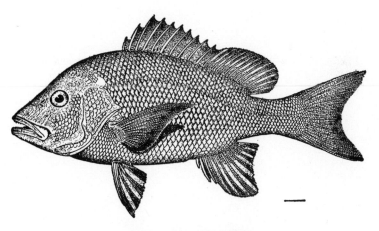

THE RED SNAPPER

Lutianus aya

serrate above; snout and lower jaw naked, rest of head scaly; dorsal and anal spines enclosed in a deep, scaly sheath; soft rays naked.

Anisotremus virginicus. The Pork-fish. Body ovate, the back very much elevated; the anterior profile steep; very much arched at nape; head $3\frac{1}{8}$; depth $2\frac{1}{10}$; eye 4; scales 11–56–17; D. XII, 17; A. III, 10; mouth small, the maxillary extending to anterior nostril; jaws subequal; outer row of teeth enlarged; about 6 gill-rakers.

THE BLACK GRUNT

(Hæmulon plumieri)

The black or common grunt is the most abundant and one of the most popular food-fishes in the vicinity of Key West. It was named by Lacépède, in 1802, in honor of Father Plumier, an early naturalist, who sent drawings of the fishes of Martinique to the museums of Europe. It belongs to the West Indian fauna, and is abundant near Key West, and not uncommon about the rocks and reefs at the lower end of Tampa Bay and other rocky localities on the Gulf coast of Florida. On the Atlantic coast it is found as far north as Cape Hatteras.

The depth of the body is a little more than a third of its length, compressed, with elevated shoulder. The head is as long as the depth of the body, with a large, curved mouth and a pointed and projecting snout. The profile is concave in front of the eye. The jaws are armed with bands of strong and conical teeth, the outer ones largest and the rear ones curving forward. Its color is bluish gray, with the bases of the scales bronze, tinged with olive, forming oblique stripes running upward and backward. The head is golden bronze, with many bright blue stripes, very distinct, a few of which extend to the shoulder. The inside of the mouth is scarlet, becoming lighter, or yellowish, on the jaws. The dorsal fin is grayish, with a yellow border on the spinous portion; the anal fin is gray tinged with yellow; the ventral fins are bluish gray; the pectoral fins are gray with a dusky bar at the base; the caudal fin is plain gray.

The common grunt grows usually to a foot in length, though more are caught under that size than over. It is often called "sow grunt" by the market fishermen, in contradistinction to the " boar grunt," as the yellow grunt is often designated by them, wrongly supposing one to be the male and the other the female. While the general remarks on its feeding habits, as given in the paragraph relating to the family characteristics of the grunts, are correct, it may be stated that they are essentially carnivorous, devouring small fishes, crustaceans, and other marine invertebrates that abound on the coralline reefs. They spawn late in the summer, on the rocky shoals and hard, sandy bars, congregating at such times in large schools. As a food-fish it is held in greater esteem than any other fish in the Key West market, and selling from a nickel to a dime for a bunch of about half a dozen, it forms the staple breakfast dish of all Key Westers, who are inordinately fond of it.

While assistant chief of the fisheries department of the World's Columbian Exposition at Chicago, in 1893, I had among other visitors a young lady friend from Key West, who never before had been away from her island home, having been educated at the convent of Key West. She could not find words to express her delight at scenes so entirely new and novel, and said that some things gave her a better idea of heaven; but there was one thing, she said, that was lacking amidst all the wonders and delights from the four quarters of the globe, and without which everything else paled into insignificance,—"fried grunts for breakfast." I made her happy by escorting her to the Aquarium and showing her the live grunts swimming in a tank, seemingly as much at home as on the coral reefs of Florida.

The methods of angling, and the tackle and baits used for grunts, are given in the opening paragraphs of this chapter, to which the reader is referred.

THE YELLOW GRUNT

(Hæmulon sciurus)

The yellow grunt was first noticed by Bloch, in 1790, from the West Indies; but owing to a mistake as to its proper identification it was named *sciurus*, meaning "squirrel," by Shaw, in 1803, based on Bloch's description and figure. The name squirrel is in allusion to the grunting noise it emits when captured, which is compared to the barking of that animal. It is abundant in the West Indies and south to Brazil, and is quite common about Key West.

The yellow grunt is very similar to the common grunt in the conformation of its body and fins, but has a rather curved profile instead of a depression in front of the eye. The teeth are similar, with about three strong canines on each side. The scales on the upper part of the body are relatively smaller than in the black grunt. Its color is uniformly brassy yellow, with about a dozen longitudinal and distinct stripes of sky-blue, somewhat wavy, extending from the snout to the anal fin; the fins are yellowish; the inside of the mouth is scarlet. It grows to about a foot in length, but occasionally to eighteen inches. It is the handsomest in coloration and appearance of all the grunts, and is often called " boar grunt " by the Key West fishermen. A black-bass bait rod, braided linen line, snelled hooks No. 1–0, with sinker adapted to the depth and current of the water, and sea-crawfish, shrimps, prawns, or cut-fish bait, will be found quite applicable for grunt fishing.

Although the yellow grunt was known to science from the West Indies as early as 1790, it was not recorded from the waters of the United States until a century later, when in 1881 I collected it at Key West. This is the more remarkable inasmuch as it is rather common along the keys, and is moreover such a striking, well-marked, and handsome species that it is difficult to imagine how it had been overlooked. The field has, however, been pretty well worked since, and many new species have been recorded.

The Florida Keys, like the southern portion of the peninsula, are of recent formation, and are underlaid by oolitic and coral limestones. These coralline rocks are formed by the action of the waves and weather on the calcareous secretions of coral polyps, those beautiful "flowers of the sea" which are still building better than they know on the outlying submerged reefs, and where may be seen those tiny "toilers of the sea," madrepores, astreans, mæandrinas, porites, gorgonias, etc., rivalling in beauty of form and color the most charming and delicate ferns, fungi, mosses, and shrubs.

The fishes that frequent the coral reefs are very handsome, both in form and coloration: silvery, rosy, scarlet, brown, and golden bodies, with sky-blue, bright yellow, rosy, or black stripes and bands, or spotted, stellated, and mottled with all the hues of the rainbow; and with jewelled eyes of scarlet, blue, yellow, or black; fins of all colors and shapes, and lips of scarlet red, blue, or silver.

THE MARGATE-FISH

(Hæmulon album)

The margate-fish, or margate grunt, is the largest of the family, growing to two feet or more in length and eight or ten pounds in weight, though usually it weighs from two to six pounds as taken to market. It was noticed by Catesby in his " History of the Carolinas," in 1742, and was wrongly identified from his description by Walbaum in 1792. It received its present name from Cuvier and Valenciennes, in 1830, from West Indian specimens; they called it *album*, meaning "white," as it is the lightest in coloration of any of the grunts. It is much esteemed as a food-fish at Key West. It is abundant from Key West to Brazil, being quite common about the Florida Keys, especially in the immediate vicinity of Key West, being usually found in deep water, except when it approaches the shallows to feed on crustaceans, etc. It is rather a warm-water fish.

The margate-fish is of much the same proportions, and of similar appearance, as the yellow grunt, but with a more elevated and arching back, and is more compressed. The teeth are in narrow bands, and are somewhat smaller than in the other grunts. The adult fish is whitish, olivaceous on the back, with faint spots on the scales of back and sides. The inside of the mouth is orange; the lips and snout yellowish; the fins dusky greenish; a broad but indistinct band extends along the sides. Younger fish are bluish in coloration of body and fins, with dark parallel stripes below.

Somewhat larger hooks, say No. 2–0, and a little heavier line, braided linen, size F, are more suitable for this fish; otherwise the same tackle and baits can be employed as for the other grunts and channel fishes.

THE SAILOR'S CHOICE

(*Hæmulon parra*)

This grunt is sometimes called bastard margaret by the Key West fisherman. The name sailor's choice is often wrongly applied to the pinfish (*Lagodon rhomboides*) and the pig-fish (*Orthopristis chrysopterus*). The sailor's choice was first described by Desmarest, in 1823, from Havana; he named it *parra* in honor of the Cuban naturalist, Parra. It is a good pan-fish, eight or ten inches long, usually, but sometimes growing to a foot in length. It is abundant from Key West to Brazil. I have taken it from the line of keys southwest of Cape Florida, and along the mainland from Biscayne Bay to Marco and Lemon Bay on the Gulf coast.

Its body is of about the same proportions, and of the same general appearance, as that of the yellow grunt, and it grows to about the same size. The radial formula of its fins and size of scales are also much the same. The mouth is smaller, but the teeth are of about the same character. Its color is dull pearly gray, belly grayish, each scale of the body with a distinct olive-brown spot, forming interrupted, oblique, and wavy streaks; fins dusky. The inside of the mouth is not so red as in the other grunts. There is a distinct black spot on the lower edge of the cheek-bone.

THE GRAY GRUNT AND FRENCH GRUNT

The gray grunt (*Hæmulon macrostomum*) and the French grunt (*Hæmulon flavolineatum*) are not so common about the Florida Keys as the other grunts, but grow to about the same size, and are often taken with them, and with the same baits and the same mode of fishing.

THE PIG–FISH
(*Orthopristis chrysopterus*)

Another pan-fish belonging to the grunt family and common to the waters of Florida, and one much esteemed as a food-fish, is the pig-fish. It is known as hog-fish in Chesapeake Bay, and sailor's choice on the South Atlantic coast. It was described by Linnæus, in 1766, from South Carolina. He named it *chrysopterus*, or "gold fin." Its range extends from the Chesapeake Bay along the Atlantic and Gulf coasts to Florida and Texas, and occasionally it strays as far north as Long Island.

It resembles the grunts very much in its general appearance. Its body is rather more than a third of its length, elevated at the shoulder, and compressed. Its head is a third of the length of the body, with a long, sharp snout and a small mouth placed low. There is a narrow band of slender teeth in each jaw, the outer ones in the upper jaw somewhat larger. The color of the pig-fish is light blue above, shading gradually to silvery below; the upper lip is marked with blue; the body scales have a blue centre, the edges with a bronze spot, forming very distinct orange-brown stripes along the rows of scales on the back and sides, those above the lateral line extending obliquely upward and backward, those below being nearly horizontal; the snout, cheeks, and gill-covers have distinct bronze spots, larger than those of the body; the inside of the mouth is pale, the back of the mouth somewhat golden in hue; the dorsal fin is translucent, with bronze spots or shades, the edge of the fin dusky; the other fins are more or less dusky, with yellowish shades.

Along the Atlantic and Gulf coasts it resorts to sandy shoals in rather shallow water, but along the Florida Keys it is found also about rocky bars, and on the Gulf coast is often on grassy flats, or wherever crabs, shrimp, beach-fleas, and other crustaceans abound, on which it feeds, principally, though it is also fond of the young fry of other fishes. It is an excellent pan-fish, of delicious flavor, and is a favorite wherever its merits are known. It grows to a length of ten inches, sometimes to twelve or fifteen inches in favorable localities, but in Florida is mostly from six to eight inches in length. It spawns in the spring in April and May.

It is much sought after in Chesapeake Bay, and is a favorite food-fish at Norfolk, Virginia, where it is known as hog-fish. It grows there somewhat larger, and is also a favorite fish with anglers. The lightest tackle must be employed for its capture, and hooks Nos. 2 to 3, on gut snells, for it has a small mouth. Sea-crawfish, crab, shrimp, beach-fleas, and other crustaceans are the best baits, though cut conch and fish will answer pretty well. It is a bottom feeder, and sinkers must be used to keep the bait near the fish.

THE PORK-FISH

(*Anisotremus virginicus*)

Another pan-fish of the grunt family (*Hæmulidæ*) is the pork-fish, a handsome and beautifully-marked species. It was named by Linnæus, in 1758, from South America, though why he called it *virginicus*, " Virginia," is not known. It is a tropical fish, its range extending from the Florida Keys to Brazil. It is very abundant in the vicinity of Key West, and is seen in the markets daily.

It has a short, compressed body, its depth being half of its length, with the back very much elevated. Its head is short compared with its height, with a very steep profile, slightly convex in front and very much arched at the nape. The mouth is quite small, with thick lips; the jaws are armed with bands of sharp, pointed teeth, the outer row enlarged. The ground color of the body is pearly gray; an oblique black bar, as wide as the eye, extends from the nape through the eye to the angle of the mouth; another broader and jet-black vertical bar extends from the front of the dorsal fin to the base of the pectoral fin; the interspace between the bars is pearly gray, with yellow spots, becoming confluent above; beginning at the vertical bar and extending backward are half a dozen deep yellow, longitudinal, and parallel stripes, the lower ones reaching the caudal fin; all of the fins are deep yellow.

The pork-fish resorts to the reefs and coralline rocks, feeding on crustaceans, small marine invertebrates, and small, soft-shelled mollusks, which it crushes with the blunt teeth in its throat. Its usual size runs from half a pound to a pound, but occasionally grows to two pounds. It should be fished for with very light tackle, about the same as used for the pig-fish, but with smaller hooks, No. 5 or 6, on gut snells, and cut-conch bait, small shrimps, and beach-fleas.

The pork-fish has been known from the time of Marcgrave, over two centuries ago, from Brazil, and from the West Indies for many years, but was not recorded from the waters of the United States until 1881, when I collected it near Key West. As in the case of the yellow grunt and the lane snapper, it is surprising that such long-described and well-marked and beautiful species should have been overlooked in our own waters until my collection of that year.

THE SNAPPER FAMILY

(*Lutianidæ*)

This family of perchlike fishes is related to the grunts on one hand, and to the groupers, or sea-basses, on the other. Those to be described here are mostly of small or moderate size, but are all good food-fishes and fair game-fishes. They are abundant along the Florida Keys, and with the exception of the red snapper are caught in a similar manner, and with the same tackle and baits, as the grunts. They are characterized by an oblong body more or less elevated and compressed; rough scales, large head and mouth; teeth sharp and unequal; dorsal fin single, with ten or twelve spines; anal fin similar in shape to soft dorsal fin, with three spines; the caudal fin concave.

Ocyurus chrysurus. The Yellow-tail. The yellow-tail differs from the other snappers in the formation of the skull, the peculiar form of its body, the large, deeply-forked caudal fin, and the presence of pterygoid teeth. Its body is elliptical, with regularly-arched back; head 3; depth 3; scales 7–65–15; D. X, 13; A. III, 9; mouth small, oblique, the lower jaw projecting, maxillary reaching front of orbit; snout pointed; caudal peduncle long and slender; eye small, 5; interorbital space very convex, with median keel; upper jaw with a narrow band of villiform teeth, outside of which is a single series of larger teeth, several in front being caninelike; a large, oval patch of teeth on tongue;

an arrow-shaped patch on the vomer; a narrow band of pterygoid teeth in the adult; gill-rakers long and slender, $8 + 21$.

Lutianus synagris. The Lane Snapper. Body oblong and compressed, back arched and slightly elevated; profile almost straight; head $2\frac{3}{5}$; depth $2\frac{4}{5}$; eye 5; scales 8–60–15; D. X, 12; A. III, 8; mouth moderate, maxillary reaching front of orbit; interorbital space gently convex; upper jaw with a narrow band of villiform teeth, outside of which a single series of enlarged ones; lower jaw with villiform band in front only, the row of larger teeth nearly equal in size, none of them canines; vomer and tongue with each a single patch; preopercle finely serrate, with coarser teeth at angle; gill-rakers rather long, $5 + 9$; 4 small canines in front of upper jaw.

Lutianus aya. The Red Snapper. Body rather deep, moderately compressed, the back well elevated, profile steep; head $2\frac{3}{5}$; depth $2\frac{3}{5}$; eye $5\frac{1}{2}$; scales 8–60–15; mouth rather large, maxillary reaching front of orbit; snout rather pointed; interorbital space strongly convex; upper jaw with a narrow band of villiform teeth, and a row of small teeth outside; lower jaw with a single row of small teeth, some of which are almost caninelike; within these is a very narrow band of villiform teeth in front of jaw only; tongue with a broad oval patch of teeth, in front of which a small, irregular patch; vomer with a broad, arrow-shaped patch; preopercle with serrated edge above, lower border dentate; gill-rakers moderate, 8 on lower arch; 4 canines in front of upper jaw.

Lutianus jocu. The Dog Snapper. Body comparatively deep and compressed; the back elevated and profile straight; head $2\frac{1}{2}$; depth $2\frac{1}{3}$; eye $4\frac{4}{5}$; scales 8–56–15; D. X, 14; A. III, 8; mouth rather large, jaws subequal, maxillary reaching front of orbit; upper jaw with a narrow band of villiform teeth, a single series of larger ones, and 4 canines in front, 2 of them very large; lower jaw with a narrow, villiform band in front only, and a series of larger teeth outside, some almost caninelike; tongue with a single patch of teeth; an arrow-shaped patch on vomer; preopercle finely serrate above, coarser teeth at angle; gill-rakers short and thick, about 9 on lower arch.

z

Lutianus apodus. The Schoolmaster Snapper. Body comparatively deep, moderately compressed, the back elevated and profile straight; head 2½; depth 2½; eye 4⅓; scales 6–43–13; D. X, 14; A. III, 8; mouth large, maxillary reaching front of orbit; snout long and pointed; interorbital space flattish; upper jaw with a narrow band of villiform teeth, a single series of larger ones outside, and 4 canines in front, one on each side very large; lower jaw with a narrow, villiform band in front, an enlarged series outside; tongue with a large, single patch; an arrow-shaped patch on vomer; preopercle finely serrate above; gill-rakers short and thick, about 9 on lower part of arch.

THE YELLOW-TAIL

(*Ocyurus chrysurus*)

The yellow-tail is a very handsome fish, and one of the favorite pan-fishes at Key West. It was named *chrysurus,* or "gold-tail," by Bloch, in 1790, from its description by Marcgrave in his "Fishes of Brazil." Its habitat is from southern Florida to South America. It is abundant in the vicinity of Key West in the channels between the reefs and keys.

The yellow-tail is well proportioned, compressed, and elliptical, being regularly curved from head to tail. Its head is as long as the depth of the body, with a pointed snout; the mouth is rather small, with the lower jaw projecting. The color above is olivaceous, or bluish, below violet; a broad, deep yellow stripe runs from the snout, through the eye, and along the middle of the body to the caudal fin; above this stripe there are a number of deep yellow blotches, as if made by the finger tips; below the broad yellow stripe are quite a number of narrow, parallel yellow stripes, with violet interspaces; the iris of the eye is scarlet; the very long caudal fin is entirely deep yellow, and the other fins are bordered with yellow.

The yellow-tail associates with the grunts and porgies about the coralline rocks in the channels, feeding on small fishes and crustaceans. Its average size is ten or twelve inches in length and nearly a pound in weight, though it sometimes is taken up to two feet, and three or four pounds. It is quite a good game-fish and very voracious, eagerly taking sea-crawfish, crab, conch, or small fish bait. Some of the large conchs, as *Pyrula* and *Strombus*, will furnish bait for an entire outing, the animal being as large as a child's forearm. Black-bass tackle, with hooks Nos. 1 to 1–0 on gut snells, will answer for the yellow-tail.

THE LANE SNAPPER

(Lutianus synagris)

The lane snapper is another beautiful fish common about the reefs and keys. It was named by

Linnæus, in 1758, who called it *synagris*, as
it resembled a related fish of Europe (*Dentex
dentex*), whose old name was *synagris*. Catesby
mentioned the lane snapper in his "History of
Carolina," in 1743. It is abundant from the
Florida Keys to South America, and not uncommon on the west coast of Florida, as far north as
Tampa Bay, and west to Pensacola.

The lane snapper resembles very much the
yellow-tail in the shape of its body, which is semi-
elliptical in outline, compressed, with the back
regularly curved from the snout to the tail; its
depth is a little more than a third of its length.
Its head is as long as the depth of the body; the
mouth is large, and the snout pointed. It is rose
color, tinged with silver below, with a narrow
bluish or greenish border on the top of the back;
the belly is white, tinged with yellow; there are
deep yellow stripes along the sides, with indistinct, broad, rosy cross bars; the iris of the eye
and the lips are scarlet; the cheeks and gill-
covers are rosy, with blue above; the pectoral fins
are pink, the lower fins yellow, the soft dorsal
pink, the spiny dorsal translucent, with yellow
border, and the caudal fin scarlet; there is a large
and conspicuous dark blotch just below the front

part of the soft dorsal fin. The lane snapper feeds on small fishes and crustaceans about the keys and reefs, in rather shallow water. It grows to a foot in length, though usually about eight or nine inches, and is a free biter at the same baits as the yellowtail.

While it is freely conceded that the highest branch of angling is casting the artificial fly on inland waters, and that the fullest measure of enjoyment is found only in the pursuit of the salmon, black-bass, trout, or grayling, it must be admitted that salt-water angling likewise has joys and pleasures that are, as Walton says, " Worthy the knowledge and practice of a wise man." And nowhere does salt-water angling offer more charms to the appreciative angler, or appeal to his sense of the curious and beautiful in nature, than along the keys off the southern extremity of the peninsula of Florida. The palm-crowned islets are laved by the waters of the Gulf Stream, as clear and bright and green as an emerald of the purest ray serene. Through their limpid depths are seen the lovely and varied tints of coral polyps, the graceful fronds of sea-feathers and sea-fans in gorgeous hues, and the curious and fantastic coralline caves, amid whose crannies and arches swim the most beautiful creations of the finny tribe, whose capture is at once a joy and a delight.

THE RED SNAPPER

(*Lutianus aya*)

The red snapper was named *aya* by Bloch, in 1790, that being the Portuguese name for it in Brazil, according to Marcgrave. It was described by Goode and Bean as a new species, in 1878, and named *blackfordi*, in honor of Eugene G. Blackford, of New York, in consideration of his eminent services and interest in fishculture. The red snapper, while not a game-fish, is one of the best known of Florida fishes, inasmuch as it is shipped all over the country as a good dinner fish, its fine, firm flesh bearing transportation well. It is especially abundant in the Gulf of Mexico, in water from ten to fifty fathoms deep, on the " snapper banks," from ten to fifty miles offshore, and thence south to Brazil, occasionally straying north on the Atlantic coast to Long Island.

The depth of its body is a little more than a third of its length, being rather deep and compressed, the back elevated and regularly arched from the eye to the tail. The head is large, its length equal to the depth of the body, with a pointed snout, large mouth, and straight profile. The color of the red snapper is a uniform rose-red, paler on the throat; fins all red, the vertical fins bordered with dusky blue; there is a dark blotch under the front of the soft portion of the dorsal fin, except in the oldest and largest fish; the iris of the eye is scarlet.

The red snapper, being a deep-water fish, is seldom found along the shores, and is of no importance to the angler. It is a bottom fish, feeding in company with the large groupers on small fishes and crustaceans. It grows to twenty or thirty pounds, but its usual size is from five to ten pounds. It spawns in summer.

The commercial fishing for the red snapper is done on the "snapper banks" in very deep water. Strong hand-lines and codfish hooks are used, with cut bait. By the time the fish is brought to the surface from the bottom it is almost exhausted, and would afford no sport to the angler. The bringing of the fish from depths where the pressure of the water is so great, to the surface, where it is comparatively so much less, causes the fish to swell up, and the air-bladder to be so filled that the fish would float; it is therefore pricked with a sharp awl to let out the air, as otherwise the fish would not sink in the well of the vessel in which it is carried alive to port.

THE DOG SNAPPER

(*Lutianus jocu*)

The dog snapper is very similar in shape to the red snapper, but is much smaller and of different coloration. It was named *jocu* by Bloch, in 1801, from Parra's description, in 1787, *jocu* being the Cuban name of the fish. It is called dog snapper, owing to its large canine teeth. Its range extends from the South Atlantic coast to Brazil. It is abundant along the Florida Keys, and very rarely strays along the Atlantic coast northward, but has been taken on the Massachusetts coast in summer.

It has a robust, somewhat compressed body, its depth a third of its length, and the back elevated over the shoulder. Its head is large, somewhat longer than the depth of the body, with a straight profile and a rather long and pointed snout. The ground color of the body is dull red or coppery, dark olivaceous or bluish on the back, with about a dozen lighter-colored vertical stripes across the body; the cheeks and gill-covers are red, with a pale area from the eye to the angle of the mouth; there is a row of small, round blue spots from the snout to the angle of the gill-cover, also a bluish or dusky stripe; the upper fins and the caudal fin are mostly orange in color; the lower fins are yellow, and the iris of the eye red.

The dog snapper, like the other snappers, feeds on small fishes and crustaceans. It grows to a foot in length and to a pound or two in weight. It is a good food-fish, selling readily in the markets. It is quite gamy and voracious, and with light tackle is worthy of the angler's skill. Hooks No. 1–0 or 2–0 on gut snells, and sea-crawfish, or a small minnow, are good baits.

THE SCHOOLMASTER

(Lutianus apodus)

The schoolmaster snapper was named by Walbaum, in 1792, based on Catesby's description and figure of the schoolmaster in his " History of Carolina," but in his figure he omitted the pectoral fins, for which reason Walbaum named it *apoda*, meaning "without a foot." Its range extends from the Florida Keys to Brazil, and is abundant in the vicinity of Key West, where it is seen daily in the markets. Under favorable conditions of temperature it has been taken on the Massachusetts coast.

The schoolmaster is very similar to the dog snapper in its general form, but differs greatly in coloration. Its body is rather deep and compressed, its depth being more than a third of its length, and the back is more elevated than in the dog snapper. The head is large, as long as the depth of the body, with a large mouth; the profile is straight from snout to the nape, thence regularly arched to the tail; the snout is long and pointed. The predominating color is orange, olivaceous on the back and top of the head, with eight or nine vertical bars across the body, equidistant, of a pale or bluish white color, the wider interspaces being red; the cheeks and gill-covers are red, with a row of small blue spots from the snout across the cheeks, just below the eye; all of the fins are yellow, more or less shaded with red.

The schoolmaster grows to about the same size as the dog snapper, usually from eight to ten inches, sometimes to a foot in length, and a pound or two in weight. It feeds on small fishes, crabs, and other crustaceans, and is a good food-fish. It is a fairly good game-fish, and on light tackle fights with vigor and considerable resistance. Sproat hooks Nos. 1–0 and 2–0 are quite suitable, and should be tied on gut snells. A sinker adapted to the strength of the tide must be used in the deep-water channels. Sea-crawfish, anchovies, or whirligig mullets are good baits.

The mangrove snapper (*Lutianus griseus*) and the mutton-fish (*Lutianus analis*) are larger snappers and better game-fishes. They are described in another volume of this series.

THE PORGY FAMILY

(*Sparidæ*)

The porgies of Florida belong to the family *Sparidæ* previously described, but not to the same genus as the northern porgy, as the scup is sometimes called. They are characterized by a deep, compressed body, humpbacked, with a large head and deep snout, and with a knob in front of the eye. The mouth is small, with strong, canine-like teeth and molars.

Calamus bajonado. The Jolt-head Porgy. Body oblong, compressed and elevated over the shoulders; head 3; depth $2\frac{2}{3}$; eye 3; scales 7–54–17; D. XII, 12; A. III, 10; anterior profile evenly curved; mouth moderate, maxillary not reaching front of eye; snout long and pointed; teeth strong, conical; anterior teeth enlarged, 2 or 3 on each side in the upper jaw, and 3 or 4 on each side in the lower; molars in 3 series in the upper, and 2 in the lower jaw; dorsal fin single with slender spines.

Calamus calamus. The Saucer-eye Porgy. Body oblong, elevated more than the other porgies; head 3⅓; depth 2; eye 3¾; scales 9-54-16; D. XII, 12; A. III, 10; anterior profile steep; outline of snout slightly curved; mouth small, maxillary not reaching front of eye; outer teeth strong, 10 or 12 in number, the outer one in each jaw, on each side, caninelike; dorsal spines rather strong.

Calamus proridens. The Little-head Porgy. Body oblong and much elevated; head 3¼; depth 2⅓; eye 4; scales 9-58-16; D. XII, 12; A. III, 10; anterior profile steep and straight; mouth moderate, maxillary scarcely reaching front of eye; anterior teeth of outer series slightly longer and more robust than those of the cardiform band; on each side of the upper jaw one of these teeth becomes much enlarged, caninelike, directed obliquely forward and downward, and strongly curved, the upper surface concave; there are usually 7 teeth of the outer series between these two canines; no evident accessory series of molars; dorsal spines slender and high.

Calamus arctifrons. The Grass Porgy. Body oblong, but little elevated; head 3¼; depth 2⅔; eye 4½; scales 6-48-13; D. XII, 12; A. III, 10; anterior profile unevenly curved, very convex before the eye; head narrow above; dorsal outline not forming a regular arch; a rather sharp angle at nape; preorbital deep; canine teeth, 8 in upper jaw and 10 in lower.

THE JOLT-HEAD PORGY

(*Calamus bajonado*)

This is the largest and most abundant of the porgies. It was described by Bloch, in 1801, who named it *bajonado*, after the Cuban name given by Parra in his " Natural History of Cuba."

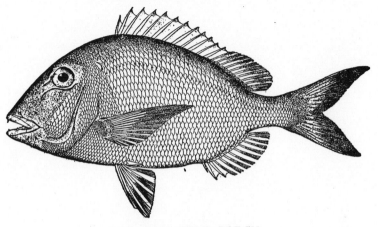

THE JOLT-HEAD PORGY
Calamus bajonado

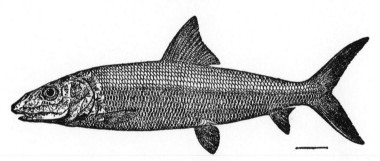

THE LADY-FISH
Albula vulpes

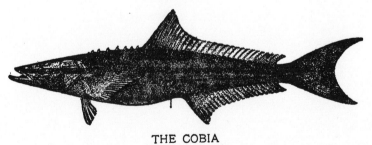

THE COBIA
Rachycentron canadus

It is not certain what the name is intended to signify. It may allude to the "bayonet-like," interhæmal bones, or to *bajio*, meaning a "sand-bank" or "shoal," in allusion to its habitat. The jolt-head is abundant along the Florida Keys, especially in the vicinity of Key West, where it is one of the commonest market fishes; its range extends to the West Indies.

It has a short, deep body, compressed, its depth being half its length; its back is more regularly arched than in the other porgies, or not so hump-backed. The head is large, with a long, pointed snout, and mouth moderate in size; the profile is more regularly curved than in the other porgies.

The predominating color is dusky or bluish, with brassy reflections; the upper fins are pale or bluish, more or less mottled with darker shades; the lower fins are plain; the cheeks are coppery in hue.

The jolt-head resorts to the rocks and reefs, as well as to hard, sandy shoals, feeding on small fishes, crustaceans, and soft-shelled mollusks. It grows usually to eight or ten inches, but often to two feet in length, and six or eight pounds in weight. It is a good food-fish, much in favor with the people of Key West, and is always one

of the commonest fishes in the markets. It
spawns in the summer. It is very voracious,
taking almost any kind of bait greedily. It is
caught in company with the grunts and snappers,
and on the same tackle, which should be light.
Hooks Nos. 1 to 2 are large enough, Sproat-bend
preferred on account of its short barb with cutting
edges and strong wire. Sinkers adapted to the
tide and depth of water must be used.

While catching porgies at a lively rate one day
I asked my boatman, a Bahama negro, why the
big porgy was called "jolt-head." He answered
in the cockney dialect peculiar to Bahama fishermen: "Vell, you see, sir, 'e 'as a big 'ed and an
'ump back, and 'e butts the rocks like a billy-goat,
a-joltin' off the snail-shells and shrimps, and 'e
goes a-blunderin' along like a wessel that 'as a
bluff bow and a small 'elm. 'E 'as more happetite
than gumption, and swallers anythink that comes
'andy, like the jolt-'ed or numbskull that 'e is.
'E is werry heasy to ketch and werry good to
heat."

THE SAUCER-EYE PORGY

(Calamus calamus)

This porgy is called "saucer-eye," owing to its
having a larger eye than the other porgies. It

TAKING BONITO BY TROLLING OFF BLOCK ISLAND

was first described by Cuvier and Valenciennes, in 1830, from the West Indies. They named it *calamus*, meaning " quill " or " reed," from the quill-like bones (interhæmal) that articulate with the spines of the anal fin. It is abundant in the West Indies, and is common about the Florida Keys, but not so plentiful as the jolt-head or little-head porgies.

It is very similar in conformation to the jolt-head, but is more humpbacked, being quite elevated above the shoulder. The body is short, its depth about half its length. Its head is short and deep, with a thin and gibbous profile, and small mouth. Its color is silvery with bluish reflections; the scales golden, forming longitudinal stripes, with pearly-bluish interspaces; the cheeks and snout are purplish, with round brassy spots; the fins are pale, blotched with orange; the iris of the eye is golden.

The saucer-eye grows to twelve or fifteen inches in length, and is considered a good pan-fish at Key West, commanding a ready sale. It is found in the same situations as the other porgies, grunts, and snappers, and is equally voracious, taking the proffered bait eagerly. The tackle for this porgy is the same as for the others, consisting of a light rod, multiplying reel, braided linen line, size F or G, three-foot leader, Sproat-bend hooks, No. 1 or 2, on gut snells, with sinker in accordance with the depth of the water and the strength of the tide.   Almost any bait will answer, as sea-crawfish, cut conch, or fish.

THE LITTLE–HEAD PORGY

(*Calamus proridens*)

This species was first described by Jordan and Gilbert, in 1883, from Key West.   They named it *proridens*, meaning " prow tooth," owing to its projecting canines.   It is abundant in the West Indies, and is quite common about Key West and the neighboring keys.   It is one of the smallest and prettiest of the porgies, and is called little-head in contradistinction to the jolt-head or big-head porgy.   It is almost identical in shape to the saucer-eye porgy, both in head and body.

It is brighter in color than the other porgies, being quite silvery with iridescent reflections; the scales of the upper part of the body have violet spots, forming longitudinal streaks; those on the lower part have pale orange spots; the sides have several dark bands ; the snout and cheeks have horizontal, wavy stripes of violet-blue ; the dorsal fin is violet, with orange border; the anal fin is blue; the caudal fin has an orange band. It is of similar habits to the other porgies, and found with them, but is less common. It is a good pan-fish, growing only to six or eight inches in length.

The little-head porgy, though small in size, is equally as voracious as the other porgies, and is well worth catching if only to admire its beauty. The same tackle will answer as for the others, or more especially that mentioned for the saucer-eye, and the same baits can be employed.

My Bahama negro boatman, alluded to under the jolt-head, continued his dissertation on the porgies somewhat in this wise: " Now, sir, the little-'ed porgy is a cute little chap; 'e gits to vind'ard o' the big-'ed, hevry time. 'E doesn't butt 'is 'ed aginst the rocks, a-knockin' the shells, but 'e 'as two long teeth like gouge-chisels, and 'e jist scoops hoff the crawlin' things from the rock-patches as 'andsome as you like. Little-'ed little wit; big-'ed not a bit!"

THE GRASS PORGY

(*Calamus arctifrons*)

This pretty porgy was first described by Goode and Bean, in 1882, from Pensacola, Florida. They named it *arctifrons*, meaning "contracted fore-head," owing to the narrow forehead. It has a more extended range in the Gulf of Mexico than the other porgies, being common in grassy situations from Pensacola to Key West; it is not known from the West Indies.

The general outline of the grass porgy is very similar to that of the saucer-eye and little-head porgies, though the back is not quite so elevated; the profile is unevenly curved, being quite convex in front of the eye. The mouth is slightly larger than in the saucer-eye. Its color is olivaceous, with dark spots, and several dark vertical bars across the body; many of the scales have pearly spots; there are several yellow spots along the lateral line; the cheeks are brownish, with yellow shades; the upper fins are barred or spotted; the lower fins are paler.

It is the smallest of the porgies, but one of the prettiest. It grows to six or eight inches in length. It is mentioned incidentally with the others of its family in order that it may be known to anglers who are so fortunate as to catch it and admire it. The same tackle and bait employed for the others are suitable. It is found usually in grassy situations.

CHAPTER XVIII

MISCELLANEOUS FISHES

THE LADY-FISH

(*Albula vulpes*)

Albula vulpes. The Lady-fish. Body rather elongate, little compressed, covered with rather small, brilliantly-silvery scales;
head naked; snout conic, subquadrangular, shaped like the
snout of a pig, and overlapping the small, inferior, horizontal
mouth; head $3\frac{3}{4}$; depth 4; scales 9-71-7; D. 15; A. 8; maxillary rather strong, short, with a distinct supplemental bone,
slipping under the membraneous edge of the very broad preorbital; premaxillaries short, not protractile; lateral margin of
upper jaw formed by the maxillaries; both jaws, vomer and
palatines, with bands of villiform teeth; broad patches of coarse,
blunt, paved teeth on the tongue behind and on the sphenoid
and pterygoid bones; opercle moderate, firm; preopercle with
a broad, flat, membraneous edge, which extends backward over
the base of the opercle; gill membranes separate; no gular
plate; a fold of skin across gill membranes, its free edge crenate;
belly flattish, covered with ordinary scales, not carinate; eye
large, with a bony ridge above it, and almost covered with an
annular adipose eyelid.

THE lady-fish, or bonefish, is the only repre-
sentative of the family *Albulidæ*. It has long
been known to science through the early voyagers
to the southern coasts of America. It was first
described by Marcgrave in his " History of Brazil," in 1648, and afterward by Catesby, in his

"History of the Carolinas," in 1737, and named *vulpes*, or "fox," by Linnæus, in 1758, from a specimen taken at the Bahamas.

It inhabits the sandy shores of all warm seas and is, perhaps, the most cosmopolitan of all game-fishes, being known from Asia, Arabia, North and South America, the Pacific Islands, etc. It is common on the coasts of the Atlantic and Pacific in the United States, and is especially abundant in Florida waters, occasionally straying in summer as far north as Long Island.

The lady-fish is allied to the herring tribe. It has a long, gracefully-shaped body, nearly round, or but little compressed; its depth is a fourth of its length; it has a long head with a projecting, piglike snout, overlapping the small mouth, which is well armed with teeth; both jaws and the roof of the mouth in front have bands of brushlike teeth, with patches of coarse, blunt, paved teeth on the back of the mouth and tongue. Its color is bluish green above, with metallic reflections; the sides are very bright and silvery, with faint streaks along the rows of scales; the belly is white, and it feeds on small fishes and crustaceans.

Its spawning habits are not well understood, though the young pass through a metamorphosis, being band-shaped, with very small head and loose, transparent tissues. I have found them abundant on the Gulf coast of Florida. The lady-fish grows to a length of from one to three feet, and to a weight of from one to twelve pounds, though it is usually taken from two to five pounds. It is a good food-fish, highly esteemed at Key West and in the Bermudas by those who know it best.

For its size it is one of the gamest fishes of the seacoast. When hooked it fights as much in the air as in the water, continually leaping above the surface like an animated silver shuttle, to which I likened it more than twenty years ago. It is now becoming better known to anglers who visit Florida in the winter season, who recognize in it much more enjoyable sport on light tackle than they can obtain with the heavy tools required for the tarpon and jewfish.

A black-bass rod, or the Little Giant rod of eight ounces, is light enough, as a heavier fish than the lady-fish is apt to be hooked. A good multiplying reel and fifty yards of braided linen line, size F, and Sproat hooks, No. 1 or 2, on gut snells, will be found eminently suitable. No sinker is needed, as the fishing is done on the surface, though a small brass box-swivel may be used to connect the snell and line, as in black-bass fishing. A leader is not necessary, but it may be used if thought best.

The bait may be a beach-flea, or a very small, silvery fish, as a sardine, pilchard, or mullet, though a small shell squid, or a trolling-spoon of the size of a nickel, with a single hook, may be employed in lieu of live bait, and is quite successful if kept in constant motion. The minnow is to be hooked through the lips and cast as in black-bass fishing, reeling it in slowly on or near the surface.

The fishing may be done from any convenient place near a pass or inlet on the flood tide. A sand-spit at the entrance, or a boat anchored just within the inlet, are desirable places, though good fishing is sometimes available from the end of a pier in a tideway. Fine fishing may also be had at other stages of the tide about offshore reefs and shoals. I have taken the lady-fish, with both fly and bait, in Biscayne Bay, in Cards and Barnes sounds, along the keys to Key West, and at nearly every inlet on the Gulf coast, as far north as Pass-a-Grille, above Tampa Bay, and usually found it associated with the ten-pounder.

The lady-fish, when hooked, will probably astonish the angler who is attached to one for the first time, by its aërial gyrations and quick movements. But the rod must be held at an angle of forty-five degrees, so as to maintain a taut line, notwithstanding its constant leaping; for if any slack line is given, it is almost sure to shake out the hook. And as the leaps are made in such quick succession, the only safe plan is to keep the rod bent, either in giving or taking line, or when holding the fish on the strain of the rod.

The lady-fish will often take a gaudy black-bass fly, in which event a black-bass fly-rod or a heavy trout fly-rod will come handy, with corresponding tackle. A heavy braided linen line, size D, is better suited for salt water than the enamelled silk line, and will cast a fly nearly as well. The flies advised for the Spanish mackerel will answer as well for the lady-fish, though I have found the silver-doctor and coachman both very taking toward dusk, which is the most favorable time for fly-fishing, though the first half of the flood tide and the last half of the ebb are usually both favorable times about the inlets.

Twenty years or more ago I called the attention of northern anglers to the lady-fish, or bone-fish, and the ten-pounder, or bony-fish, as game-fishes of high degree, and accorded equal praise to both species as to gameness. I have never been able to convince myself as to which is entitled to the palm; but they are both good enough, and comparisons are indeed odious as between them. I am glad to note that they are coming to the front and their merits at last recognized. Of late years northern anglers are having great sport with the lady-fish on Biscayne Bay; but judging from their communications in the sportsman's journals, they are confusing the lady-fish with the ten-pounder. This is easily accounted for, inasmuch as they are usually of about the same size, and have very much the same general appearance in form and bright silvery coloration; and moreover there is a confusion attending their vernacular names, as the lady-fish is sometimes known as bony-fish. It should be remembered that the lady-fish has an overhanging, piglike snout and larger scales, while the ten-pounder has a terminal mouth with the jaws about equal, and smaller scales. Moreover, the bony-fish, or ten-pounder, has a bony plate under the lower jaw, like the tarpon, which is absent in the lady-fish. Both are cosmopolitan, inhabiting the warm seas of both continents. They have been known to science for a century and a half, and have been described by many naturalists from different parts of the world. The current specific names were both bestowed by Linnæus. Catesby, in 1837, called the lady-fish (*Albula vulpes*) of the Bahamas " bone-fish," while Captain William Dampier, one of the early explorers, called the bony-fish (*Elops saurus*) of the Bahamas " ten-pounder." The fishermen of Key West usually know the lady-fish as bone-fish, and the ten-pounder as bony-fish. The best plan for anglers is to adopt the names lady-fish and ten-pounder for them, and relegate or ignore the names bone-fish, bony-fish, and skip-jack.

THE TEN-POUNDER
(*Elops saurus*)

Elops saurus. The Ten-pounder. Body elongate, covered with small, silvery scales; head 4¼; depth 6; eye 4, large; scales 12-120-13; D. 20; A. 13; dorsal fin slightly behind ventrals, its last rays short, depressible into a sheath of scales; anal fin smaller, similarly depressible; pectoral and ventral fins moderate, each with a long, accessory scale; opercular bones thin, with expanded membraneous borders; a scaly occipital collar; gular plate 3 to 4 times as long as broad; pseudobranchiæ large; lateral line straight, its tubes simple.

The ten-pounder, or bony-fish, belongs to the same family, *Elopidæ*, as the tarpon, and both are allied to the herring tribe. The ten-pounder was first described by Linnæus, in 1776, from specimens sent to him from South Carolina by Dr. Garden. He named it *saurus*, or "lizard," but there is nothing lizard-like about the ten-pounder. I imagine that Dr. Garden sent the fish under the name of "lizard," from hearing it called by its Spanish name of "lisa," which is pronounced much like lizard. The ten-pounder was mentioned by some of the old voyagers to the West Indies and Carolinas. Like the lady-fish, the ten-pounder is a cosmopolitan, existing in the warm seas of both hemispheres. In the United States it is common to the southern portions of the Atlantic and Pacific coasts and the Gulf of Mexico.

In the general aspect and contour of its silvery body the ten-pounder has much the appearance of the lady-fish, and has been often confounded with it by anglers. Its body, however, is more slender than that of the lady-fish, with smaller scales and a very different head and mouth; the lady-fish has a piglike, overhanging snout, while the lower jaw of the ten-pounder projects slightly. The depth of the body of the ten-pounder is only about a sixth of its length, and the body is not much compressed, being nearly round. The head is long and pointed, with a very wide mouth, with upper and lower lips nearly equal, or terminal. The eye is large, hence one of its names, big-eyed herring. There are many series of small and sharp cardlike teeth on the jaws, tongue, and roof of the mouth. There is a bony plate beneath the lower jaw.

The color on the back is greenish or bluish, the sides silvery and bright, and belly white; the top of the head is greenish, with bronze reflections; the cheeks have a golden lustre; the lower fins are tinged with yellow, the others dusky.

Its habits are not unlike those of the lady-fish, and they often associate. It feeds principally on crustaceans and also on small fishes. It frequents sandy shoals and banks in shallow water at high tide, also grassy situations where its food abounds. Its breeding habits are not well understood, though, like the lady-fish, its young pass through a larval form, and are ribbon-shaped. It grows to a length of two feet or more, and weighs several pounds, sometimes ten or more. It is quite bony, and is not considered a good food-fish, but excels as a game-fish, being equal to the lady-fish in this respect.

The same tackle as that recommended for its
congener, the lady-fish, answers just as well for the
ten-pounder, and it can be fished for in the same
locations.   It frequents shallow water on the
grassy banks and sandy shoals rather more than
the lady-fish, and can be sought there accordingly,
as well as at the inlets when the tide is making.

Both the ten-pounder and the lady-fish are
warm-water fishes.   They are to be found in
Biscayne Bay and along the neighboring keys
during winter, and as the water becomes warmer
they extend their range northward on both coasts.
After the disastrous frosts that occurred during
the winters of 1886 and 1895 in Florida, I saw
windrows of dead ten-pounders, lady-fishes, and
tarpon on the beaches about Charlotte Harbor.
They had become chilled from the sudden lowering of the temperature.   I have caught both the
ten-pounder and lady-fish as far north as Tampa
Bay on the west coast of Florida, and Indian River
Inlet on the east coast.   My fishing was mostly
done from the points of inlets and passes, on the
flood tide, and usually with the artificial fly, in
shallow water, the time and places mentioned being the most favorable for fly-fishing.   At other
times I have fished on the shallow bars and grassy

banks, using such crustaceans as fiddlers, beach-fleas, and shrimps for bait, alternated with small minnows. When beach-fleas are used a fly-rod is preferable and the hook should be smaller than where other bait is employed; No. 4 is about right, if of the Sproat or O'Shaughnessy pattern, they being of larger and stronger wire than other patterns. If beach-fleas are used with a bait-rod, a small sinker must be added to give weight to the cast.

The ten-pounder snaps at the bait or fly in the manner of most fishes, and is off immediately in a wild whirl, skimming through the water, if shallow, in a way to astonish the angler who hooks one for the first time. Then follows a series of brilliant leaps and aërial contortions that commands the admiration of the coldest-blooded fisher. The lady-fish, however, owing to the position of its mouth, being underneath its projecting snout, does not at first take the bait with the vim and snap of the ten-pounder, but apparently nibbles or mouths it for a while, but when hooked displays the same energy and desperate efforts to escape as its congener. The consistent angler may truly exclaim with Pope: —

> " How happy could I be with either,
> Were t'other dear charmer away."

THE SNOOK, OR ROVALLIA

(Centropomus undecimalis)

Centropomus undecimalis. The Snook. Body elongate, with elevated back and straight abdomen; head 3; depth 4; eye 7; scales 9–75–16; D. VIII–I, 10; A. III, 6; head depressed, pikelike, the lower jaw projecting; villiform teeth in bands on jaws, vomer, and palatines; tongue smooth; dorsal fins well separated; preorbital faintly serrated; subopercular flap extending nearly to dorsal fin; maxillary to middle of eye; gill-rakers 4 + 9.

The snook belongs to the family *Centropomidæ*, which embraces a dozen or more species, most of which inhabit the West Indies and the southern Pacific coast, and are all good game-fishes. The snook was first described by Bloch from Jamaica, in 1792; he named it *undecimalis*, or "eleven," as the soft dorsal fin has eleven rays. The name snook was mentioned as the name of this fish by the early explorers, among whom was Captain William Dampier, who also mentioned several others, as "ten-pounders," "cavallies," "tarpoms," etc. Snook is derived from "snoek," the Dutch name for the pike, which it resembles slightly in the shape of the head, though it is more like the pike-perch in its structure and appearance. On the east coast of Florida this fish is known as the snook, and on the Gulf coast as rovallia, the latter name being a corruption of its Spanish name *robalo*, by which it is known in Havana. It is sometimes called sergeant-fish, from the black stripe along its sides. It is common along the shores of the Gulf of Mexico, from Texas to the West Indies, and is especially abundant in the bays and lagoons of both coasts of Florida, often ascending the rivers to fresh water.

It has a long, robust, and nearly round body, its depth being a fourth of its length; the back is slightly elevated and arched. The head is long and depressed, or flat, and is more than a third of the total length of the body; the mouth is large, with a projecting lower jaw; the gill-cover is very long; there are brushlike teeth on the jaws and the roof of the mouth, but no sharp or conical teeth as in the pike or pike-perch.

The color of the back is olive-green, the sides silvery, and the belly white; there is a distinct and very black stripe along the side, following the lateral line from the head to the caudal fin; the dorsal fins are dusky; the lower fins are yellowish.

The snook is a very voracious fish, feeding on fishes, crabs, and other crustaceans, and resorts to sandy shoals and grassy flats where its food is found. It grows to a length of two or three feet, and a weight of twenty or thirty pounds. It is a fair food-fish, though not held in much favor in Florida where so many better food-fishes are common. It is better flavored if skinned instead of scaled.

It is a strong, active game-fish, that, when hooked, starts off with a rush that is dangerous to light tackle, and its subsequent manœuvres require very careful handling when it is of a large size. It has smashed many light rods in the hands of anglers who were not aware of its pugnacity. It will take any kind of natural bait, and rises well to the artificial fly.

A rather heavy black-bass rod or a light striped-bass rod is required for the large fish of the bays and estuaries, though ordinary black-bass tackle will answer for those of less weight at the mouths of streams, or in fresh water, to which it often resorts. A good multiplying reel and fifty yards of braided linen line are sufficient, though one hundred yards will not be amiss, as large fishes of other species are very apt to be hooked in Florida waters. Sproat or O'Shaughnessy hooks, Nos. 1–0 to 3–0, on heavy gut snells are required, with a brass box-swivel to

connect the snell with the reel line; a sinker
may be used or not, depending on the strength
of the tide, though the fishing is usually practised in quiet water, and not in the tideways.

A small fish, mullet or sardine, or fiddler-crab
bait, will prove very enticing to the snook,
though the minnow is better adapted for casting.
The fishing is much like black-bass fishing in
fresh waters, and the snook takes the bait in its
mouth in much the same way as a bass, starting
off at once with a great commotion if near the
surface. Its desperate and vigorous spurts and
rushes are apt to put one's tackle in jeopardy if
the fish is large, and it must be handled with
caution and skill.

For fly-fishing, a rod of nine or ten ounces is
not too heavy where the fish run large. A heavy
braided linen line, size D or E, is best for casting
the fly in salt water. Black-bass flies of showy
patterns, on hooks No. 1 or 2, as coachman,
silver-doctor, polka, oriole, red ibis, professor, etc.,
will answer. The most favorable time is on the
flood tide near the inlets, or toward evening if
in quiet coves or lagoons. The fly should be
repeatedly cast and then allowed to sink a foot or
two. If fishing from a boat, it must be kept in

the deeper water, and the casts made under the mangroves, or to the edges of sand-spits, shoals, or mud-flats, which abound in all bays on the west coast of Florida.

The snook is easily captured by trolling with hand-line and the spoon or minnow, though it is a questionable style of sport at best. Along the edges of shoals and mud-flats and over grassy banks the snook will be found at home. A landing-net should always be used for any kind of fishing with the fly.

THE TRIPLE-TAIL

(*Lobotes surinamensis*)

Lobotes surinamensis. The Triple-tail. Body oblong, deep, compressed and elevated; head 3; depth 2; scales 47; head small; snout short; mouth moderate, oblique, with thick lips; profile of head concave; upper jaw very protractile; the lower, the longest; maxillary without supplemental bone; jaws with narrow bands of villiform teeth, in front of which is a row of larger conical teeth, directed backward; no teeth on vomer or palatines; preopercle strongly serrate; maxillary reaching middle of orbit; scales around eyes small, those on opercles large; eye small; small scales running up on the base of soft dorsal, anal, and caudal fins; caudal rounded; D. XII, 15; A. III, 11; soft rays of dorsal and anal fins elevated, of nearly equal size, and opposite each other; anal spines graduated; branchial rays 6.

The triple-tail belongs to the family *Lobotidæ*. It is allied to the snapper family, but differs in having no teeth on the roof of the mouth. It was first described by Bloch, in 1790, from Surinam, South America. He named it *surinamensis*, from the name of the locality whence his specimens were procured. There is another species on the Pacific coast, *Lobotes pacificus*, that is quite abundant at Panama, where it is known as berrugate.

The triple-tail is known in all warm seas. Its range on the Atlantic coast extends from South America north to Cape Cod, though it is not abundant. I have taken it on both the east and west coasts of Florida. At Tampa it is called black snapper, and in South Carolina it is known as black perch. I have never heard it called flasher, which is said to be its name in the markets of New York.

It is a short, thick, robust fish, nearly half as deep as long, with an elevated back, and with the ventral outline corresponding with its dorsal curve. The head is a third of the length of the body, its profile concave, the snout prominent, and the lower jaw projecting; the mouth is of moderate size, with thick lips.

The color of the back is dark, or greenish black, the sides silvery gray, sometimes blotched and tinged with yellow; the fins are dusky gray or yellowish. In life these colors are very bright, but after death they become almost black.

It feeds on small fishes, mussels, and crustaceans and grows to a length of two or three feet, weighing from ten to fifteen pounds, though its usual size is not more than one-half of this length and weight. Its breeding habits are unknown. It is found in northern waters only during the summer months, but from South Carolina to Florida it is common all the year.

It is a strong and vigorous fish, but rather slow and sluggish in its movements, and not remarkable for game qualities, though it pulls steadily and strongly when hooked. It will take shrimp, clam, fiddler, or small fishes as bait.

A light striped-bass chum rod is very suitable for the triple-tail when of good size. A multiplying reel and fifty yards of braided linen line, hooks No. 1–0 or 2–0, on heavy gut snells, and a brass box-swivel, make up the rest of the tackle. A sinker will probably not be needed as it is usually found in quiet coves about sandy shoals or grassy flats. I have taken it on both coasts of Florida, though it is more common on the east coast. I have also caught it in Chesapeake Bay and near Charleston, South Carolina, but never over five pounds in weight, though I have seen it taken in nets up to about ten pounds. Its short and rounded caudal fin, with the soft portions of the dorsal and anal fins, together, give the appearance of three tails, hence the name triple-tail, by which it is generally known.

THE COBIA

(*Rachycentron canadus*)

Rachycentron canadus. The Cobia. Body elongate, fusiform, subcylindrical, covered with very small, smooth, adherent scales; head $4\frac{1}{4}$; depth $5\frac{2}{3}$; D. VIII–I, 26; A. II, 25; head broad, low, pikelike, the bones above appearing through the thin skin; mouth wide, nearly horizontal, the maxillary reaching front of eye; both jaws, vomer, palatines, and tongue with bands of short, sharp teeth; lower jaw longest; premaxillaries not protractile; preopercle unarmed; two dorsal fins, the spines of the first depressible in a groove; soft dorsal long and low, somewhat falcate, similar to, and nearly opposite, the anal; caudal fin strongly forked; no caudal keel; no finlets; gill-rakers short and stout; pectorals broad and falcate.

The cobia, or sergeant-fish, is the only fish of its family, *Rachycentridæ*. It was first described by Linnæus, in 1766, from a specimen sent to him by Dr. Garden from South Carolina; it is allied to the mackerel tribe, and is found in all warm seas in the old and new worlds. On the Atlantic coast it is common from the Chesapeake Bay to Florida, but occasionally strays north to Cape Cod in the summer. It is rather rare on the west coast of Florida, but common on the east coast.

It is a long and round-bodied fish, quite gracefully formed, with a depth of about one-fifth of its length. The head is broad and flat, something like that of the pike, with a wide mouth, and with jaws, roof of mouth, and tongue armed with bands of short, sharp teeth; the lower jaw projects. The back is olive-brown, or dusky, the sides lighter and silvery, and the belly white; a distinct broad and very dark stripe extends from the upper jaw and through the eye to the caudal fin, with an indistinct one above and below, and parallel with it. Owing to this dark stripe the cobia is sometimes called sergeant-fish, thus confounding it with the snook.

The habits of the cobia are not unlike those of the pike, or mascalonge, of fresh waters, in that it is solitary and lies in wait for its prey, and is almost as rapacious. It lies under the mangroves and cocoa-plum bushes along Indian River and other streams of the east coast of Florida, watching for stray fishes and crabs on which it feeds. It is commonly seen of a length of two or three feet, but grows considerably longer, with a weight of fifteen to twenty pounds. The largest I have seen was at Key West; it was fully five feet long. It is not uncommon in the Chesapeake Bay, and like most of the mackerel tribe it is a fairly good food-fish. It spawns in summer, but its breeding habits are not fully understood.

As might be imagined from its shape and habits, it is a good game-fish, and quite strong and vigorous on the rod. It requires all of the angler's skill to land it safely, especially when it is taken about the mangroves, among whose arching and numerous roots it is sure to take refuge if it can do so. It will take a small fish bait or a crab, going for it with a pikelike rush. I once took one on Indian River with a large red ibis fly, but never succeeded in catching another with the same lure.

A strong, rather heavy rod is necessary for the cobia, which the Key West fishermen call cobi-6. A striped-bass chum rod of natural bamboo is a good and serviceable tool for the work, with multiplying reel and braided linen line, to which is affixed a Sproat hook, No. 3–0, on gimp snell, by a brass box-swivel. A sinker should not be used about the mangroves.

A fiddler-crab, a mullet, or other small fish is hooked through the lips, and is cast from a boat to the edge of the mangroves or other bushes, in the same way as in casting for mascalonge in northern waters. I have never tried casting with a spoon, which might be successful, but a minnow is better by far. The cobia takes the bait with a fierce lunge, and turning quickly endeavors to return to his lair, a proceeding that must be thwarted by the angler at all hazards to his rod or tackle, for once under the arching roots of the mangroves he is as good as gone. The boat must be rowed to open water at once, while a strong strain is maintained by the rod on the fish. With open water the angler can play his fish with leisure, though he will be severely taxed by the struggles of as game a fish as he is likely to meet during a winter's sojourn in Florida.

THE SPOTTED WEAKFISH

(*Cynoscion nebulosus*)

Cynoscion nebulosus. The Spotted Weakfish. Body rather elongate, compressed; head 3½; depth 4½; scales 10–70–11; D. X–I, 26; A. II, 10; eye 7; snout long and acute; mouth large, maxillary reaching to posterior edge of eye; lower pharyngeals narrow, each with 7 or 8 series of short teeth, the inner enlarged; maxillary, preorbital, and lower jaw naked; canines in upper jaw strong; lower jaw without canines, other teeth in narrow bands, sharp, but closely set; membrane of preopercle serrate, the bone entire; pseudobranchiæ well developed; caudal lunate; soft rays of dorsal and anal scaleless; gill-rakers short and thick, 4 + 7.

This fish is closely allied to the northern weak-fish, and belongs to the same family, *Sciænidæ*. It is known very generally in Florida as trout, salt-water trout, or sea-trout, owing to its spots. It is, of course, not a trout at all, and these names should be set aside; moreover, the name sea-trout is preoccupied by the sea-run brook-trout of the Gulf of St. Lawrence. Its present specific name, *nebulosus*, or "clouded," was bestowed by Cuvier and Valenciennes, in 1830, displacing the earlier and better name *maculatus*, or "spotted," conferred by Dr. S. L. Mitchill, in 1815, for reasons that it is unnecessary to refer to here. It is abundant from Virginia to Florida, and along the Gulf coast to Texas. It occasionally strays as far north as New Jersey.

It is almost the counterpart of the common weakfish in the form of its body, the depth of which is about a fourth of its length, and with a similar head, eye, and mouth, but with somewhat smaller scales, and a few less rays in the second dorsal fin. Its mouth is large, with narrow bands of sharp teeth on the jaws, and two long canine teeth in the upper jaw.

Its color is bluish gray on the back, with steely reflections, the sides are silvery and the belly white.   The upper half of the body has numerous black spots, as large as the pupil of the eye, with smaller ones on the soft dorsal and anal fins; the other fins are plainer, and the anal fin is dusky.

The spotted weakfish is a better food-fish, and also a better game-fish, than its northern cousin. It is abundant in the bays of Florida during the entire year, often ascending the streams to fresh water.   Its usual weight is from two to four pounds, often of six to eight, and sometimes of even ten pounds or more.   It appears in schools in March and April, often in company with the Spanish mackerel, and runs into brackish water for the purpose of spawning.   It spawns in the spring; the eggs are buoyant, quite small, about thirty to the inch, and hatch in two days.   It feeds on small fishes and crustaceans.

All things considered, it is one of the best game-fishes of Florida.   It is a surface feeder and takes the artificial fly eagerly, as well as natural bait, or the artificial squid and trolling-spoon.   With light tackle it affords good sport, being a strong and determined fighter.   It is a great favorite with all anglers who are acquainted with its merits.

When of the usual weight of from two to four

pounds, black-bass tackle is very suitable and serviceable in rod, reel, line, hooks, or flies, though a rather heavy braided linen line is better adapted for salt water than a silk one. To be more explicit, an eight-ounce rod, multiplying reel, line size F, Sproat hooks Nos. 2–0 to 3–0 on gut or gimp snells, will be found to be just about right for bait-fishing.

For fly-fishing, a rod of eight ounces, click reel, braided linen line, size E, leader of three or four feet, single gut, and black-bass flies such as silver-doctor, red ibis, Abbey, soldier, oriole, coachman, etc., on hooks Nos. 1 to 2, will be found to answer in skilful hands. A heavier rod may be used when the fish run larger, and also flies on hooks a size or two larger. Very small phantom minnows, spoons, or squids may be often used with success when the fish are running in schools in the spring.

Fishing, either with fly or bait, can be practised with good results at flood tide from the end of long piers that extend to deep water, or at the points of inlets during the running season. The piers at Port Tampa and St. Petersburg, on Tampa Bay, also at Mullet Key and Egmont Key, or Pass-a-Grille, in the same vicinity, are

famed fishing resorts in March and April.   I prefer to fish from a boat moored to the pier, rather
than from the pier itself, as the fish are not so
likely to see one, and they are more conveniently
landed.

During the winter the best fishing will be found
in the bays and bayous, or in the streams, in the
vicinity of sand-shoals or mud-flats, at almost any
stage of the tide, which usually rises but a foot or
two in the bays of the west coast.   At the inlets
and passes, at the first of the flood and last of the
ebb tide, the fishing is also good during the winter
months.

The spotted weakfish takes its prey at the surface with a snap of its jaws that is quite audible,
especially at night when one's yacht is at anchor.
It takes the angler's fly or bait in the same way.
It will remind him forcibly of the bite of a large
brook-trout, and its manner of resistance when
hooked is very much the same as with that fish —
one reason for the name sea-trout.

The fishing is especially good in Tampa and
Sarasota bays, and the upper portion of Charlotte
Harbor, on the west coast; and on the east coast
at the mouths of streams entering Halifax River,
Mosquito Lagoon, or Indian River.

THE DEEP-SEA WEAKFISH
(*Cynoscion thalassinus*)

This species was first described by Dr. Holbrook, in 1859, from the coast of South Carolina. He named it *thalassinus*, or "pertaining to the sea," from its supposed habit of living in deep water. It is either a rare fish or it has been confounded with the common weakfish. It has been recorded from several places on the South Atlantic and Gulf coasts, in Virginia, South Carolina, Florida, and Mississippi. It is supposed to inhabit the deep water of the sea and Gulf, though this is by no means certain.

Its form is very similar to the spotted weakfish, with a more pointed snout and somewhat larger eye; otherwise it is much the same. Its color is brownish above, lighter below; the middle of the sides is marked with many dark dots; there is a dark blotch on the upper part of the cheek; the first dorsal fin is black, the second dorsal and anal fins are dusky, and the other fins pale. The same remarks as to fishing for the spotted weakfish will apply as well to this species, if the opportunity should occur to the angler. It is a doubtful species at best, and may eventually prove to be an aberrant form of the spotted weakfish.

THE BERMUDA CHUB

(*Kyphosus sectatrix*)

Kyphosus sectatrix. The Bermuda Chub. Body ovate, somewhat compressed; head $3\frac{3}{4}$; depth $2\frac{1}{8}$; scales 10–55–16; D. XI, 12; A. III, 11; head short, with blunt snout; mouth small, maxillary reaching front of eye; each jaw with a series of narrow incisors, implanted with compressed conspicuous roots posteriorly; behind these a narrow band of villiform teeth; fine teeth on vomer, palatines, and tongue; teeth 35 to 40 on each side; preopercle weakly serrate; top and sides of head finely scaled; interorbital region gibbous, below which point snout is truncate; soft dorsal and anal very low; second anal spine highest; caudal well forked, the lower lobe longest; gill-rakers long; dorsal spines depressible in a groove of scales; small ctenoid scales entirely covering the soft portions of the vertical fins, and extending up on the paired fins.

The chub belongs to the family of rudderfishes, *Kyphosidæ*. It was noticed as *sectatrix* by Catesby in his "History of the Carolinas," in 1738, and was so named by Linnæus in 1758. *Sectatrix* is the feminine of *sectator*, meaning "one who follows," in allusion to its habit of following vessels. Its range is along the South Atlantic coast to the West Indies, sometimes straying as far north as Cape Cod in the summer. It is common on the west coast of Florida.

It has an oblong, elliptical body, its depth being more than a third of its length. The head is short, with a blunt snout and small mouth, and a curved profile. There are well-developed incisor teeth in each jaw, with peculiar horizontal bases. Its color is bluish-gray, with steely lustre; the sides have numerous narrow, indistinct, yellowish or brassy stripes, alternating with bluish ones; there is a pale stripe below the eye, and a yellowish one above and below it; the fins are dull grayish.

The chub feeds on barnacles and other small mollusks, and is found wherever they abound, sometimes in rather deep water. Its usual size is six to ten inches, weighing from one to three or four pounds, but it occasionally grows to fifteen or eighteen inches in length in favorable locations. Its spawning habits have not been studied. It is an excellent pan-fish. Light tackle is needed for the chub and pin-fish, both being usually found together. The hook should be small but strong, with gimp snell; Sproat hooks, No. 1 or 2, are very suitable. The best bait is fiddler-crab or hermit-crab. It is quite a game little fish.

I was once staying for a few days' fishing at the Quarantine Station on Mullet Key, in Tampa Bay. The station is built on piles in water twenty feet deep. There was a trap-door in the floor of one of the rooms, through which many

kinds of fish could be seen swimming about in the
very clear water. These fishes could be readily
taken with the hook or the spear, as they were
unable to see any one in the dark room above.
I was much interested watching the chub and
sheepshead pinching off the barnacles from the
piles with their chisel-like teeth. A dozen could
be easily taken in as many minutes with fiddler
bait, and the table was kept well supplied with
chub, which was the favorite food-fish during my
sojourn.

THE ANGEL–FISH

(*Chætodipterus faber*)

Chætodipterus faber. The Angel-fish. Body much elevated and
compressed, its outline nearly orbicular, the anterior profile
nearly vertical; head 3; depth 1 to 1½; scales 60; D. VIII–I,
20; A. III, 18; jaws about equal; no teeth on vomer or palatines; teeth on jaws slender, somewhat movable; preopercle
finely serrate; two dorsal fins, somewhat connected; vertical
fins falcate in the adult; first soft ray of dorsal filamentous;
ventral fin with a large accessory scale.

There are a number of angel-fishes in Florida,
remarkable for their bizarre and beautiful coloration, but of no importance to the angler as
they do not often take the baited hook, their
very small mouths and weak teeth being only
adapted for feeding on the minute organisms
about the coral reefs. The common angel-fish,

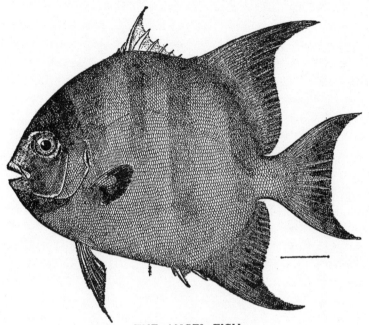

THE ANGEL-FISH
Chætodipterus faber

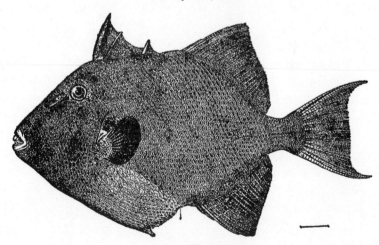

THE TURBOT
Balistes carolinensis

or spade-fish, is more sombre in hue than the others, and belongs to a different family, *Ephippidæ;* it has a somewhat larger mouth, and is more widely distributed. It was described by Broussonet, in 1782, from Jamaica, who named it *faber*, or "blacksmith," though why is difficult to imagine, except that it is dark in its general hue, with smutty cross bars. It is very abundant from the South Atlantic coast to South America, and is not uncommon, occasionally, as far north as Cape Cod. It is very common on the east and west coasts of Florida.

It has a short, very deep body, nearly round in outline, and very much compressed; it is almost as deep as long. Its head is short and deep, with its profile nearly vertical. The mouth is small, with slender, movable teeth, on jaws only; the soft dorsal and anal fins are quite large and winglike, extending far backward nearly to the tail; they are quite scaly, which adds much to their thickness and stiffness; the caudal fin is broad and nearly square.

The general color is usually gray or slate color, often bluish with iridescent tints; there are several dusky, broad vertical bars across the body, becoming obsolete or faint with age.

It feeds on small marine organisms, and grows to a length of two feet, occasionally, though its usual size is ten or twelve inches, and average weight from one to three or four pounds. It is an excellent food-fish, though its good qualities in this respect are not generally known. It spawns in the spring.

It is usually taken in seines in the bays of the Gulf coast, and salted with mullet and sheepshead by the fishermen. It can be caught by the angler with a very small hook, No. 5 or 6, and cut clam or conch bait. It is a fair game-fish on light tackle, which may be the same as advised for the Bermuda chub.

THE PIN-FISH

(*Lagodon rhomboides*)

Lagodon rhomboides. The Pin-fish. Body elongate, elliptical; head 3⅛; depth 2½; eye 4; scales 10–65–17; D. XII, 11; A. III, 11; mouth moderate, maxillary not reaching front of orbit; head flattened; snout pointed; profile not very steep; 4 incisors in each jaw, all deeply notched; two series of molars in each jaw; dorsal fin single, with high spines; caudal fin deeply forked.

The pin-fish, also called sailor's choice and bream in some localities, belongs to the family *Sparidæ*, and is closely related to the sheepshead of that family, having incisor and molar teeth. It differs from it in the conformation of the skull.

The pin-fish was first described by Linnæus, in 1766, from specimens sent to him by Dr. Garden from South Carolina. He named it *rhomboides*, meaning "rhomboid," from the shape of its body. It is abundant on the South Atlantic and Gulf coasts, extending south to Cuba, and occasionally north to Cape Cod. It is found in all bays on the east and west coasts of Florida.

Its body is symmetrical, being rather evenly curved on both dorsal and ventral lines, and rather deep; its head is large, with a depression in front of the eye. Its color is olivaceous, darkest on the back, with bluish silvery sides, and narrow horizontal stripes of blue and gold, alternating, and six faint, broad vertical bars; it has a dark spot on the shoulder at the top of the gill-cover; the dorsal fin is bluish with gilt edge; the anal fin is bluish with yellow band; the caudal fin is yellow, faintly barred; the ventral fins are yellowish; the pectoral fins are plain.

It is a pretty fish, and is usually abundant wherever found. It feeds on small mollusks and barnacles, resorting to old wharves and about the mangroves where such food abounds. It grows to a length of six or eight inches, and though small, it is a good pan-fish. It spawns in the spring. The same light tackle used for the pig-fish and pork-fish can be utilized for the pin-fish, with small, strong hooks, as Sproat bend, No. 4 or 5, on gut snells. The ends of piers and wharves, in comparatively shallow water, are favorable localities for fishing.

THE SQUIRREL-FISH

(*Holocentrus ascensionis*)

Holocentrus ascensionis. The Squirrel-fish. Body oblong, moder-ately compressed, the back a little elevated; head $3\frac{2}{3}$; depth $3\frac{2}{5}$; eye 3; scales 5-50-7; D. XI, 15; A. IV, 10; head compressed, narrowed forward; opercle with a strong spine above, below with the edge sharply serrated; preopercle with a strong spine at its angle; mouth small, little oblique, with the lower jaw pro-jecting somewhat; eye excessively large; upper lobe of caudal fin the longest; soft dorsal fin pointed, as high as the body; third anal spine very strong, as long as longest anal ray.

The squirrel-fish belongs to the family *Holo-centridæ*, the species comprising that family hav-ing very rough or spinous scales, a single dorsal fin, deeply divided, with the spines very tall; the caudal fin deeply forked; the anal fin with four spines; and a very large eye.

The squirrel-fish belongs to the West Indian fauna, ranging from the Florida Keys to South America. It was first described by Osbeck, in 1771, from Ascension Island, who named it for that locality. It is not uncommon along the reefs, where I have taken it a number of times. Its body is oblong, moderately compressed, its depth about a third of its length, with the back slightly elevated, and the ventral outline nearly straight. Its mouth is small, the eye enormously large, and the caudal fin deeply forked. Its color is bright crimson, with a darker shade on the back, and a somewhat lighter tint below, with silver streaks along the sides. The fins are also red, some bordered with olive; the head is red above, with an oblique white bar running back and down from the eye. It feeds about the reefs on small fishes and marine invertebrates, and grows to two feet in length, occasionally, but is usually found smaller. It is a good food-fish and sells at sight in the market. It is a remarkably handsome and attractive fish in appearance.

In one of Stockton's stories, John Gayther, the gardener, tells of the curious and beautiful things to be seen on a coral reef in the tropics, with the aid of a long box with a glass in the end. His description applies just as well to the vicinity of the Dry Tortugas, where I have often viewed the wonders of the sea-floor through a sponge-glass, a wooden pail with a glass bottom: —

"Where the water is so clear that with a little help you can see everything just as if it were out in the open air, — bushes and vines and hedges; all sorts of waving plants, all made of seaweed and coral, growing in the white sand; and instead of birds flying about among their branches, there were little fishes of every color: canary-colored fishes, fishes like robin-redbreasts, and others which you might have thought were blue jays if they had been up in the air instead of down in the water."

THE TURBOT

(*Balistes carolinensis*)

Balistes carolinensis. The Turbot. The fishes comprising the family *Balistidæ* are characterized by an ovate body, much compressed; small and low mouth, with separate incisor teeth; eye very high; gill opening a small slit; the absence of ventral fins; the dorsal fins widely separated, the first with but 1 to 3 spines. The turbot has a very deep compressed body, covered with thick, rough plates or scales; head $3\frac{1}{4}$; depth $1\frac{3}{4}$; eye small; scales about 60; about 35 scales in an oblique series from vent upward and forward; D. III, 27; A. 25; third dorsal spine stouter than the second and remote from it; plates on head similar to those on body; caudal lobes produced; soft dorsal high; ventral flaps large, supported by several pungent spines; lateral line very slender, undulating, and very crooked, showing only when scales are dry; a groove before the eye; larger plates behind the gill opening.

The turbot, or leather-fish, belongs to the family *Balistidæ*, or trigger-fishes. It was first described by Gmelin, in 1788, from Carolina, from one of Dr. Garden's specimens, Gmelin being a coadjutor of Linnæus, to whom the specimen was sent. The locality from which the type specimen was sent accounts for its name.

The turbot, as it is called by the Key West fishermen, is an inhabitant of tropical waters, and is abundant on the South Atlantic coast and along the Florida Keys; it is known also from the Mediterranean Sea. Like all of the trigger-fishes it has a curious form and appearance. It is as deep as long, and slants both ways from the dorsal fin above and from the ventral flap below, presenting somewhat of a diamond shape. The head is triangular, and the fins are thick and leathery. The first dorsal spine is locked when erect by the second, or "trigger." The soft dorsal and anal fins are opposite each other, and are of similar size and shape. The color is olive-gray, or slate color, with some purplish spots on the back; two obscure cross bars are under the second dorsal fin; a ring of blue spots alternating with greenish streaks are about the eye; there are violet marks on the sides of the snout; the first dorsal is spotted and clouded with bluish; the second dorsal has pale yellowish spots, with rows of blue ones, separated by greenish reticulations; the anal fin is colored like the second dorsal; the pectoral fins are bluish with olive spots.

The leather-fish, or turbot, resorts to rocky shoals and coral reefs, feeding on the small marine organisms that are abundant in such localities. Nothing is known of its breeding habits. It grows to a foot in length and is considered a good food-fish by the people of Key West. The thick skin and rough scales are pared off together with a sharp knife by the fishermen when delivered to a customer. It is caught, with the grunts, porgies, etc., in the channels among the keys and reefs with the baited hook, and also in wire traps. Very small hooks must be used for the turbot, as it has a very small mouth. Cut crawfish, conch, or barnacles are good baits.

CONCLUSION

IN closing this account it occurs to me to say that the angler who has a genuine love for the finny tribe, and who has never visited the sunny waters of Florida, has in store an experience of joy and delight in the wonderful variety of its fishes. Some idea may be formed of their number from the fact that I have collected nearly three hundred species in the fresh and salt water of that sub-tropical wonderland. And the fishing lasts the year round, and is always good, except when an unusually cold "norther" is blowing. The warm-water species, like the tarpon, lady-fish, and ten-pounder, are more plentiful, and extend their range farther northward in the summer. At that season all of the inlets and passes of both the Atlantic and Gulf coasts abound with them; but the winter visitor will find them in Biscayne Bay, Barnes Sound, Cards Sound, and southwest along the keys to the Dry Tortugas. The brackish water species will be found all winter in the bays and estuaries of either coast.

A just idea of the fishing resources of Florida twenty years ago — and it is much the same to-day — may, perhaps, be gathered from the following excerpts from my "Camping and Cruising in Florida": —

"At flood-tide the channels under the mangroves teem with redfish, groupers, and snappers, while near the beds of coon oysters are schools of sheepshead and drum. In fact, all of the passes and inlets of the Gulf coast are fairly alive with fishes, from the mullet to sharks and sawfish. While lying in his bunk, one can hear all night long the voices of the deep, under and around him.

"The hollow, muffled boom of the drumfish seems to be just under one's pillow; schools of sparoid fishes feeding on shell-fish at the bottom, sounds like the snapping of dry twigs on a hot fire; while a hundred tiny hammers in the hands of ocean sprites are tapping on the keel. Then is heard the powerful rush of the tarpon, the blowing of porpoises, and the snapping jaws of the sea-trout among the swarms of mullet, which, leaping from the surface by thousands, awake the watery echoes like showers of silvery fishes falling in fitful gusts and squalls.

"Sanibel Island, at the entrance of Caloosa Bay and opposite Punta Rassa, is renowned for its fine fishing. The angler can here fairly revel in piscatorial abandon and cover himself with piscine glory and fish scales. If ichthyc variety is the spice of the angler's life, Sanibel and its sister keys are the Spice Islands. Sharks, rays, and devil-fish, tarpon and jewfish, redfish, snappers and groupers, Spanish mackerel and kingfish, sea-trout, bonito and cavallies, ladyfish and sergeant-fish, sheepshead and drum, a host of smaller fry — spots, grunts, and porgies, and the ever-present and ubiquitous catfish — can here be jerked, and yanked and snaked, and pulled and hauled, until the unfortunate angler will lament that he was ever born — under the last but not least of the zodiacal signs."

The foregoing excerpts relate to fishing on the Gulf coast, but on the east coast, while the variety of fishes is not so great, the angler will find enough and to spare, and many that are worthy of his best efforts. Large-mouth black-bass are plentiful in Tomoka River, near Ormond on the Halifax, and in Elbow Creek, Turkey Creek, Sebastian River, Taylor's Creek, and the St. Lucie

River, all tributaries of Indian River. At the mouths of these streams, brackish-water fishes will be found in more or less abundance, comprising most of the species inhabiting the Gulf coast. Some of the best localities are at Daytona, New Smyrna, Rock Ledge, Indian River Inlet, Gilbert's Bar, and Jupiter Inlet. Still farther south the fishing is much better, notably at Lake Worth, and on Hillsboro' and New rivers. Mangrove snappers, bluefish, amber-jacks, and barracudas are especially abundant south of Indian River Inlet, more so than on the Gulf coast. In all of the fresh-water lakes in the interior of the state the angler will be amply rewarded, as large-mouth black-bass, calico bass, warmouth perch, and bream are in most of them. As a matter of fact, one can hardly go amiss for some kind of fishing in Florida, wherever there is water, salt or fresh, provided one proceeds with patience and intelligence, and with a due regard for the amenities of the gentle art.

Perhaps the queer descriptions and homely comparisons of some of the fishes as given by my negro boatman from the Bahamas, whom I have before mentioned, may not be uninteresting. I always employed him when possible, for he was a good fisherman and sailor, and had a never-ending fund of anecdotes; and being a close observer, he had a good general idea of the fishes of the locality. I always encouraged him in his quaint and original remarks about fishes, and in this way obtained considerable knowledge of their habits from this faithful Achates. Some of his observations, as I remember them, and which seem very odd in his Bahamian lingo, were as follows: —

"Vell, sir, it's curious 'ow some fish is made; but w'atever their model in length, beam, and draft, there is some good reason vy they is built so."

"Yes," I would answer, "they are all endowed by Nature with the shape best fitted for their mode of life and environment."

"Vell, 'wironment or not, as you say, and I'm not gainsayin' it, there's as much diff'rence in their model as atween a man-o'-war 'awk and an 'ummin'-bird. Now, sir, just look at the stingaree and the wipporee; they is flat as pancakes, and goes a-skimmin' along like a turkey buzzard, or a-wabblin' like a jolly-boat in the breakers, and then they flops down on a sandbank like a flounder, when feedin', 'cause their mouth is hunderneath like a shark. And they crawls along on their belly a-gobblin' hup the periwinkles and fiddlers, and crounches 'em vith a set of teeth like a pair o' mill-stones."

"Yes," I assented, "the rays are curious creatures, and have very remarkable teeth."

"Now, on the hother 'and, sir, look at the moonfish. They is all length and draft and no beam, like the 'ind weel of a vaggon; it couldn't cast a shadder if it was facin' the sun. And the angel-fish 'aven't much more beam to swear by. Now, sir, hall these slimjims 'ave small mouths and pinchers for teeth, and goes a-nosin' 'round the rocks, and a-vorkin' of theirselves thro' the narrow crannies, and a-pinchin' hoff the coral-bugs and sea-lice. Now, sir, a flounder is wicey wersy from a moonfish, it 'asn't hany draft, and don't carry any sail to speak of, and so it 'ides in the sand a-waitin' for sumpthin' to turn hup in the vay o' grub."

"That's true," I would say, "they lead a very lazy, humdrum life, and don't hustle much for a living."

"But for a real racin' yacht," he would continue, "give me the kingfish, or Spanish mackerel, or boneeto; they ketches their food on the run and jump; and speakin' o' jumpin', sir, look at the tarpon, and bone-fish, and skipjack; they is the kankeroos o' the sea."

"Many fishes," I would observe, "have their analogues; that is, they seem to bear some fancied resemblance, either in habits or appearance, to some object or animal of the land."

"Vell, sir, it's as true as gospel; a man is like a fish out o' water; 'e puffs like a porpus and drinks like a fish. And the butterflies are the yellow grunts and pork-fish and little snappers and cockeyed pilots; and the red snappers and squirrel-fish are the fillimingoes and pink curlews; and the yellow-fish and conies is the le'p-ards; and the blowfish and puffers is the 'edge'ogs and porkupines. And then there's the poll-par-rots, red, blue, yellow, and green, from the puddin'-wife to slippery-dick; if they'd vings like the flyin'-fish, we'd put 'em in cages."

"True, enough," I would assent; "and up north we have fish that go into hiding and sleep all winter, like the bears; and some that make nests for their eggs, and guard them, and take care of their young ones like a hen broods her chicks. And in some countries there are fish that crawl out on the land, and climb trees like squirrels."

He listened to this apparently very doubtfully,

and frowned fiercely, but kept silent until he filled and lighted his pipe ; then, after scanning the horizon, he said meekly : —

" I think we'll be goin' 'ome, sir; it looks werry squally in the sou' east."

INDEX